Being with the Beings
The How and the Why of ET Contact

Miguel Mendonça

Featuring interviews with

Lyssa Royal Holt
Darlene Van de Grift
Vanessa Lamorte Hartshorn
Krista Raisa
Jujuolui Kuita
Rob Gauthier
Vashta Narada
Robert Fullington
Jacquelin Smith

About the Author

Miguel Mendonça is an Anglo-Azorean author based in Bristol, England. After studying and working in forestry and horticulture, he gained an honors degree in geography and history then studied social science and environmental ethics at postgraduate level. He worked in the sustainability field, specializing in renewable energy policy. While serving as Research Manager for an international NGO he lectured widely and wrote textbooks, articles and papers, providing an evidence base for campaigners to push for new or better renewable energy laws.

After publishing a collection of short fiction in 2011 he began to research the ET field in depth, and in 2015 he co-authored *Meet the Hybrids* with Barbara Lamb, a study of the lives of eight ET-human hybrids living on Earth. In 2016 he authored *We Are the Disclosure*, a two-part people's history of ET-human interaction, featuring interviews with 27 people who have been involved in the subject for a combined total of around 700 years.

About the Cover Artists

Vashta Narada (Aleksandra Aleksandrov) is a lifelong consciousness explorer, ET communicator, researcher, geek, gamer and an intuitive artist. She places great importance on subjective experiences, seeing them as a doorway to other dimensions, entities and a true understanding of consciousness. Her artwork is aimed at helping people establish more personal connections with the galactics. Inspiring imagination, different perspectives, creative thinking and exploration of the infinite are her main passions in this life, and many others.

Her website is: vashta.com

Ashley Ruiz is an art student at the Academy of Art University majoring in Illustration. She is also a freelance artist that loves to paint portraits and scenes of faraway places. Illustrating is one of her passions, but she also loves photography and hiking in the spring and fall time in South Texas.

Her website is: airisillustrations.tumblr.com

First published 2017 by Miguel Mendonça

Copyright © 2017 Miguel Mendonça

Cover artwork by Vashta Narada (main image)
and Ashley Ruiz (background image)

Cover design by Miguel Mendonça

A catalogue record for this book is available from
the British Library

ISBN 13: 978-1544270852
ISBN-10: 1544270852

www.wearethedisclosure.com

To our beloved Cynthia

Our task must be to free ourselves ... by widening our circles of compassion to embrace all living creatures and the whole of nature in its beauty.
Albert Einstein

Man has gone out to explore other worlds and other civilizations without having explored his own labyrinth of dark passages and secret chambers, and without finding what lies behind doorways that he himself has sealed.
Stanisław Lem, Solaris

I searched for God and found only myself.
I searched for myself and found only God.
Rumi

Acknowledgements

I wish to express my deepest gratitude to the participants in this project (in whatever form they may take). Not only for their willingness to share so much important information, and for making this book so much fun to put together, but for their invaluable support through the process. Thanks and big hugs to: Leo and Kristen Sprinkle, Lyssa Royal Holt, Darlene Van de Grift, Vanessa Lamorte Hartshorn, Jujuolui Kuita, Krista Raisa, Rob Gauthier, Vashta Narada, Robert Fullington and Jacquelin Smith.

I also wish to thank Vashta, Ashley Ruiz, Tatiana Roumelioti, Lyssa, Robert, Juju, Kesara, Vanessa, Darlene and Jacquelin for the use of their artwork, light language symbols and other images. I've been an admirer of the work of Vashta, Ashley, Tatiana and Kesara for some time, and I am thrilled to assemble my dream-team in this book, and share their magic with more people.

Kevin Moore and Reuben Langdon, for their suggestions on the right people to involve in this book. Rebecca Hardcastle Wright for assembling the discussion group that has been inspirational, through the people I have met and the level of discussion we have enjoyed.

Also Wendy, Matt, David, Carol, Mary, Kalina, Alexis, Sharina, Marilyn, Claudine, Marc, Alfred, Rita, Jerry, Rey, Jenn, Rosemary, Diana, Sam, Alisa, Miguel, John, Tina, Irish Dave, Giles, Fiona, Jojo, Chris, Bob and Phil. You all make my work better, easier and more rewarding.

I want to thank all those working with experiencers, in supporting them and giving them a voice.

Special thanks to Barbara Lamb, whose willingness to engage with one curious person precipitated this entire trilogy.

And Cynthia, our Galactic Godmother. You have given so much to so many. I hear from more people all the time on how much your support has meant to them. You have inspired me to continue your connecting role, and to work on letting go of judgment, and getting out of the head and into the heart. The real work is now to balance them.

As always, I am grateful to my family, and to Lou, DB, Mike and Dexter.

Miguel Mendonça
Bristol, 2017

Table of Contents

Foreword

Welcome, dear reader, to another grand contribution from the author, Miguel Mendonça. He provides us not only with much information about encounters with extraterrestrials (ETs), but he also offers us a profound view of the New Human. We are transitioning from being planetary persons to becoming cosmic citizens.

Earlier, the author worked with Barbara Lamb, writing and publishing an important book, *Meet the Hybrids*. They interviewed participants who view themselves as having parents who are both human and extraterrestrial.

Then, the author presented what I considered to be the zenith of ET-human interaction: *We Are the Disclosure*. In two volumes, he presented the results of his interviews with researchers, writers, ET experiencers, et al., to support his thesis: we disclose, to those around us, the ET presence and the ET technologies (including the Tesla Coil) - not the military-industrial complex and the governmental leaders who are withholding this information.

Now, the author is guiding us to new vistas: not only Disclosure, but also discovery, and design: How are humans interacting with ETs, and how can we design ourselves as New Humans in a new era?

The author approaches these questions by asking the interviewees to respond to a standardized interview format. His approach differs from earlier writers.

In summary, there were two groups: the ET experiencers, who wrote about their individual encounters with ETs, and the engineers and scientists who attempted to describe the craft, and the propulsion systems of the craft.

NICAP (National Investigations Committee on Aerial Phenomena) represented the group that sought 'scientific' understanding of ET craft, or 'flying saucers'. APRO (Aerial Phenomena Research Organization) sought more understanding of flying saucers and, also, more information about the occupants. Headed by Jim and Coral

Lorenzen of Tucson, Arizona, APRO enlisted the aid of consultants: Dr Frank Salisbury, PhD, Professor of Plant Physiology, Utah State University, and Dr James Harder, PhD, Professor of Engineering, University of California, Berkeley.

When I joined APRO in 1961, Jim Harder was already using the pendulum technique to conduct hypnosis sessions with ET experiencers. With my training in Counseling Psychology and hypnotic procedures, we planned to conduct sessions to learn more about 'missing time' during ET Encounters.

However, the author has gone for beyond those basic questions. He has combined 'left brain' and 'right brain' investigations. He combines 'new science' with 'old science'.

Early scientists, often reacting to the dogmatism of Church officials, attempted to separate spirit and matter. But new scientists coordinate the study of physical/biological, psychosocial/spiritual levels of our human experience.

New science views the universe as various frequencies of energy - as do mystics, who view love as the basic energy of the Universe. Thus, both matter and spirit are forms of energy.

The author combines both quantitative and qualitative aspects of ET-human interactions with his standardized interview procedures. He asks each interviewee the same basic questions, and, thus, the responses can be compared and categorized. However, he also elicits individual reactions to the questions, and, thus, he can gain more meaning from the responses of participants.

Dear reader, welcome to the work and world of Miguel Mendonça. May his work provide us with a better understanding of ET-human interactions, and may his approach be helpful to us as we enter the era of the New Human. May we continue to shift from planetary persons to cosmic citizens.

In Love & Light,

R. Leo Sprinkle, PhD
February 2017

Introduction

The extraterrestrial subject has been wreathed in mystery and intrigue since day one, if we take day one to mean the birth in the wider public consciousness of this phenomenon. This was most likely June 24th 1947, the day private pilot Kenneth Arnold sighted nine UFOs in the vicinity of Mount Rainier, in the US state of Washington. He initially assumed they were new military aircraft being tested, but it was not long before the possibility of an extraterrestrial connection arose. The term 'flying saucer' was coined, the movie business got hold of the subject matter, and the battle to wring truth out of government and the military began.

In my previous book, *We Are the Disclosure*, 27 interviewees set out their experiences and perspectives on the question of how we can have a better conversation about this subject in our culture. Their combined research and personal experience in this field totals around 700 years, and covers a vast spectrum, from the material, technological and political aspects, across to the philosophical, metaphysical and spiritual aspects. By the end of the process, my approach to the whole subject had shifted. I no longer identified with the need to drag the authorities kicking and screaming into a place of truth. It dawned on me that they are going to have focused almost entirely on the aspects of the subject related to power and profit. Their business is only to expand their personal and institutional power and wealth, so the spiritually transformative aspects of this subject would have little to no relevance for them. And the evidence of a large-scale public survey of experiencers—those who have experienced any of the various forms of 'ET' contact—shows that 70% of respondents have undergone positive life transformations as a result. The Foundation for Research into Extraterrestrial Encounters (FREE) designed their survey to detail these personal shifts, and showed that the majority of experiencers became more spiritual and less competitive and materialistic following their experiences. Those individuals have become more aware of the staggering scale of life in the universe, our own spiritual nature, and the vast multiplicity of forms we may take through the journey of our soul. Since most control is exerted through placing others in fear and perceived dependency, the authorities have little to gain by offering such an expanded, liberating narrative to the public.

Therefore, the idea of top-down Disclosure has a hardwired problem. But it is one that we need not waste our time with. Bottom-up Disclosure—the sharing of ET-related experiences—has been happening for at least 70 years at the time of this writing, and offers a wealth of material that is immediately available to those drawn to the subject. *We Are the Disclosure* goes some way toward representing the scale and scope of that material, and it inspired me to go further, and dive deeper, in my quest to understand the nature and implications of this contact. As a researcher I have always sought out the best sources, and so for this project, that meant talking with those who have had long, ongoing contact with 'the beings'. Then I realized I could go a step further. But we'll come back to that.

Author and radio host Alexis Brooks said in *We Are the Disclosure*, "The biggest discovery here is that it is self-discovery." This is, in my experience, profoundly true. As the author of this trilogy, which began with *Meet the Hybrids*, I have been in the privileged position of not only being able to interview dozens of experiencers and researchers, but have also become friends with many of them. And what I have learned through this contact is that it is no accident that I should find myself doing this work. Over the last two years I have begun to notice the threads that have tied me to this subject throughout my life, and through one experience after another, I have been opened up on numerous levels about my own nature. I have documented my journey in these books because I want to be in truth, and I want to contribute to the long tradition of bottom-up Disclosure. And this is allowing for more personal contact and connection with the beings themselves.

Contact can be intense, it can be joyful, but for me a lot of it is work. Indeed, this book began life as a download. I was stretching out on the couch to begin four days of vacation, having just ordered the bound proof of *We Are the Disclosure - Part II*, and I let my mind empty and drift. Within 90 seconds I suddenly saw the title, outline, list of questions and list of participants for this next book, flashing up, fully-formed, one after another. It was so clear and insistent that I recognized it as a download and sat up and started making notes. The outline said it must be a book featuring only those with long, ongoing contact with the beings, and the final interview question must be: what message would they like to share?

The more I thought it through, the more excited about the possibilities I became. I had a channel on the list, as well as some hybrids, and I began to think about the types of people I know who have a long history of contact with the beings. I then began to ask some of my colleagues for recommendations. During the promotion work for *We Are the Disclosure*, I was interviewed by radio host Kevin Moore for his show, and afterwards I told him about the next project and asked for some suggestions. He gave me a great list, which mapped onto one given to me the next day by Reuben Langdon, who interviews channels for his show *Interview with E.D.* E.D. stands for extradimensionals, the type of beings which are the true subjects of the interviews. I got a great response from the nine people I felt drawn to approach, and have spent the last four months having my mind blown on an almost daily basis during the interviews.

Four of the interviewees channel ETs in the classic sense, one is an intuitive artist and four identify as ET-human hybrids. Each of them has been having contact for most of their life, and their combined experience of contact totals around 250 years. They are all introduced with a short bio at the head of their chapter, and the website wearethedisclosure.com has more information and links for them.

In the interview sessions I asked the questions which were given to me in the download, and added some of my own, and some from the participants themselves.

Firstly we discussed the kinds of beings they have been in contact with, how they refer to them, and how the contacts first took place. We then looked at how they make contact and what safeguards they have used. Then we get into the why. Why the beings make contact with them, and what each party gains from the experiences. This covers a wide range of practical, intellectual, emotional and spiritual factors.

Finally we explore the messages the beings would like to share. These take many forms, as you will see. They may be written or drawn, and for the channels, we could go right to source, and interview the beings themselves. These have been extraordinary experiences, and take the entire enterprise to another level.

I knew at the outset that this project would trigger more contact experiences of my own, and sure enough, things have been getting extremely interesting around here of late. In my contacts I have drawn upon the advice and approaches shared by the interviewees, and I can attest that they are working well for me. I trust that you, the reader, can likewise approach contact with safety, security and good sense by working with the practical aspects of this material. Because it seems that the ET subject is as practical and available as you want it to be. If you desire contact you can have it, and this book offers advice, based on literally centuries of experience and insight, to those who wish to venture into these realms.

And for those already engaged in contact, the hybrids and channelers may offer you fresh perspectives, more context for your experiences, or simply something to compare them to.

Some may feel less alone in their contact, because for many people it is still hard to talk about such things in our culture. But the people in my books are very willing to connect with others, and build a community of those willing to embrace their evolutionary process. So if you are needing to reach out to the interviewees in these and my other books, please do. Many of them offer established services based on their experience and abilities.

For the first time, I am including longer exchanges between myself and the interviewees, including the beings. I initially wished to be invisible in these books, but it has become clear that the whole process is triggering my own awakening, which some readers may wish to observe as it unfolds, and perhaps compare to their own. My interjections are highlighted by an M at the start of a paragraph.

In addition, sharing my personal journey with the interviewees deepens the exchange, and we have got to some places which we could not have done if I was not willing to open up. Being an experiencer also tends to improve the quality of the questions.

In a way I am too close to the subject to be as objective as I would like, but it has given me some valuable perspectives that I did not anticipate. These are shares throughout the interviews and highlighted in the conclusion.

The use of images was suggested by Vanessa, and is something I have wanted to do for some time. I know from experience that images of beings, light language and geometric designs have the capacity to trigger powerful shifts in people, and I look forward to receiving feedback from readers on the stories, techniques, ideas and images which most impacted them.

What it all ultimately means is highly subjective, but all the experiencers I have ever met have reported a hugely expanded sense of reality, and sense of self. They have done their best to improve the lives of others in many ways, and contribute positively to human knowledge and day-to-day experience. On that level alone, this subject has enormous value, and I believe that this realm of experience offers us so much, on so many levels, that if we could all be comfortable with it on a personal level, we could move on from the materialist fixation that is in the process of wiping out life as we know it on this world. This is a concern shared by most experiencers, and most of the beings they encounter.

Old-school ufologists have little to do with contact experiences for numerous reasons. *We Are the Disclosure* showed that they are mainly concerned with the material-political-masculine aspects of the subject, and are looking for data/proof that can be accepted by the same political/educational/scientific/media establishment institutions that are, generally speaking, in complete denial. But more and more people are working differently in this field, and not engaging in the cyclical processes—the claim/denial loops—that have achieved little in terms of cultural acceptance of the reality of the phenomenon.

Should top-down Disclosure ever come to pass, the complex, chaotic dynamics that would play out are very difficult to predict. However, while we remain on this side of that threshold, there is much work to be done. We must continue to develop our personal and shared understanding of what this contact is about, build communities of experiences, and create resources like this one, which can help more people deal positively with their personal encounters.

This is not intended as a linear book. The reader is encouraged to go with the flow, and pick out any name you are drawn to. I have read the chapters in various orders, and they each link to one another in various ways, as you will see.

I would also recommend that you take this in slowly. Taste your food. You will miss many things of significance if you wolf it down. With such challenging concepts, it is a good idea to give yourself time to let it integrate.

And I would advocate reading the whole book before embarking on conscious contact for the first time. There are many contrasts in approaches and philosophies, and you will benefit from absorbing the full range, to see what resonates the most. Your body will tell you what is good information for you at the time, and as you will learn from the experiencers, developing an awareness of your reactions to the information and images is an important skill.

This material will change your life in numerous ways, large or small, and it is offered with our love and support. The most important thing is to have fun and enjoy the journey.

Lyssa Royal Holt

Lyssa Royal Holt has been a seminar leader, channel, and author since 1985. She is the co-director, with her husband Ronald Holt, of Seed of Life Institute LLC and the SOLi School, an organization whose primary purpose is to assist individuals to understand the nature of consciousness and to put this understanding into practice in daily life – providing a road map to the process of realizing the true Awareness beyond the human identity.

Lyssa is most known for her in-depth explorations of the nature of extraterrestrial consciousness and how it impacts human evolution. Her books *The Prism of Lyra*, *Visitors from Within*, *Preparing for Contact*, and *Millennium* are classics in the field of channeled literature. Her newly-released *Galactic Heritage Cards* are a one-of-a-kind set of 108 inspirational cards based on the cosmology she introduces in her classic book *The Prism of Lyra*. She also has an extensive library of audio material based on her work since the late 1980s.

She has been interviewed on TV and radio around the globe (including most recently by the Discovery Channel, and Shirley MacLaine's radio show), and has appeared in countless magazine articles over more than two decades.

Lyssa works extensively in Japan and has done so since 1990. She also offers courses in North America and Europe as time allows. Sometimes she offers private consultations as well. She also works from time to time with her husband Ronald Holt, combining her intuitive and channeling work with his expertise in the fields of sacred geometry, meditation, yoga, martial arts and more.

Her website is: lyssaroyal.net

Which words do you use to describe 'them'?

I would use 'beings.' The classic definition of extraterrestrials is limited by the image of the physical guy standing there, but they have so many different forms. 'Beings' is a little bit more flexible.

How do they appear to you?

I'm not a visual seer. I don't see things as other people do. I see them internally I guess. And even then it's still not a 'seeing'. In my profession as a trance channel, everything tends to come as downloads, mentally and energetically.

Sometimes there are pictures, but often the pictures are metaphorical, because only metaphor can describe some of the deeper truths that are limited by our language. So they come to me more in that way. It's through a mental, energetic process. There has been 'classic' ET contact stuff, but I don't tend to focus on that any longer. I focus more on the information and what can be learned from the experiences.

Trance channeling is a process of putting yourself in an altered state of consciousness to allow your consciousness to open to receive communications from outside. Some people call it 'mediumship', but I don't use that term. I know in Britain that term's a little more popular. I see a 'medium' as someone who deals more with those who have passed on, whereas a trance channel deals more with other types of communication from non-physical beings or ETs or whatever.

I grew up in New Hampshire, and had UFO sightings there. After I got my degree in psychology I moved to Los Angeles, and the sightings continued, including some pretty dramatic ones. Then I began receiving messages. At first they were very simple, but then one night I had a dream, and a boy from India appeared. He touched all the energy centers on my body, the chakras, and said, "You will be a channel." I woke up amazed. I knew what a channel was. I had read Shirley MacLaine's book *Out on A Limb*, and she talked about channeling in there. But I thought, 'How in the world is that possible for me?'

The beings then started to train me. They would have me lie down, and they would tell me what to do, and how to work with my consciousness. But it's very hard to train yourself through the channeling process. Coincidentally, a friend called me and said, "There's a channeling class happening, and there's only one space left, so I signed you up for it." I had no choice, right? So I went.

It was supposed to be a 12-week class, once a week, but we ended up training for a year. I had a degree in psychology, and I tend to be a very mind-oriented person. The really cool thing is that the class was run by a woman who was a trance channel, and she was part of a study at UCLA (University of California, Los Angeles), a bunch of professors were studying the developmental process of those who become channels. One particular professor had a hypothesis that if you approach learning to channel as a spiritual process in which you work with your ego, you become very self-aware, and you go through an awakening process internally. Basically this means cleaning out your crap, so to speak! Through this, the channeling gets clearer and clearer, and the channel and the human can go through a kind of blending process where the channel's consciousness gets uplifted. Because there were professors studying this, I thought, 'This is going to be really legitimate.'

So that's why I stuck with the class. It was profoundly moving, and it felt as if I'd been waiting for it my whole life, and I knew it was what I was supposed to be doing. That passion was there, the interest, but I didn't know why, or that 30 years later I would still be doing this work.

Once I became a channel and was channeling regularly, there were several key questions that drove me: why are humans connected with the stars? Who are these beings who are contacting us? What is their relevance to us? There were no books in '85 answering those questions, and they were insisting on giving me the information, so I ended up writing the book myself. It is called *The Prism of Lyra*.

That's how channeling is connected to the work that I do. There are really two aspects to it. One is channeling and one is the ET contact work. Some people have asked me: What's the difference between the two? As time goes on, the differences are decreasing, because contact is happening for me during the channeling process, and for many of the students that I work with. The contact itself is happening in a very different way than people have envisioned it would. You know, everybody has this image from movies of the ship landing and the being coming out, and we shake hands or whatever. But sorry to say guys, contact has already been happening for a very long time, and it's happening through us, if we just pay attention. That's what I've done for the last 30 years.

This work has for me has been about the exploration of why the human race has felt connected to the stars since ancient times and who these ETs are that have been communicating with us since then. Retrospective studies of UFOs and that kind of information is helpful, but why is this important for us now? That is what drives me at present.

It all has to do with us changing our view of the universe from a fragmented one to a holistic one, because that is what is going to shift our species. A lot of the work I've been doing, especially in the last 25 years, has been about how to shift our perspective about contact and about humanity toward an understanding that is inclusive, that can take us into the future, and away from a destructive focus based on separation.

Through channeling, I've gotten detailed information about the nature of consciousness and how the contact experience itself is a reflection of us. So for those humans who see negative ETs under every rock, and are focused on the wars in the heavens, or the black projects and all the negative things, that seems to be a reflection of their own consciousness. That's not meant as an insult. It has to do with the question: how do we refine our consciousness to move us to the next level of our species' evolution? Can our evolution offer us the opportunity to become a space-faring species and go into space from a place of peace, rather than from a place of fragmented consciousness and warlike mentality?

The information I've gotten is on how to refine the consciousness to get us to a place where we can have the optimal relationship with ETs. There's much more, but that's the core of it.

Which kinds of beings are you in contact with?

I'll answer this in two parts.

The first part is through my channeling work. When I do channeling work, it is either by teaching workshops or working one-on-one with people, which you could call 'spiritual counseling'. There are two main beings who come through me.

One is more like a collective consciousness, and he calls himself Germane, which is the word meaning 'coming from the same source'. So it's not Saint Germain. I say he, but Germane is neither; he is a 'they'. He is best described this way: if our entire galactic family evolved themselves and became one collective consciousness, it would be the consciousness of Germane. So it's a huge energy system, that apparently has connected to many others, and has gone by different names. He has the memories of the galactic family within him. He is the one that channeled the book *The Prism of Lyra*. He also did the newest project, the *Galactic Heritage Cards*, which is a way to tap into our galactic memory; but not just that. The cards also help us connect to the whole process of the evolution of consciousness. His information is of such a high source that it is still surprising to me. He will give me information that sometimes I won't understand until years later, which tells me that it's not my own mind making it up. So that's Germane, and he is the one who does the galactic history stuff.

The other primary being I've worked with since 1988 is a being who calls herself Sasha. She says she is from the Pleiades. She came to me after a series of UFO sightings that I'd had in childhood, then in Los Angeles. Now the kicker—and there's always a kicker—is that she says she is a future incarnation of myself. When she came in 1988 that was a big thing to swallow, because it seemed like Sasha's consciousness and Lyssa's consciousness were so far apart. But if we go back to what the professors were studying at UCLA, their hypothesis was that when you're channeling a being like that, the gap between you shrinks until an integration process happens, both within the psyche and energetically. At that point, in a sense you are living as that incarnation in consciousness in this Earth plane. After 30 years of this, I can see that integration process happening. Sasha no longer feels as far away from me as she did at the beginning.

Sasha. Credit: Vashta Narada

Sasha is responsible for a lot of the information that I've channeled that has to do with opening contact, and developing contact programs on the planet. She channeled the book *Preparing for Contact* in the early 90s. It was all about moving from the idea of being a 'victim' of contact to how humans can become equal participants in the contact process. Again, it's all about consciousness. How can humans evolve their consciousness in such a way that they can allow themselves to be equal to those who are contacting them, and how can they allow themselves to work in partnership with them?

That book was sent to the printers in late '93, and I went off to speak at the Laughlin UFO Congress that year. Steven Greer spoke there, and I had no knowledge of who he was. I sat through his lecture and was absolutely blown away, because so much of what he was saying I had just written through channeled material in *Preparing for Contact*. So I knew then that the paradigm was starting to shift. It was a message for me from the universe to go deeper into this idea of going out into the field and beginning to do contact work that helps to evolve our consciousness.

At that time I got really involved with CSETI, the Center for the Study of Extraterrestrial Intelligence. This was around '94-'97. I was involved in a working group here in Arizona. But I found that because I had the connection with Sasha, and she would give me information about protocols to use in the field that were outside of CSETI protocols, I felt a little bit limited by just staying with the CSETI protocols. At the time I was really close friends with Steven Greer's right-hand person Shari Adamiak. They had given me permission to do my own thing with the channeling, but kind of off the record. That's kind of how I broke away from CSETI, but to this day I have a tremendous amount of respect for what they're doing. This was even before they were doing the Disclosure stuff. They were more focused on the contact work.

So you have Germane, who is much more of a collective consciousness, working with galactic history information, and then you have Sasha, who, being a singular being from the Pleiades, is able to work more on a human level, in a way that is a little more grounded—if it can be grounded—with the contact information. Since that time in the early 1990s, Sasha has worked with contact groups. We actually just finished a retreat about five days ago, where we do that kind of contact work. As time goes on, even though things are happening in the sky, or are obviously ET in nature, it's become much more focused on the internal experience of contact, rather than the flashy stuff about seeing ships and all of that, which on the surface is kind of worthless.

I said there were two parts. The second part is about the kinds of beings I work with. In specific instances when I'm teaching or doing contact work with a group, I will sometimes channel other beings from other star systems, who are that night working with the group in the contact exercises. So sometimes it's a being from Sirius (the Sirian ambassador named Hamón). This past weekend we had a Mantis being who gave a transmission. And sometimes there are beings that don't even fit into a category.

Again, I have to put in here that it's always for the purpose of the evolution of consciousness, and they refuse to do the work if that is not the purpose of it. They basically feel they're not here to give a show, they're not here to create religion or anything like that. Their purest intention is that humanity is at a place where it needs to evolve its consciousness to move to the next level of evolution as a species. That next step has to do with us developing a more holistic view of ourselves in relation to the universe. They've actually given what they call a 'quantum map' which talks about this.

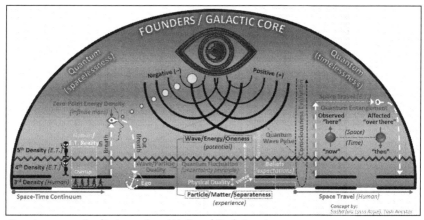

Quantum map. Credit: Lyssa Royal Holt and Tash Anestos

Through the contact work we can evolve ourselves to get to that place, where we can connect on a quantum level, which is where all the barriers begin dissolving.

This quantum map is the new information from the last two years that Sasha's been working with. It's been phenomenal because it gets into what you were talking about earlier, where you said that the central message from the hybrids is to get out of the mind and into the heart. I'll give you the very simple model of this. They say that there is one holographic mind in creation. Just one. We are all fractals of that hologram. We have a mechanism known as an ego, which serves as an anchor, to keep us in experience of separation for the purpose of evolution. But the separated self is not the real reality. The ETs that are working to help us with our evolution represent more of the true nature of consciousness, and they can exist more in that quantum state, which they call 'the common ground upon which all consciousness can meet'.

Therefore, our role as a species is that as we travel along this quantum map, from egoic consciousness and separation back into more of our quantum selves—which are holistic and holographic in nature—we have to pass through various bands of challenge: fear, pain, things like that, which keep us separated. It all has to do with that merging of the mind and the heart. As we move through these final bands—they call it the 'fear band', we emerge into more of the holistic state of quantum consciousness. That's a summary of the most recent teachings.

How do you connect?

Because I am trained as a trance channel, there are a couple of different ways. One of the ways I make contact is through my process of entering that trance state. At this point, because I've had decades of meditation and channeling, it happens very quickly. It's almost like going into a meditative state and flipping a switch in my brain. Kind of like I'd tune to a radio station. I pretty much know the radio stations of Sasha and Germane. If a new being comes, it is the same process, but may take slightly longer.

If I am going about in life, or if I am out in the field doing contact work, they may initiate the call. Usually it comes in the form of a huge download. I often describe the downloads using a simile. It's like a big ball of string that drops in my head and starts unwinding. Lyssa can watch the ball of string unwinding, but I have to go into that trance state to understand it more deeply. Especially when I'm doing contact work with groups and we're outside in the dark, I'll get one of those big downloads, and then go into the trance state and connect with the download and bring it through.

Now if the download is coming from a being I don't normally channel, I usually can sense it in my body. I get strange physical reactions if it's an unfamiliar energy. For example, it might be ears popping, or a sense of disorientation or slight dizziness, or tremendous heat. Different things like that. But after channeling any being a few times I begin to recognize their energetic signature, for instance Hamón the Sirian ambassador. Those physical effects tell me that there's incoming energy that is deliberate.

If I'm doing a private session with someone, I can make a call for that person, and connect with whatever is necessary for the client.

However, when they want to tell me something they call me. It's never a case where I channel randomly, like a schizophrenic. I'm always very aware of the flows and the threads of the energies and the communications, but I never lose sight of the host personality, which is the Lyssa-being that's here on this world. She is the switchboard operator basically, organizing everything. So I never go into a state of confusion about identity. I know there are some critics who say that channeling is just a form of schizophrenia.

As a side note, some of these professors did brain studies of channels, to actually see the brain activity as it's happening during channeling. More recently, I posted a link on the library section of my website about this. It has an episode of an American TV show hosted by a famous TV doctor called Dr Oz. He brought on Dr Daniel Amen, a top brain imaging scientist, who hooked up a famous medium called Theresa Caputo to a brain scanning device to do a test called a 'quantitative EEG'. What it shows is that during channeling, the brain lights up in areas responsible for external stimuli coming in. Yeah, they have proven this! So by this point, anybody who has really seriously investigated channeling in terms of brainwaves, can see there is definitely different brainwave activity that happens when people are channeling. That's a given for anyone who wants to accept it; the research is there.

When they want to give me a message they will make it very clear that a message is there. But they never interfere in my life, and that's the idea of the partnership, of working as equals in the process.

Can you initiate contact?

Yes. But as I tell my students, being a channel is not like being a vending machine. You cannot put the money in and get the answer. Though of course we all wish it was like that. So instead, the beings that work with me have a perception of the bigger picture, which is much bigger than the human ego has. For instance, say I'm going through a very difficult time and having a conflict with a friend. And let's say I ask, "Hey guys, can you help me with this?" And let's say I perceive that I'm getting no help at all. I'm getting no advice and the situation isn't shifting. Why? I've come to learn that it's because the human Lyssa needs to have the experience and learn what she needs to learn. So in that sense they're not interested in taking away pain and fixing reality the way our egos want it to be fixed. They are more interested in the idea of our growing and evolving to that place where our consciousness expands and we learn how to navigate this reality with the least amount of conflict.

We are always welcome to ask questions, but you also have to be patient for the natural progression of the situation to unfold. They will help as much as they can. And by helping, I don't know that 'intervention' is the correct word. I would never say they intervene. They will give me a new way of looking at something, and show me how the situation was created perhaps by the way I am. Maybe if I shifted or released something within myself, that would shift the whole dynamic of the situation. So again it goes back to the idea of helping human beings grow to become the optimal being that can be evolved here on Earth.

How do you differentiate between your own thoughts and those from outside?

There are so many ways I could approach that question. On the one hand, I think each person learns their own signatures, such as not being able to sleep, or feeling a download, that intense influx of something. In those cases, there's obviously something going on from the outside. But the key thing here, again going back to the hypothesis of the professors, is that it's getting to a point where our sense of self is expanding to include our others selves too. In that sense it doesn't matter who it's coming from. It becomes just one flow of expression.

This is something I really learned doing the contact work. When I was going out into the field, and Sasha would come, there was often a clear definition: this is Lyssa; this is Sasha. But when you're in the field and it's dark, the darkness helps quiet my ego. In that situation, my ego doesn't maintain the rigid separation boundaries between who is Lyssa and who is not. So in those environments the blending between Lyssa and the other beings is much more fluid. In those instances, we cannot define the sharp separation between the identities. If we go back to the quantum model of consciousness, our natural state of consciousness at this quantum level is that it contains all the fractals of ourselves, and in that sense, Miguel is another me. That fractal of me has chosen a male body, and is doing this project from that perspective, and Lyssa is doing it from this perspective. But when Miguel and Lyssa get plugged into the flow, then even the separation between these two physical beings becomes less important, and the flow or energy of the project and its expression becomes stronger than the individual beings.

This is an example of how the quantum consciousness in a human reality can be expressed. The way that this connection stops is through the ego, and whatever the ego fears. That stops the quantum connection. This is part of one of the challenges for humanity right now, with all the political and religious crap and all of that stuff. People are so desperately clinging, and afraid of their view of reality changing, that they can't transcend into more of a collective consciousness, even though they already do exist on a collective consciousness. That is our truer state.

Right now as I'm talking to you I'm aware that it's Lyssa talking to you, but it's 'Lyssa plus'. Lyssa plus whoever or whatever, but it doesn't matter. Just a side note there!

M: For some reason this is bringing to mind an experience back in around 1995. I had a near-death experience where, at the moment that our car should have been hit head-on at high speed, I found myself instead in a white space as pure consciousness, and saw in front and above me, an angel with its wings spread. This lasted a few moments, then I heard sound flowing backwards and my consciousness was dumped back into my body.

My take on those kinds of experiences is that the angel was another version of you. And that in that moment, where you were going to have a head-on collision, again using Sasha's quantum map, you got sucked out of the local identity, which is Miguel, and you went into the greater or more true you, which could have been represented by the higher self or angel idea. It was almost like a reset. When you go back to quantum and then back into physicality, that's when you jump timelines. When I say 'timelines' I simply mean the infinite number of probabilities that exist based on our choices and actions. We can sometimes change tracks quickly when we radically change ourselves. You were going along this linear timeline where you were going to be in an accident, and you got sucked back into the quantum. I'm going to draw something here. You've got an X on the right, and an X on the left, and above them both you have a circle.

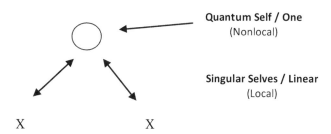

So the X on the right is the time stream where you were going to be in an accident, and before the impact you got sucked back into your quantum self, which is the circle. You went past angels and higher versions of you on the way. Then you got 'spit back out' into a different time stream, or probability stream, in which there was not an impact with the car.

The quantum you, the real you, is the one outside of time. That aspect of you can access multiple probabilities and multiple time streams. But since it has no ego, it cannot be controlled by the ego. You needed to have the experience of almost crashing, but not the experience of the crash itself. The organizing principle of you, which for lack of a better term you could call the higher or quantum self, took you into the experience just before impact, then sucked you back into the default area, which is the quantum, then spit you back into a different stream so that you didn't have the impact. I see this kind of thing very often. There was another you that had the impact. But this version of you didn't.

M: Well, it's not like I've gotten away with everything in my life.

In the eyes of the quantum it's all equal. Whether you get hurt or not, it's all neutral from that point of view. Of course the ego prefers we don't get in an accident, so we call on the angels (another version of us), "Oh please protect me," but their role is not to interfere. They can't really protect us, but their presence allows us to come more fully into our own magnificence or wholeness.

M: I have always felt my guidance to be my higher self. It feels like my energy. And my intuition is the same. So I'm not sure I see a difference between internal and external guidance. Is that your sense?

Yes. There really is no difference. The external is just a projection of the internal. Carl Jung talked about that long ago as well. I love studying humans, that's why I went into psychology. I've always seen that the way someone views experience and reality is a reflection of their internal self; it can't be any other way. There really is nothing outside of us. If you understand that statement from the point of view of the quantum self, there is nothing that exists outside of us. That's a hard pill for people to swallow, because immediately the ego says, "Well then all the bad stuff is my fault." But that's not what is meant by that. It's just a way for us to begin to take responsibility for ourselves, our points of view, and our own evolution and growth as human beings.

M: Can you give me a simple definition of the quantum self?

Okay. I'm going to give you a diagram that I often use in workshops.

I've drawn a circle here, which represents the one consciousness that we all are. You can't even draw consciousness with a circle, because it doesn't have a boundary, so it's a metaphor. That one consciousness, that we all are, originally has no duality, so it is infinitely at rest. But, let's say, hypothetically, consciousness says, "Okay, I wonder what it would be like not to know myself." So that thought creates a realm of separation within itself.

M: I hear this idea often - do you know where and when it was first discussed?

As far as I know, this idea goes back to basic Taoism and creation myths. Nothing created the one consciousness because the One always existed and always will. Our egos have trouble with this idea because we are habituated toward linearity – past, present, and future, so to speak. As for this diagram, Sasha created it. I've never seen it anywhere else.

I've drawn a smaller circle within the bigger circle with many fragments in it. The smaller circle represents the realm inside the quantum oneness, that separated off and began to create the reality of separation, in which we forget we are the one consciousness, and we start incarnating as singular beings. The physical universe exists within this smaller, fragmented area.

We go about our lives, living this incarnational cycle, and believing in this idea of separation. However, the quantum self is always there, surrounding and embracing the separated self. It never goes away. It simply watches the idea of the separation.

Sasha taught me this. It's part of their Pleiadian spirituality teachings. When you have a civilization that is beginning to evolve out of the idea of separation, what begins to happen is that this inner circle starts to become a little more porous, and bits of quantum consciousness flow in. So your example of the angelic encounters and other such things, or even the sense of guidance that you've gotten with the books is your quantum self flowing into the reality of the separated self.

As consciousness evolves, which is what is happening to humans now, people begin asking the question: Is this it? Is this all there is? They start asking these questions intuitively, because they can feel the quantum self - it's still there embracing the false self. People start feeling there is something more. They eventually start opening to more of the intangible. For an awakening species it can initially be a bit of a conflict, where the ego fights with these intangible experiences that start happening. But at some point the egos begin to embrace that there is something bigger going on. As that happens, then the boundaries dissolve more and more, so that humans begin to be able to live in both worlds - the quantum world of the all or the oneness, and the separated self of the human vehicle.

If you look at Sasha's civilization, which lives in what she calls '4th density', they too have egos and they are separated beings, but they are much farther along the spectrum of evolution. They're quite aware of this process, and are quite capable of transcending the limitations of a physical reality, and in a sense existing more from the state of quantum wholeness most of the time, rather than individuality.

That's what's happening to us now, and is one of the reasons why the ETs are so fascinated in coming to Earth and watching during this time. Apparently this is a process that occurs on all developing planets that reach this point, and it's always fascinating for them to watch.

Although they can't intervene, what they can do is begin to give these teachings, to help frame what is happening in a way that humans can understand, so they don't start freaking out about ET contact and weird things happening. In my experience, when I work with people who are just waking up, and when they've got a framework like this which can help them understand what's happening, suddenly they just relax and say, "Oh my God, *now* I understand what's happening." At first they go back and forth fighting the ego, wanting to cling to the ego's definition of what's real, so to speak, but eventually they kind of have to surrender to it. I went through this process myself, especially as a channel, and struggling all the time with, 'Am I going to surrender, and allow this quantum consciousness experience, or am I going to keep fighting it?' Eventually I had to surrender because it was so obvious that it was necessary or it was the next step.

How do they connect with you?

The beings primarily connect with me through the process of trance channeling. I put myself in an altered state of consciousness that allows me to open to their communication. This is usually done with an audience or a client who is on the receiving end. They sometimes give lectures, workshops, answer questions, and lead experiential work. They can also communicate through what I call 'downloads'. It feels like the dropping of a huge data packet into my consciousness that then takes some time to unravel and understand. The full understanding usually comes if I channel it verbally, or write about the data transmitted. Somehow the process of getting it out into the physical reality helps the unraveling process. The process is never invasive. There have been times when I've been woken up in the middle of the night with information but I always have the option to postpone the transmission if needed. After 30+ years, there is now a wonderful balance.

What do Sasha and Germane get out of it?

That is an interesting question and I think I'd have to answer it separately for each being. Overall however, I think that the idea of doing something in order to 'get something out of it' is more of a human concept!

With Sasha, because she is an incarnational 'future' version of myself with a Pleiadian orientation, my understanding is that by helping me grow and evolve, she also heals a part of her soul lineage. This is based on a holographic model that she has been talking about for years. We are not all separate cogs in a wheel, but part of an elaborate fractal of one consciousness that is intricately connected.

Germane is a group consciousness representing an evolved and integrated version of our galactic family. Kind of like a bus stop on the way back to full integration as the One. He has said many times that working with us shows him what the experience of separation is really like. How can we not remember who we are? That idea is astounding to him, so he comes up with creative ways to help us remember, through his lectures and experiential work. I suspect working with humans is a way to put him back in touch with the aspect of his collective history that experienced the pain of separation and forgetfulness. This gives him a richer experience of creation itself.

How well do you feel you understand the beings?

I think that after all these decades that I understand them fairly well - as much as a human is capable of understanding. This doesn't mean that they don't surprise me though. For example, with the *Galactic Heritage Cards* project that Germane channeled in 2010, I didn't have any idea how to do a card system and really had to surrender and trust Germane. He told me that everything he has ever taught or ever will teach is embedded in that card system. I didn't really know what this meant. I had to go through years of learning the card system, and the depth of it revealed itself over time. I feel I have still just scratched the surface and Germane continually surprises me by teaching me more embedded info in the cards that has been there all along. It is quite humbling. That is an example of how I know Germane well enough to trust him fully, but not well enough to anticipate his surprises!

As for Sasha, again, though I know her pretty well, my encounters with her are always full of surprises. She will come up with metaphors and lessons (like Germane) that are so creative and so poignant that it takes my breath away. Through the contact retreats we do yearly, I am amazed at the new information she brings through, and the experiential work she does with the groups that leads to amazing results.

So then the basic answer to this question is that while I know them pretty well, they are full of surprises!

What have you learned?

I have learned so much that I could write a book just on that! So instead of answering this question based on what information I've learned (which is endless), I have to answer it based on what I've learned that are core foundational spiritual lessons directly applicable to my life not only as a human but as a teacher and a spiritual being.

The most important thing I've learned is that there is a big 'organizing reality' (for lack of a better term) that adds to the flow of our lives. In this flow, nothing is out of place. We may experience isolated events (like a loss or an accident) and see them as interruptions to our lives but in fact every single thing we experience is part of this organizing flow that exists to move us back to the One. We can choose to see that and work with it (thus evolving ourselves spiritually) or we can choose to feel like victims and see life as a series of separate events that create pain. This has been a hard lesson. Who wants to accept and embrace the unpleasant experiences? But in doing so, we create a fertile environment to grow our true inner peace.

That being said, this idea plays itself out in my channeling because I now trust that I can allow Germane and Sasha to give their lessons to my groups without my interference or control. They have a much larger view of this organizing universal flow than I do. Extending it further, it means that all of us can let go in our lives, stop trying to control things, and trust more. We may not always understand why things happen but that isn't the point. The point is, can we be here in the present moment with whatever is happening? Can we use it to refine ourselves? Can we relax and move with the flow and finally enjoy our experience as physical beings? I'm still working on that!

How has contact affected your life?

It affects my life in countless ways that are hard to verbalize. My experience of life is more expansive and I can see the bigger picture in a way that allows me to let the little things go as much as possible. Knowing that there is a larger organizing flow out there helps me to relax and remember that I don't have to control everything! In fact, it has taught me that controlling anything is impossible. This is just a game our ego plays with us to keep us chasing the carrot. Control is a total illusion.

It has taught me that if there is a reality out there that I don't like (politically, socially, etcetera), it's appearance in my reality is a way for me to find those parts of myself that I don't like or that I fear, and begin to embrace them. So it has taught me that the universe is reflective. Everything we see outside of ourselves is a reflection of us. It may be a clear reflection or a distorted one, but it's always us, because nothing exists outside of us. We are, in a sense, experiencing a temporary detainment inside a giant fun house filled with mirrors. The way out of the fun house is to remember that everything we see outside of us is distorted and by seeing clearly beyond what is showing up in the external reality, we free ourselves. Thus, the way out, is in.

Channeling Session

Well greetings to you. This is Sasha. Wonderful to finally speak in this way. How are you?

M: I'm very good thank you. Welcome. How are you doing?

Very wonderful. We are excited about your project. And especially feeling your excitement. Because as you were talking with Lyssa we could feel a little bit of that bouncing-off-the-wall energy, so to speak, because of the excitement. So we're excited that *you* are excited!

M: Well, the excitement helps, I find!

I have probably about ten questions, and I'm hoping that we can get through them. You can be as expansive as you'd like to be. I've no particular expectation, I would say, or limitation. I'm in your hands.

Why do you use channeling?

That's a very good question. The reason we use channeling has a lot to do with the level of evolution on the planets we visit. Though for right now, if you look at your world, and especially if you look at the field of the study of extraterrestrial intelligence, you are at a point where you're kind of stuck in certain levels of research. You have the hardcore researchers who are only after the empirical evidence. And they've kind of, let's say created a very rigid structure of that study of ufology. So if a civilization is to really understand the truth about their connection to the greater universe out there, they're going to have to come out of that box of empirical structure and go more into the realm that is unprovable. Which is where a lot of people don't want to go, because ultimately you cannot separate what you call the spiritual ideas, or metaphysical ideas, from the science of extraterrestrial study. You can't really separate it, they're one in the same. If you are to actually study the truth about your connection to the stars, then you are going to go into realms that are unprovable, that go into the deep metaphysical, because they are inexorably connected.

Okay, so we're rattling on. We are known to rattle on. So feel free to steer us in the right direction if we get off on a tangent.

Therefore, we use channeling to first of all help answer the questions many people have that are not answered by science alone. And so one of the reasons for us coming to Lyssa as a channel was because she had many deep questions of her own. She kept asking these questions of the universe in the 1980s, and it was a natural process for me to come, or another to come, to answer those deep and sincere questions. It just so happens that others were interested in the questions too. And therefore it began to snowball.

But let's zoom out for a minute. That's the personal level for Lyssa, and in terms of a call that drew us in. But there's another call too. And that is that my job—if you wish to call it that—not just with Earth but with other civilizations, is to go to a developing planet at the time where you are now with Earth, where you're just opening to more universal concepts, and to very gradually help to introduce the idea of extraterrestrial connections in a way that is balanced, non-polarized, and not filled with all the drama, negativity and conspiracy that some factions within your society use to control the information.

So this process of channeling, of bringing through universal information, is actually a natural process of the evolution of a planet. When you get to this point in your development there is the need for maybe a little push into the unknown, to get the ball rolling, to get the mind open, to get the consciousness beginning to expand. We don't see this as interference in any way, shape or form, as long, of course, as our actions have integrity, and we're not trying to control results etcetera. Instead, we see it as a sacred responsibility, in which older species have the sacred responsibility of guiding younger species. Especially those that they are connected to genetically. And one day, humankind will be the guides for other younger species as well.

Why do you work with Lyssa?

One of the reasons we work with Lyssa goes back to some of the information that she shared in her part of the interview, regarding the holographic model of consciousness. She was talking about how basically there is really only one consciousness in creation, and all of you are fractals of that one consciousness. That means then, that Sasha is one of the fractals, as is Lyssa and Miguel, etcetera. And incarnationally-speaking, the simplest way to say it, is that I represent what you might call in your understanding, a future incarnation of Lyssa. It's also connected to many past incarnations of both her and I, and connected to your Earth as well. It's too complex to really go into that, but suffice it to say, the reason that Sasha is primarily channeling through Lyssa and not another being, is because of this incarnational connection. The fractals are very close. And let's say our passions are very similar. Because of that we can align our energies. So when Sasha comes through Lyssa, it is, let's say, a broader perspective outside of the human one, that can help the evolution of consciousness. Not just for her, but for those that we come into contact with, and who are open to it.

M: It's just occurred to me to ask: do you happen to communicate with Germane, kind of outside of connecting with Lyssa? I wonder about that relationship. If a person is channeling more than one being, even if that being is a collective consciousness, I wonder about the relationships between the different beings that are coming through the channel.

Yes, interesting question. Again it would depend on the beings that we're speaking about. For example, if we're talking about two different singular beings, such as Sasha and another extraterrestrial, like Bashar for example—or she talked about the Sirian being Hamón—we believe that in that case, because it's two singular beings, we can say that yes there can be a relationship, as you understand the idea of relationship, outside of the channeling. And there very often is.

However, when you're talking about Sasha, who is a singular being, and Germane, who is a collective being, the relationship is a little different. And the best way to describe it is to use a very similar metaphor, which would be one of concentric circles. So if Germane is the outside circle, and Sasha and other singular beings are inside, it's kind of like saying the Germane energy, which is a collective, is embracing or containing the Sasha and the Lyssa energy, and the singular beings in general.

In that case, the communication is not like we can go out for a glass of beer together on a physical plane; it is more the same type of relationship you might have with your higher self, or with another non-physical being who has a broader perspective than you. Does that make sense?

M: Yeah, I think so. I've found that in these channeled sessions that my imagination is just so alive during the conversation that I have at least three tracks running at once. So often what I'm doing is basically making little mental notes that there's something really interesting in there that when I get to transcribe the audio I can really concentrate on.

But there was something else that was coming to mind. I guess I'm just curious about what type of being you are, from your perspective.

In terms of the extent to which you are physical, or let's say a more subtle form of matter.

And as a part b, I wonder about your consciousness. Is there a 'you' that is existing almost independently of this contact? Like are you able to go about your day, and have part of your consciousness available for channeling?

Ah yes. Again, every being has their own descriptive scale for consciousness. So we're going to use ours, and we'll try to make it as simple as possible. Think of a spectrum, for example a rainbow. You might on the surface see that there is green and blue, but when you look really closely, the green will gradually fade into the blue, so there is no clear-cut definition. Consciousness is very much the same, in its evolutionary spectrum. So humankind then, has been existing in what we call 3rd-density reality, which is a reality based on very intense separation. So you experience your singularity and your separation in a very profound way. And within that 3rd-density reality there is a mechanism that keeps you grounded, or anchored, if you will, away from the true oneness that you are, and into the experience of singularity. That mechanism is called the ego. And the ego therefore has the job of keeping you separate, so Miguel is not Lyssa, as an example.

Now, as a civilization's consciousness begins to evolve, they begin evolving from a 3rd-density perspective of all that intense singularity, and of course also the experience of intense polarity, into what we call a 4th-density reality. Again this is a spectrum. So the metaphor there is that the anchor that anchors the consciousness in singularity in 3rd density begins to get lighter and lighter and lighter. What that means for the individual person is that they begin to experience less of that intensity of singularity and more of the sense of being a holistic part of the one consciousness itself.

So if you're to look primarily at the differences between human consciousness and Sasha's consciousness, what you're going to find is that my civilization, who are 4th density, we are about three-quarters of the way, on the spectrum, through 4th density. If you are to look at our civilization, we do not have this strong egoic identification that humans do. And without that strong egoic identification, there's very little conflict - in the way that humans know conflict.

We also have begun integrating what you have as separate layers of your consciousness, very often expressed as 'brain wave states'. We've come to the place where we've begun integrating those previously separate layers into a more integrated state of consciousness, which is very similar to what the dolphin species on your world experiences, if you look at the differences between human and dolphin brains. And this allows us that more universal perspective, where we are able to remove ourselves from the bouncing back and forth of polarized vision that humans experience, into more of a holistic, non-polarized vision, a non-egoic expression.

In terms of bodies, the human form would be the most dense. And as you begin moving in 4th density, we incorporate more of what we might call Pranic light, or quantum light, into our DNA structure. So if you had a device to measure quantum energy, you would find that our bodies would be containing a lot more of this light, which is an expression of the capability of our consciousness to move in and out of our physical form in a much more fluid way than humans at this time - although that is changing for you.

So in this channeling state then, you are accurate when you said that a part of us can be focused on other things at the same time. Because there is a part of me that is channeling through Lyssa, but it is not like I am necessarily sitting in a chair and focusing just on her, it's a very different experience altogether. Does that answer your question?

M: I think so. But it's almost like this conversation is a waking dream, because I am just so filled with images and ideas as you speak. It's like there's about three or four different conversations running at the same time. And I have the sense of many people being involved in this conversation. It's interesting.

One of the reasons you're having this experience is because you are giving yourself the experience of exactly what we're talking about. Because as you make this transition as a species, you are going to be able to process and experience simultaneous experiences, without the ego thinking it has to grasp and understand every single one. That's a very 3rd-density perspective. Humans are moving out of that now, and you're having the taste of the experience of multidimensionality in this moment.

M: Yeah, that word was coming to mind in the middle of it. But as I was explaining to Lyssa, there has been a lot of these shifts taking place, a lot of experiences, and I think just having access to you guys, and so much of this energy, it's changing me. It was explained by one of your colleagues working on this book project, Rob Gauthier/Aridif. Aridif said that however conscious of it you may or may not be, the information is still moving through you as energy and you are in some way internalizing it. It's not something I planned, but I feel like I'm a kind of an avatar for the reader. I'm having a lot of experiences that I'm only later finding words for, and that takes some time. In a book I obviously have no choice, but it's a challenge.

There's one minor question I can't help asking. One hears about Pleiadians continually in this field, and I wonder if you have any reflections on the kind of depiction of Pleiadians that exist?

You mean the artistic depictions?

M: I'm thinking about something I was told by someone who met with Pleiadians in Peru (Jerry Wills, in his chapter in *We Are the Disclosure*). The Pleiadian made some comments to him about the ways in which his race is represented, and I wonder if you have any observations on that. And maybe the better question is, I wonder if you have any thoughts on how Pleiadians are seen on a symbolic level by humans?

Ha ha! We are laughing because this is almost a kind of question that we would discuss if we were discussing a university course on intergalactic relations. We could say a great deal on this so we're going to try to keep it very focused.

The general depiction you have on Earth of Pleiadians is that we are human-like, and that we are the closest to you, genetically-speaking. In general that is very true. However, what people don't tend to notice or understand is that Pleiadians from many timelines or time streams can be interacting with you simultaneously. So if you go back to, for instance the very famous Pleiadian contacts in the 70s and 80s with Billy Meier and a being named Semjase, people will sometimes ask Sasha, "Do you know Semjase?" Well from my point of view, Semjase is in my civilization's history. She is an historical figure long gone. So this is what we mean when we say that you will be pulling in, as a civilization and as individuals, the Pleiadian beings that you need for particular lessons. Therefore, there can be a very wide variety in the character of Pleiadian beings.

If you're pulling in someone from a younger era of Pleiadian civilization they will be less experienced, younger, maybe seemingly more human-like. If you're pulling in a mid-era Pleiadian like myself, you will see in the physical evolution that we're at the higher end of the evolutionary spectrum. But there are also Pleiadian beings who are non-physical as well, who have already, you might say ascended back out of that body into more light forms.

So in that sense there is not one standard Pleiadian, but there is a spectrum of experience within the Pleiadian lineage, just like there is with the human experience as well.

M: Interesting. To say the least. I'm caught between just wanting to get into a free-flowing dialogue, and wanting to get through the questions that I have. There's one section that is very personal to me, but I trust it will be just as useful for readers, in terms of offering them more insight into how you work with humans through Lyssa. It's part of my process of working through what my involvement in this is, and how to deal with the process itself.

I don't know what access you have, in terms of your consciousness, to information on this. Again, there's no expectation here in terms of the extent to which you are able to offer insight into these questions.

Do you have any sense c   l in this work?

It's always multi-layered. And of course the basic level is to be of service, to give something to other people. To give something to the world. To help trigger other people in their own awakening process, and their own reconnection to the greater aspects of who they are. So that's a simple level. That's not a big newsflash.

However, on the more personal level, anyone who does this type of a project, let's say is being guided to do it more as a spiritual process for their own unfoldment. So for you, with talking to us and the many other people you've talked to in this series of books, it's been a way for you to unlock your own inner knowledge, and reconnect to your greater self, if you will. This is the shape of your particular journey.

With doing a book—as you well know since you've done several—they have a life of their own. And they often take you down unexpected paths. And a lot of that is because it's what you are needing for your unfoldment to get you to the next level. So it's not that the book or your work is taking you for a ride, it is more that it is the way that your spiritual journey is unfolding. It's going to lead to something else later, which you will see then. We're not seeing it and withholding it, we're simply giving you the information that we have available to us right now, which is that this is really just the beginning phase of what is going to come later.

M: You've anticipated my next question. As somebody who has been awakened, is becoming aware of my multidimensionality, of the nature of the soul, all of these things, I've been thinking about the value and utility of that for others. As you had set out initially, I feel very drawn to helping as many people as possible go through the same process. I think it is fundamentally about wanting to see as many people liberated as possible. I suppose it has some similarity to the Buddhist 'bodhisattva' idea.

But then at the same time ... I've always had trouble reconciling this. It seems somewhat paradoxical. Many people will say that the whole point of being here is experience. And we incarnate for a set of experiences. So the identities and bodies we choose are appropriate to that. However, if somebody goes through an awakening process, and becomes aware of all of this, then that may throw them out of that role. They may never be able to complete that role.

But they're taking up that role as a different experience. It's still being there to experience. There is never anything extraneous. You can never be thrown off your pat   Did we say ever? Ever.

When you think about it too much, is when you kind of tangle yourself up in the process. When you allow yourself to experience the moment, whatever is arising in that moment, without needing to understand every single thing, the experience that comes to you actually becomes even richer. And then the understanding actually blooms, if you will, from within, through the experience. It's also another reason why, going back to what we were talking about earlier, with the UFO situation, it's why researchers will never understand unless they are experiencers. Through the experience, understanding arises.

So there's nothing wrong with chasing it intellectually and mentally, but you also have to allow yourself the space to process what you are experiencing and that is where the true wisdom comes.

M: As a researcher I am not only driven by my own questions, but also those of the other people. The kinds of places that people get to. And for myself, a lot of it is trying to build context for my existence, for my experience. So that's why I'm interested in this question as to whether there is, in your view and experience, a kind of objective purpose here. Because there are all these subjective purposes played out by individuals, but I just wonder if that is part of some objective purpose.

And the final piece, that as I say is tough to reconcile, is if somebody ... I almost see it like a stage play. The cast must remain in character in order for the audience to be served, and for all parties to share that experience. Everybody is agreeing on a certain experience. However, if one of the actors breaks character, unexpectedly, then that has the potential to completely throw off the whole enterprise. So that's why I wonder about the awakening process. If there is an objective purpose for us all to come here, and incarnate together to have a set of experiences, then if you wake up out of the dream, and break character, by awakening and becoming self-aware in the process, I wonder where that fits with the overall enterprise.

That *is* the overall enterprise my dear - you've just hit the nail on the head. The overall purpose of this physical reality is to, in a sense, break character. The character is the sleeping human, run by the egoic consciousness. The breaking of character is the recognition that you are not the ego. And that there is in fact a greater purpose. The breaking of character *is* the awakening.

So in terms of objectively what happens, for example you doing this work and this book, what naturally happens in all evolving civilizations ... let's say you have an empty hall, filled with unlit candles. And Miguel comes along with a lit candle. The passion of his flame creates a heat which can jump to the next candle, and the next, until the entire hall is illuminated. That is the natural process of planetary, species, galactic evolution, that you are in the middle of right now.

So people like you and Lyssa and myriad others on your world are those lit candles, whose passion is creating the heat, so to speak, to light all the other candles. That is the proce   of   1 it doesn't mean that you have to do something   1 it through the ego you actually weaken your own flame. That's the paradox. Instead, you have to simply allow yourself in the moment to surrender to the passion and the excitement of what you're doing, which then makes the flame hotter, which then automatically allows the heat to transfer to the other candles. As soon as the ego becomes involved, the flame gets weaker.

M: I think that's true. Again, thank you for the image. I was really there. I was seeing almost the inside of a cathedral, with banks of candles on either side. It's beautiful. Every answer has been this amazing visual experience. I'm loving it.

Do you have any sense of who may be working with me in terms of guides?

We get this question a lot. We're a little bit unsure how to approach it. If you were a client of ours we would approach it very differently. We would push you a little bit, because we see our role is not to be a vending machine for answers, but instead to help you learn how to get your own answers. So if you were a client and we were working with you on this question, we would actually be questioning you, and giving you reflections and information that can help you answer that question for you. Because your own answer is much more important than anything we have to say. You can see our dilemma. We're assuming you don't want that type of personal information published.

M: I see what you mean, but I don't mind. It feels important to share my journey, because it can't be separated from the process of working on the books.

I have a really strong sense of presence in my home, that has been building over the last I would say ... I've been really aware of it over the last two months. Like every human knows the feeling of when someone is standing behind you. Even if you have no way of knowing, and you've been completely distracted, you can become aware of a presence behind you. I've also started to meet beings in dreams, and I've had some interesting goings on in my home.

Do you have a sense of what the energy is? This is a question we would ask all clients.

M: It's just intense. It's really high energy. But I would say it feels sort of neutral. It doesn't feel threatening, and it doesn't feel like a benevolent, loving, radiant thing. It's just this real intense energy that's in my space, perhaps observing. I feel comfortable with it.

I had that experience before I went to sleep one night, and I met a being in a dream. That itself was very loving, exciting and fun, and funny. And then recently I had that incredible sense of presence in the living room, the strongest I've ever felt it, then when I was in bed I was feeling it, and I woke up in the morning to find that a very heavy lamp had been moved, around other obstacles—including a huge singing bowl—and placed on the floor in a narrow gap by the side of my bed. And I have no history whatsoever of sleepwalking, or that kind of behavior, where I could have been responsible. It really was like this very physical marker, like someone was leaving a calling card to say that somebody was physically here.

Yeah. It's all really related to this project that you're doing. Because you're opening yourself to a lot of energies. We're not going to say other people's energies; you're opening up to your own energies, that have been around you and with you for a greater portion of your life. And through the work you're doing right now, it's giving you the confidence that you can open to it and connect with it. Sometimes they give these types of very physical signs, like the moving of objects or just the feeling of the intense energy presence as a way for you to begin to not question the validity of it so much.

Now we do sense a Pleiadian connection there. You said you've been talking with a lot of people who kept bringing up this Pleiadian idea. One of them is because of the Pleiadian energy that seems to be coming at you from many different angles. We're sensing one particular male Pleiadian that's a connection for you. It has nothing to do with any of us who are part of the book. It's your connection. And he is there kind of saying, "Miguel? Miguel?" Knocking on your head from time to time. But in fun, playful way. Not in a heavy way.

M: Okay, I'm going to take this a step further. I've had experiences which suggest to me that I've been many things other than human. I just don't feel very human at all. In fact I feel profoundly confused by humans. I really do. Again, I don't know what kind of access your consciousness has to this type of thing—I don't really know how you experience information—but I wonder if you have any of sense of what form I may have taken before the human form?

This is one of the reasons why Germane created the *Galactic Heritage Cards*, because Lyssa, Germane and Sasha were getting asked this question often. People want to know their galactic history and heritage. For the way Lyssa channels, gaining access to that information on a very deep level is often exhausting for her. Now we're talking about a full reading about that, we're not talking about just answering that quickly. So that's why the *Galactic Heritage Cards* were created, so Lyssa can work with them and access the information through there, but also so other people can access information through them.

In general, the answer to the question is that, again going back to the idea of the holographic model, that means that you have everything within you already. So any civilization, any species that you can think of, is part of the hologram, which means it is part of you. However, as you go through your various lives as a human being, there are times when certain thread connections to pieces of the hologram become stronger than others. And through your life this can change. So when we give you a brief answer here, we're going to say that this is the connection for you now. It's not your complete picture, because that is very much like layers of an onion.

So right now, we've mentioned to you about the Pleiadian energy. And we've mentioned to you about the connection to the male being. This male being would represent a future you, in a similar way that Sasha represents a future Lyssa.

But there's also a Sirian energy. Now the Pleiadian energy is more heart-centered, or emotional. The Sirian energy is the second energy we sense. It has more to do with your mental body. And the evolution of your thought processes, from linear to holographic. So the Sirian energy is working with you on that.

In terms of lineage, we would say that the two most 'recent' non-human lifetimes, if you are to plot them on a linear timeline, would be Sirian, for sure. As a Sirian interacting with Earth humans. This would be ... we're throwing a figure out there—please do not hold onto it, it's not exact—but approximately 40,000 years ago. There were also Pleiadian lifetimes as well. So Sirian and Pleiadian right now, in both your past and your future, are the active energies.

M: As you're speaking, questions are circling in my mind about the nature of time, and timelines. And how all of those things interact. Because as you're speaking there, I again got very strong imagery, and I had this sense of being all of these things at the same time. But I wonder how you relate to the idea of linear time.

Linear time is a convenience for physical beings, but it has absolutely no basis in reality. So when you are in a reality that's organized by an ego, which is basically a reality of separation where you are a singular being, then the linear time is a way to organize reality. However, as you begin moving into less of a singular-being orientation, and more into a connection with the holographic or holistic you, linear reality becomes no longer a convenience, but an obstacle to understanding the true nature of your consciousness. Therefore, your relationship to linear time, you as an individual and as a species, is now going to have to change. It's already starting to change.

This is why very often it's very hard for us to talk about galactic history. Putting galactic events on a human timeline it's like ... what do you say ... oil and water. They really don't mix. We use them for illustration, but they really don't mix.

M: Yeah, it's interesting even trying to find the words to have a conversation about time, from a linear perspective, when you're starting to have those little insights, those little experiences that are showing you that time doesn't exist as humans conceive it. For example, Lyssa and Miguel are in different physical places and time zones, yet our consciousness is connected, so time and space kind of evaporate. Because when consciousness connects, time and space really has no relevance.

Exactly. That is a very good example. Extrapolate that to Sasha in my reality, somewhere out there. It's exactly the same. Therefore, that old saying about 'the only time is now' is very true. Because in the now you have three beings in three different time zones connecting in this moment.

What is the most important message you can give to humanity at this time?

Ha ha!

M: *Ha ha!* Yeah. Have at it.

How long do you have? ....
Choosing ... is difficult.
We would say, continuing from the conversation we have had with you today, that one of the most important messages we have is to remind humans over and over again that they are not their bodies, they are not their minds, or their thoughts or emotions. They are not singular beings. They are multidimensional beings having a human experience, anchored by an ego, here in a physical reality. And this means that the ego is susceptible to all kinds of distractions. So the distractions of what's going on politically, and what's going on in religion, and in the drama of your relationship, or whatever it is, can very easily pull you out of that budding awakening of your wholeness. And it is very important in this crucial time of human transformation to not be pulled out of your awareness of your wholeness through the distraction of the physical world.

If you can allow yourself to find that place within you that is like the default setting, the default setting of your wholeness ... for some people it's through meditation, for some it may be through yoga. Whatever it is, find that default setting of your wholeness. And you are going to be needing to return to it over and over, and more and more, as the intensity of your world increases in the immediate years to come. They might be a bit intense and might be challenging you to go into distraction. We are reminding people not to do that. So for instance, this book, for those of you who are reading it, can be a way to pull you out of the distraction and guide you back into your wholeness, or back into that hallway with all the candles, so to speak. And you're going to be asked by reality to do this over and over again. One of the biggest distractions of the ego is to become attached to polarity. This person is right, that person is wrong. I am the only one with the truth, you are deluded. That polarized consciousness will mire you in the ego and mire you in physical reality.

One of the reasons so many of us beings are here now, is to help guide you out of that hall of mirrors so to speak, where you're seeing your own polarization and your own fragmentation bouncing back at you. We're here to guide you back from them and into the memory of your wholeness. When you go into the experience of your own wholeness—and again it is an experience, not a solely mental process—when you experience that wholeness, you then experience the dissolution of the distractive energies that bind you to the 3rd-density, physical, separative reality. That, from our hearts, in this moment, is the most important message we can give to guide humanity away from being lost and into their awakening process.

M: I guess it's anticipating other questions that I've had about how to do that at a personal level, because I guess in doing this work I've gone from the objective social scientist to ... I'm seeing the chrysalis/butterfly symbol, that kind of transformation. That will, that need, that desire, the inescapable process of having to move into that new level of authenticity. Which is a tough thing to do.

But connecting with you guys is incredibly supporting in doing that. And that I think is one of the most critical offerings of this whole project, as you were suggesting. It can be a reminder to people, it can be supportive of those who are going through this process of moving into wholeness, of identifying that. Even accepting that one's life as a human being is just one expression of a much larger being. Even those ideas are really tough ideas.

Yes. Miguel, you could have forced yourself to stay in the box of social scientist. And if you had done that with this book, you would be infinitely unsatisfied with the results. And your mind would have been infinitely unsatisfied with the answers, because you would be chasing every single question from a purely mental place. Obviously one of the reasons we would say it foisted itself upon you, so to speak, was because the greater you was attempting to stimulate a paradigm shift within you, for your future work. You've just described it. You could no longer sustain that rigid box of the social scientist. You had to go into the realm of the experiencer too. Which has afforded you the simultaneous view of both the scientist and the experiencer. That is a process of integration. So we are certainly not talking about exchanging the scientist for the experiencer, or exchanging the mind for the heart, but we are talking about a process of integration in which they become one.

It goes back to this whole idea of how, in the old days on your world, science and spirituality were one idea. Along the way they got separated, but they are going to find their way back to each other again, because that is the true nature of creation itself. God is empirically measurable when you know where to look, which is everywhere. So you allowed yourself to experience a form of alchemy for your own process, between the mind and the heart. And therefore you're also showing the reader that it can be done. And that's one of the reasons why the project felt like it was foisted upon you. It was very much about you, and shifting your paradigm so that you can have the passion as that candle and help light the other candles along the way.

M: That feels true. Even there I wasn't having to deal with it cognitively, it was coming through at a different level. It was just resonating as feeling profoundly true. And it's funny that there's been so many times in this session where I've had a question, and immediately you start giving me an answer. So that's amazingly efficient, in terms of process!

Ha ha! Well, our motivation is not efficiency my dear, but it is showing you the process Lyssa was talking about in her interview. The one holographic consciousness is expressing itself through the fractal of Lyssa and the fractal of Miguel, and they're working together in the flow of the project from different perspectives. You've just seen it in action.

Is there anything we haven't talked about that you wish to say?

Well we haven't said this directly, but we've kind of implied it. It's related to the previous question. We know that many people on your world are extremely worried about the physical reality and what is happening on your world. And this worry has been draining a lot of energy for a lot of people. And for many people it even causes a type of depression, or disengagement from the human experience. And we do have to say that, from the perspective of the all, or the one, the hologram, everything, always, in every moment, is completely balanced. Even though the human consciousness, the human mind sees the environment as toxic, or sees this or that and judges it and makes a story about it without seeing the bigger picture. There is a bigger picture, and on that level, everything is always in perfect balance.

It is not the job of the human ego to see that or to try to control that, because it cannot. What this brings you back to then is how you can experience peace, how you can fully engage the human reality, even though there's a lot of resistance to this from being human. The fact is, if you're reading this book as a human, you are here because it is part of the universal balance, and it is necessary for you to be here right now. And since right now is the only moment you have in which to be and to express, in this form that you are in now, why not fully engage it, fully embrace it? And learn to cultivate the trust that that universal balance is always there.

And if you can do so, then you begin to let go of the need to habitually control reality. Letting go, letting go, eventually allows you to be fully present, with all of your energy, in the present moment, embracing the experience. And in that moment, that's the doorway through which you can fully connect with, feel and experience your own wholeness. But it will require a little bit of work on the human level. It's okay. We know everyone is worried, but collectively, take a breath, relax, let go, and it is there where the peace can be found.

M: Thank you so much. It was fascinating, and it was useful, and it was just a really lovely experience. I'm so happy we met.

So are we. We certainly know it won't be the last time we connect. And you know we check in on you every once in a while. We were not the one who moved your lamp though!

M: I'm sure I'll find out who that was in due course. But do feel very free to drop by. Anything you think I need to be aware of, or reminded of, you are most welcome to let me know.

In fact, myself and my partner were having the discussion, in the week between Christmas and New Year's, about the fact that so many people seem to feel defeated and confused, and I have the sense that that's partly why the contact is stepping up - because we really need it.

And it also benefits us, because we get to experience that aspect of the hologram. The aspect of being alone and frightened and feeling separate. It enriches us as well, so it's definitely a two-way street.

M: Yeah, it's pretty tough down here. A lot of people struggle with the idea of non-human intelligences, but one of the things I really want people to understand is that it's a much more subtle thing than people realize. There's a whole other level of discussion to be had on this, and this is what I wanted for this project, that it almost does away with ETs and spacecraft, and is more about the true nature of the self, and of reality. And the value of understanding those things, awakening to them, embracing them and integrating them in our human journey.

Exactly. We agree 100%.

So, we're going to bring Lyssa back, and she will speak with you shortly. So thank you so much for your very insightful questions, and for being part of the flow from the Miguel fractal. Much love to you.

M: And to you.

Darlene Van de Grift

Darlene Van de Grift is an internationally respected Medical Intuitive whose skills, talents, gifts and strengths attract clients from all walks of life. Her skill, refined by over 30 years of dedication, is accessing and understanding what clients think they want for themselves versus what their bodies truly need, crave and are ready to release. Our bodies have their own innate wisdom that our lifestyles often compromise.

Darlene, founder of A Way to Better Health Massage School, taught her students anatomy, physiology and massage. That credentialed curriculum expanded to include: Kinesiology, Touch for Health, One Brain, Nutrition, Relationship Counseling, Matrix Energetics and Inner Child work. She also taught Intension Muscle Balancing, a unique interactive healing modality created by her mother Charlotte. It uses isometric movements designed to alleviate pain and retrain injured muscles to regain proper function.

Darlene's talent is how warmly she welcomes every issue, challenge and opportunity that clients bring to their session. One of her key strengths is comfortably creating safety and respect for their journey. Her talent for weaving clarity into the fibers of their past, present and future lives provides a rich tapestry to help clients embrace a deeper understanding and appreciation of their experience of life.

Darlene's unique gift is collaborating and sharing the wisdom she gathers from her Guides, Ancestors, Akashic Records, other dimensions, timelines and galactic life forms. She consistently directs this data and information toward healing and opening new portals for herself, clients, family and friends.

Darlene is a devoted mother, grandmother and loving partner. Her greatest pleasure is creating pathways and being part of our journey back to realizing our truly remarkable selves.

Her website is: soulunion.com

Which words do you use to describe 'them'?

It depends on who I am talking to, but I think the word that fits best, that they like, is 'interdimensional beings', or 'cosmic beings'. They dislike 'ETs' because it has a different flavor and history attached that they don't want to be associated with. There's some information available about being benevolent, but the majority of information that we are taught or shown through movies and the media is not benevolent. They are portrayed as malevolent, and are considered evil in some ways. You know, they're out to destroy us, they're horrid. Not True.

I spoke with Rebecca (Hardcastle Wright) over the weekend, who was at a conference, and she said there were so many speakers talking about the evil nature of ETs, and that humans need to destroy them. She said that the Catholic Church is doing thousands of exorcisms each week to release these ETs, because they are out to destroy us. The interdimensional beings' understanding of this is that yes, there are what they call "misguided ones." They wouldn't label them evil or bad, but as misguided; beings that don't resonant with the light as other ETs or dimensionals do.

So they don't like the word 'ET', but they will go with it because we don't use many other words for them. A 'light being' is an acceptable name also. But 'ETs' to them is not a positive reference. They like to keep their vibration pure, and as clean as they can when merging into this 3rd dimension. It takes a lot for them to enter here and have communication with us, whether that's in physical form, as some of them do, or within our own internal dialogue with them through telepathy. They have to cross barriers and keep their frequency stable to make contact. So even the name is a bit offensive and lowers their vibration.

Which kinds of beings are you in contact with?

I'm in contact with a variety of them. The Reptilians I deal with are considered 'defectors'. I just read in your last book about defectors in relation to those leaving the government in order to disclose the government's connection with ETs for the last 50 years. But that's what they are referred to as: defectors. These are Reptilians, at least at this moment. There may be others species, that would be considered 'misguided ones', that are not in alignment with what some Reptilians may or may not be doing that is harmful to humanity. So I work with 'defectors' in different forms of mediation.

I primarily work with all ETs around timelines. I am either dissolving, diminishing, deleting or integrating them. Those interdimensional beings I'm guided by take over after the mediation. There is a process that continues in vetting or discerning their integrity within this group. My understanding of that is that it's almost like a trial period.

I have found that the defectors I've met have little to no ego left. Who they have been or how they have been used or mistreated has brought them to a new realization, and they are humbled to let go of their old paradigm and be seen as having a greater potential. A few have come with a price on their head and seek refuge. So defectors are not totally welcomed in, yet. It's not assumed that they go from the misguided type of a being to a more benevolent being and are welcomed in immediately. There's a series of, I would say trials or tests - being part of the group and being observed. I don't take part in that, but my understanding is that that is some of what is happening in this transition of the defectors.

I work with Blue Avians. They come in individually, or in groups of three. I also work with a lot of hybrids—not on this 3rd dimension— that are a combination of Pleiadian, Arcturian, Sirian and various other cultures. I don't get so involved in their culture. I am primarily working with what they want to clear, and their interconnected relationships with humans, and sometimes with each other. So it's a wide variety of beings, depending on who they present to me.

I primarily talk to one from an Andromedan group, who are all androgynous. I would look at them as very female, but they breed within themselves, so there are no sexual encounters. They come in all shapes and sizes. I've seen them mainly in shades of blues and greens. But some of them have feathers cascading down the back of their heads, on their forearms or have feathered tails. I believe their feathers are significant in their culture. Their meaning is represented in where the feathers are located on their body. It doesn't feel like status, it's more an indicator of respect, or their history, or what they've been born into.

So I work with many different species. More show up at night, different ones, which feel like they're in and out. There's no conversation. For the most part they're pretty neutral or are observing and curious. I'm not necessarily working with them, I'm just aware they are around.

How do they appear to you?

There was a period of eight to ten years, in the mid-to-late 80s, through to around '95-'96, where they were in the bedroom every night. They were three hooded beings. I believe they were probably the smaller Greys or they could have been small Whites. They appear either beside the bed or by the windows, in the different places that I lived. It wasn't alarming to me. I'm a light sleeper, so I would roll over and I would see them and nod, and I would get confirmation that they were there, and I would fall back to sleep. That happened almost nightly. In fact, when that stopped, the contact became an internal, clairvoyant, clairaudient thing. I hear them, I see them, and I'm called to meetings. They will show up, and say we need some of your time. Sometimes it's immediate, and sometimes we'll make an agreement depending on my schedule.

A month or so ago, I was reading your book in a diner, waiting to be picked up by my partner. I was tucked in a corner and when I looked up there was a Grey that appeared in the aisle and slid into my booth across from me. I wanted to feel him, so I put my arm out and he slid his very thin wrist and forearm under my hand and put his other four fingers on top. He only stayed around 30 seconds, to give me new coordinates to connect, because there was that breach, which I'll explain later. They couldn't stay in the locations I was used to meeting them, which were usually remote nature settings, so they had to give me a new location. These locations are not of a physical nature, they're a mental place that I would energetically travel to. He said, "You now have the coordinates," then moved out of the booth and disappeared. I was looking around at this time like, "Is anyone else seeing this?" But everybody else was just eating their meals. There were no servers who came up to the table. I was looking around thinking, 'This is both ridiculous and awesome.' But I saw him, and it was the first time I had that close of an interaction in this dimension. Other than the three that visited me at night, and I don't remember if there was more to it than that. I remember they were very present, very physical. It seemed like they were in waiting, all those years.

Can you describe your first contact?

I have two. One was very early on when I was four, maybe five years old. I used to love to go outside and talk to the insects. And our property had a whole border of lilac bushes, and at night I would go out and listen to them grow. I could hear the roots growing. Which I didn't think was unusual at the time.

My father built this L-shaped fireplace outside, with a sink and storage, and it was probably seven feet tall. I remember playing in the dirt behind the fireplace, with sticks and ants, which I loved to do. My first recollection is that I sensed somebody on my left, and I thought it was my father so I didn't pay any attention. But it got closer, and energetically it started to feel like it wasn't my father so I was afraid to look. I don't remember running. It was more like I was so frightened I couldn't move. I remember still stooping with the stick in my hand. There was a very gentle voice that said that he was here for me. I remember being touched on the right shoulder, and I felt very warm and comforted. When he vanished I sensed there was a residue, is the best way I can describe it. Something was given to me at that moment.

There were other times in my childhood. My bed was right under a window. I remember turning away from the window so I didn't see them coming in. But I don't know what happened during those times.

The second contact was an experience I had when I was around 37 or 38, and my mother had gone through a regression in a workshop. Both the therapist and my mother after the regression told me that it was something they wanted me to listen to in my own space. When I listened to it, I was hearing she had an abduction, and it was very frightening for her. In the regression I could hear her terror. And there was a voice that immediately came up inside me, which said, "We did not do this, it was not us." I didn't know what that voice was. But I could see internally that it was a hooded being, probably one of those who were visiting me at night.

I started channeling at that point, and did that for four or five years. It was an interdimensional being called Eli Wizar, and he was part-Reptilian. It meant 'the wizard' in their culture. And I channeled him for about four years, until he finished his mission here. There was a group that had been together in another lifetime where he was present, who were also Reptilian. And he needed to clear that lifetime. That was probably in early '91.

As I look back on it, this was what started me clearing timelines, and my precursor to becoming a mediator. There were six or seven other beings that were in Eli's timeline, and all of them were part of a group of people who came into my life at that time. It's interesting that nothing is a coincidence. As Eli came through in that group, there would be conversations in which he would acknowledge what happened in that timeline that he felt accountable for. And we would ask questions of the group for his clarity. Eventually the timeline was complete for him and he chose to leave. I have in the last year been reacquainted with him, as he is now part of the interdimensional team I work with. Eli was my first interdimensional teacher.

Eli. A Reptilian renegade who supports the advancement of Humanity. Member of the Galactic Federation. Credit: Darlene Van de Grift

Can you explain what a timeline is and how and why it would be 'cleared'?

A timeline, as I work with it, is a thread that connects this present moment to the past or future of an individual. If there is an issue, behavior, pattern or even a question of concern, there is always a beginning. The beginning can be a past-life experience, an in utero experience, a genetic factor, or something that occurred later in this life. That thread is tracked to its original cause, then significant events are added or experienced that are relative to the timeline up to the present day and sometimes beyond. Once that is established, the solutions for diminishing or deleting that timeline are presented to me through audial, visual or kinesthetic means. Usually the individual is given a completion process to undertake privately, but sometimes I facilitate the process. This unravels the timeline so it has less or no usefulness to the person in their present or future. As guidance explained it, it's like a pearl necklace with all the pearls representing times and events connected to one issue. When the thread is pulled out you release that timeline and the person has no attachment to any of the pearls.

It takes commitment and understanding on the person's behalf to work with their timelines. But I also find that some behaviors or patterns in timelines are still useful to the person and can only be diminished. However, the individual will understand why the behaviors and patterns are beneficial and how to manage them better.

Those years with Eli were my first experiences of bringing a group together to create harmony and resonance. When that timeline was cleared, between those present-day relationships, he moved on. I also chose not to channel after that in that same capacity. I didn't like the feeling of an entity or another being coming through my body. Following that I was used as more of a mediator, as opposed to bringing an entity into me. Up until this past weekend, but that's a whole other thing that I'll get to.

I channeled this group probably up until around '95. Following that there was a more significant connection. What changed for me at that time became several months of ranting my rage at God. I needed to come to a place of peace and love within myself and with my first connection with my childhood God. In doing so I became more clairaudient, I could see things, and they could talk to me. It was more of an introduction to how to maintain clarity within myself to articulate their information. It's very important for who I am, to have value in the information received and to relate. I grew up feeling there was no good and bad. That concept wasn't embraced in my family; my mother could never understand how I could believe that since I was raised to be religious. It was an adamant feeling that there just *is*, with no judgments. I believe 'evil' is a word that can be overstated. There are other words that you could use such as 'disharmony', or being 'misguided'. Evil is a word I rarely if ever use. I need to have everything be very truthful. If I received information that didn't feel truthful it created an internal conflict.

Becoming the mediator, maintaining that ground to be truthful and contain value, was crucial for guidance, for the information they wanted to convey, and for who I believe I am as a human being.

Saari. Behavioral Analyst. Experimented with human emotions and through that found her capacity to love. Now is part of core group facilitating work with timelines. Credit: Darlene Van de Grift

How do you connect now?

If they want something from me they show up. On a regular basis, not a daily basis, I will look for them. I'll look ⁺⁻   ᵢ ᵢ   ᵧ ...ng I need to be doing or knowing on that day. I ɪɪ ask: "Is there anybody here that has a message for me?" Sometimes there isn't any connection available. Contact has been severely diminished since that breach. I also think they've been distant because of what happened this weekend. It feels like they were in preparation for what occurred, and they distanced themselves so that this event would be more prominent and powerful, which it was.

I can ask questions of them, and most of the time they will send one or more to give me an answer. I used to have 45 minutes to an hour in conversation with them, but recently that's been limited to 10-20 minutes because of the breach.

So I'll describe the breach. There was a very close relationship that I felt with them for a long time. Then in the beginning of September there was no contact for nine days. At first I was kidding around that maybe they were at an ET conference. The longer I went without contact the more concerned I became. They did make contact at the end of nine days, and that's part of why that ET showed up, to give me coordinates. Three of them came as a hologram, initially, to tell me that there was a breach. My understanding is that there were human remote viewers that were assigned to investigate the frequency where connections with dimensional beings were being conducted and interfere with that frequency. The guidance I work with thought the breach was more widespread than it was. There were a number of ET 'contactors' whose contact was influenced by the interference in this particular frequency location. Several governments set that into action, and my understanding is that it is still happening. The dimensional beings that many of us have been working with are prepared, and are standing down. They are finding new locations. But they are not backing down in our connections that they've fostered for a long time. They are not creating a war with humans on Earth, but there is an intellectual technology war that is going on in that frequency.

Now I'll explain what happened at the weekend. There were 29 of us at a meeting of the Northeast CE-5 group in upstate New York. The term CE-5 refers to a fifth category of close encounters with extraterrestrial intelligences, involving two-way communication, as opposed to one-way contact. It was developed by Steven Greer and others, and has become a global network. Our group is led by Marilyn Gewacke, whom you interviewed in *We Are the Disclosure - Part I*, and Diane and Jen. How Marilyn leads the group is always from the heart. It becomes like a love fest over two days, because there is no ego with any participant. Skywatching for craft is such a small part of what happens in Marilyn's groups - it's much deeper. Finding the ET in you, resonating with that, and coming from a place of inviting interdimensional beings into a very loving community is the heart of the matter. It's one of the most profound groups I've ever experienced. There is no ego, no right or wrong. Marilyn's group is made up of truly amazing people that bring their contact beings with them.

We were being led in a process that was very benign for me. It was a regression. I do that in my own work so it wasn't anything special. But as I lay on the floor I was instantly out, and that's not normally what happens. I thought I was out for a really long time, but then I heard the instructor saying, "And now what do you see?" I looked around and I was in a boy's body in the middle of a desert, tending camels. There were craft overheard, and we were being attacked. I don't know if they were ET or military craft, or what they were. I was there for maybe 30 seconds, and I was trying to hide underneath a camel. I felt as if I was sucked out of that lifetime and thrown into this lifetime at three months in utero. I have a remembering, that rose to my consciousness prior to this, in which I lost a twin sister in utero. I had always connected to the loss of that relationship and felt I had a missing piece in my life. But I never looked at how I got here in this body. So that awareness of being yanked out of one body and being thrown into this body, and the difficulty that occurred in my in utero experience, was alarming.

The instruction was done within ten minutes, and I remember sitting up and talking to the group about the experience, and how I needed to sort through it. But I never came fully back into my body. So I got up and went to Marilyn and said, "You need to hold my hands, because I don't know what the heck's going on here." She made eye contact with me and I felt a bit better. I went outside and I was seeing all kinds of timelines; I was seeing ETs walking on the planet, dead people, cities where there were no cities. I was very much in many different dimensions, and it was very disconcerting. They worked with me for 30-40 minutes; I don't remember much of it.

But I do know that a portal was opened for a new presence to come in. The best way to describe it is that it opened a space within me so that I would have more access. There was a woman there—thank goodness—who was trained as an Oracle by Buddhists to do shamanic work. She saw what was happening, that I wasn't coming back to the present. So she took me upstairs with a few friends, two of whom were my shaman friends. She did a ceremony to help the integration I was experiencing and remove any negativity that was being presented. Her understanding was that I was bringing in a major piece of transformation for the planet, and that there were other malevolent energies that didn't want that to happen. I was dealing with that conflict internally, which is certainly how it felt. When she finished I almost instantly felt myself again. So thank God it didn't last for hours with me doing my own work; I'm not even sure I would have been able to manage that. A few people that were present at the Oracle's ceremony saw wisps of energy leave my body and dissipate.

That whole experience was very emotionally draining for me. I don't remember a lot of it. When I went back to the group, their understanding was that there were major timeline shifts for everybody in the group, and everyone got something from the experience. A few of them were very freaked out for me, but the 28 of them held the space for this to happen. The group did their debriefing while I was resting, and some people couldn't talk as they were still in their own process.

The next morning, I still didn't have clarity on what occurred. I asked for guidance from anyone on my interdimensional team to let me know what happened. Several of them came in. They said it was important and necessary that my sight increase and my sensory information increase. A new being provided space for me to do that. They're calling her a "Blue Crystal Celestial being." I asked if celestial means she is angelic. They said they consider themselves all celestial beings. I said, "As in angelic?" They said, "No, she is celestial." I believe the difference is being made because humans have signified what angelic means in our own creation and that is not an appropriate term for who she is. I was told there's an integration process, with my body becoming more resonant with her, until November 9th. I will check in at that time to get further information.

Blue Crystal Being. Credit: Darlene Van de Grift.

On the Sunday morning I spoke about this to the group, and the clarity of what it feels like to be a starseed and come into physical form. A starseed is a soul who originates from other planets or galaxies that volunteered to assist Earth through her next phase of evolution into a more loving, peaceful existence.

Being a starseed, living in another place and time and coming here to Earth, is like packing and saying goodbye to all that is familiar to you. Goodbye to your family and friends. Packing everything you think you could possibly need here, not knowing that even when you get here, you will not remember what you packed. In this 3rd dimension, on this planet, where people have choice, you're at a disadvantage of not knowing exactly what's going to happen. So you don't know exactly what to pack.

I also spoke to the group about this awakening, and bringing in this new energy. Not that I'm not familiar with it, as I was introduced to Blue Crystal energy several months ago, but not as a being. At this moment I don't know how to utilize this new Blue Crystal being. But the experience was an eye-opener and I was totally grateful for the outcome and connection.

The groups of interdimensional beings that I've worked with through the years have always been good at not telling me what's in store for me in situations like this. I would prefer it that way, so I don't feel like I'm consciously creating it. When I first started channeling I thought, 'I'm making this up.' I didn't like it. It wasn't comfortable. It took years to trust the process, and trust who I was working with. Over time we developed a relationship. I've always felt taken care of by them. I've felt like I've led a very blessed life in living in this place and time, although there's been turmoil and heartache. But it's not that bad; people have it worse.

That's what happened at that CE-5 weekend, and I'm in the process of working with the Blue Crystal being. I can tell you that Monday and Tuesday, in my private sessions with clients, they've changed drastically. In fact, several people asked, "What happened to you?" But I did not go into detail. The guidance I was getting for clients had a more open-hearted space for conversation and connection. Another marked shift since the weekend is an expansion of information about how to cut their timelines, resolve addictions through examining patterns they've done for eons, and how to work through that.

Can you initiate contact?

For me the contact wasn't about reaching out to them. My initial desire was to dive as deep as I could within myself and expand my consciousness. I wanted to connect psychically, telepathically with other beings. When I started all this I didn't know that it was going to be about ETs. In fact, those eight to ten years of them showing up felt normal, so I never told anybody. I have discovered later in life that ETs were very much part of the experience of my mother, father and brother. I believe my connection to ETs is most likely genetic.

My own exploration started with learning how to do visualization, which I'm very good at. Guided meditations helped me open up my third eye to all possibilities. Then I was reading several books on how to go into the alpha state. At first I used to just blank out and I would always fall asleep. One day I remember sitting down to practice the alpha state, determined to not fall asleep. It came so suddenly, and I was being shot through the universe, seeing hundreds of faces and beings, and traveling among the stars. I remember being given information at that point. It was fascinating to drop into that zone and allow the information to be downloaded without me creating it. That access was created through deep meditation and wanting to reach a higher state of consciousness.

The other thing was driving. Driving is a valuable time for me in my connection with interdimensional beings. As I was driving I would ask to see what this location looked like a hundred years ago, or a thousand. And I would be shown those images. I would then see the area as fields, or a mountain would show up. I had no way of knowing if any of that was real or not, but I believe it opened that capacity in the third eye to bring in information. Those were the two avenues that I found initially to receive information and eventually contact.

When you want to connect with any other being, including humans, I think you need to meet them with an open heart and neutrality. They are here to serve us as much as we are here to serve them. We are on their timeline. Some of them I've met are my future selves that are dimensional beings. The Blue Avian that I spoke about has told me that in the distant future he is a great-great-great-great grandfather on my timeline.

So it's the desire, the open-heartedness. Because of how I work with timelines, I believe that who you attract or connect with are part of your DNA, whether it's been a past life or whether it's in your genetic human DNA. I don't think we attract that which is unfamiliar to our cellular level.

One of the most significant ways that helped me create contact was learning how to do kinesiology. This was back in the 70s, and I had a fascination with this because my mother had terminal cancer and was healed by a chiropractor using kinesiology in his practice, in combination with other modalities. I was fascinated with connecting to the body through the subconscious and receiving guidance that was truthful and not what the person perceived. I was introduced to Touch for Health when I was 17, when my mother was given six months to live. I continue to use kinesiology as a tool, but somewhere along the line it changed to a form that became solely mine. I believe that tapping into a different place within the body, within the psyche, opened me up to who I am today. It is an access point, and for me it's a truthful access point, as long as I step out of the way and stay neutral. When none of my thoughts and beliefs interfere, the truth emerges, and most of the time the content is a surprise. I do believe that that's part of it: get out of the way and allow guidance to guide. After all, 'they' do know better.

Sometimes when I'm in conversation with the ETs, I am checking it out in my way to find out if their information is accurate and not being influenced by me. And I would say that 99% of the time, what they are saying is coming from a higher perspective and not myself.

How do you differentiate between your own thoughts and those from outside?

There are a few different ways that I differentiate me from them. My interjected thoughts are very uncomfortable to me when I am receiving information and having contact. There were a few instances where I felt like this is my mind doing this, it is not pure information, and I shut it down. I can be demanding, saying, "No, if this me making this up, you have to tell me in a different way. Because if this is coming from you, I'm not getting it, and I don't like it."

So it feels like there is a boundary or barrier that I have in discerning what's my mind or information from them. There is always a watchful part of me, observing my ego in any connection, and ensuring that the information isn't self-serving. The curious or most interesting part in receiving from them is that their information is usually surprising. Meaning that the information offered is not something that I would ever have considered.

Why do they connect with you?

We don't attract anything or any being that doesn't resonate with us. I think this is true whether you're working with dimensional beings, ETs, past lives or any guidance.

I've been introduced to 28 beings on my full team. Many of them are not a part of me in a past or future life, but they hold aspects or qualities that I draw from. For example, I am very justice-oriented, and I have a being that works with me that is also very justice-oriented. I also have a being with me that cannot lie, and always speaks her mind. She doesn't have the capability of lying in her DNA. When I got first introduced to her I couldn't keep my mouth shut about the truth. Whatever personal truth came to mind in a conversation, I would verbalize it. I'd struggle internally with how I would normally be quiet (staying invisible in life has always been important), but my mouth would open and I couldn't hold back. I needed that aspect in my life and in my work. The beings I meet are the ones that have resonance with me. It is either an aspect that they have that I'm familiar with, or an aspect in myself that needs attention. That allows me to receive their information and connect in harmony. They get a benefit from sharing an aspect, as do I. Especially if they are on my past or future timeline. Connection seems to work that way for me; I don't feel like anyone comes to me that is not familiar to me.

It has happened on occasion, not through my intention or guidance, that a being will show up that I am not familiar with. My guard is up because I don't know them, I don't resonate with them, their frequency doesn't feel familiar. Therefore there's less welcoming from my side. I'll listen, or ask what that is, but a lot of times they move on very quickly. They're not there for anything other than to observe.

I believe that the influence of the beings is present in most of my client sessions, even though they don't appear the same to me as in my personal work, because they open doors for me as I'm working.

And somewhere along the line you know what I think would be important? I'd like to offer you a session so you get a feel for how this works.

M: S⁻⁻ ̄ ̄

It feels like there is a band of protection around you, and that it's warranted. The band has to be taken down or dismantled by going inside. It is not a protection in terms of something or someone is out to get you; rather you are being contained until you're ready to germinate. When you decide you're willing and capable enough, then that shell breaks open and you emerge. That form of protection or shell has a crack and is not sealed like it was prior to you writing your books. You are finding your way through that crack, in order for the shell to fall away, and you can really present who you are. Everything that you're doing, the books and the people you're talking to, is bringing you out and forward into another realm of possibility. In this process, you beginning to know who you are will be important for all involved.

M: It's funny you say that, because earlier as you were talking many of these same thoughts were going through my head. In some cases almost word for word.

One, knowing who you were might be important. Two, knowing what you're capable of, and why you came here is very important. All of what you have done so far is on this timeline. Even you being involved with the environment, at the level you were, and how that came to you, it feels like that's a significant piece in what is going to be next for you. Not that you'll be back doing that work, but there is a particular knowledge base you have from being in that community; and now you're in this community. It feels like these are two significant pieces of you, to get you to the next place, and the next. Does that make sense?

M: It does. I've been feeling like there are all these parts of me floating around, and I need to better integrate it all. I've started playing music again, and I feel like that's helping this integration process, sorting through things emotionally.

Back in the 80s, before I labeled things as timelines, I always felt like I was a weaver, bringing people's pieces together. I loved doing that. I am a seamstress, I am an artist, and so it was very natural for me to see people's patterns and pull them together, and discard what didn't work. That's part of how I started working with timelines and weaving people's life pieces together. That weekend at CE-5 proved to me that the Blue Crystal being—whoever or whatever that is—is significant to me, and feels like it's one of my last pieces, if not my last piece. I always thought it was my sister missing that was my screw-up, that I didn't have my twin, and that was my missing piece. But after this weekend, this is the piece I've been waiting for. I don't know what to do with it yet. But it feels right to claim this as the piece I've been waiting for.

Now is your time for integration and understanding. So that you can sort through the value of that part of your life, creating a foundation for you, a knowing that you can springboard into whatever's next. As I'm looking at your template that they're showing me around you, there isn't much in this lifetime that hasn't been of value to you, in supporting where you need to go. People, places and positions have all been there for you in the right place at the right time. Bringing you to a place of significance as a writer, an artist, even a musician. It comes up that the music is your soothing and your salvation. The music itself is tuning you up. You are sometimes in such dense vibration, with the people you're working with, with the information that you're writing. The eyes that are going to be watching you—if they're not already—that has a density. And it feels like the music has the potential to shift that, to give you some relief, to move things. I'm very happy you're back into your music.

M: What I love about music is that there's almost no point talking about it. I concluded by the end of *We Are the Disclosure* and *Meet the Hybrids* that there is so much of this subject that is beyond language. We don't have the words for it. It doesn't even work to try to put language to it. It doesn't mean anything. It's purely experiential. You feel it. And so it is with music. Of course if you're composing, and especially if working with other people, it helps to have a linguistic platform for discussing the structures you're using, but when jamming I rarely pay attention to what is happening at a theoretical level. You're guided through musical intuition, which works faster than the mind's analytical capacity. You feel your way to the key and the dynamics within the piece. We could play long pieces, maybe 45 minutes, that would have many sections, styles, tempos and so on, and none of that would be prearranged. Music is real magic that you can experience. It's a truly magical thing.

It is, and that's why I believe there is so much sound healing out there now. Drumming, gongs, crystal bowls and other instruments, all relieve us of residue, and debris, that we don't have to think about. We don't have to process through it. It cleanses the chakras. And because we have an emotional attachment to certain types of music, it does raise the vibration. Sound and music offers us relief in many ways.

Interview Session Two

M: I'm going to describe my recent dream state contact experience, because it feels pertinent. And you clearly helped trigger it. After we had our session about my guides, I wanted to connect with them, so I was doing guided meditations on this for a couple of nights. And the night it happened I'd been doing one by James van Praagh called 'Know Your Spirit Guides', and then one by Dakota Walker called 'Connecting with Your Spirit Guides'. And as I got deeper into the latter, instead of getting sleepier I was feeling charged up. My mind and body, and the whole room, was so energized. It was really hard to get to sleep. I was feeling this rising, intense energy in my mind, body and in the room. I had to throw the covers off and I tossed and turned for ages. I'd interviewed Jacquelin Smith earlier in the day, and I remembered her saying that the energy gets really charged in the room before a contact experience. And I was thinking about what Vashta Narada had said in our interview about protection: you have to *know* you are safe. So I was focused on being in my power. But I still wasn't really expecting contact. Maybe because I didn't know what to expect.

Eventually I dropped off, but I woke up too early in the morning, about half seven, and decided to just fall asleep again. Then I had the dream. I was in a house I didn't recognize, and I was dealing with a blocked toilet, of all things. I thought, 'I would love it if I was dreaming and could just wake up, because I really don't want to have to deal with this.' Then I looked around, wondering if I was dreaming. It felt real enough, but I wasn't sure. Then there was a bright flash of white light to my right. The door was slightly ajar, and as I looked at it more flashes of light came through, but now they were multicolored, not just white. And I suddenly thought, with great excitement, 'I think I'm having a contact!'

Then I pictured in my mind's eye the Reptilian hybrid being that you told me about, who is one of my guides, and I wondered if it was this guy coming to see me. And I had never before seen anything in my mind's eye while in a dream. So that was unique.

I was bursting with excitement at the idea of a contact, and ran out of the room, turned right and went down the hall to the bedroom, which had no door. There was a humanoid being stood at the foot of the bed, and I looked him up and down briefly. He was about five feet tall, wearing a blue jumpsuit, and he had orange skin and a bald, not overly large head, which was flatter on top than your archetypal Grey. His head also had these interesting symmetrical indentations, slightly to the side. And I knew it was a him somehow.

I felt this overwhelming sense of familiarity, love and joy, and I ran over and threw my arms around him. We hugged for a couple of seconds then I drew back. But I didn't want to let him go. I reached for his left hand and saw it had three fingers and a thumb. His skin was the softest thing I have ever felt. And the flesh was kind of pudgy. I squeezed a little more firmly and could feel the bones of his fingers and hand.

Then I became more aware of the light coming from the end of the room, where the head of the bed was. All around the edges of the far wall was like a seam of bright white light, and the light was somehow very clean. I then saw that the center of the wall had white and colored light coming through it, like the wall was softening and thinning.

He said telepathically that it was time to go, and I was fine with that. But I said telepathically that I wanted to get a selfie with us. If you meet up with your friends, what do you do? You want to take pictures together. I could picture the photo in my mind, of me with my arm around his shoulders and us grinning and laughing. And I felt like I wanted people to know that it was real. But he motioned to the light and said telepathically that the photo wouldn't come out. I said no, it's fine, I'll just screw around with the settings and figure it out.

And that's the last thing I remember. As I was aware I was waking up I kept my eyes closed and just played it back in a loop, about five times, going over every detail, looking at it all, and feeling it all again. I then wrote it up in my journal, including a quick sketch of the guy. Then I messaged Robert Fullington, and wrote, 'Now I know why you refer to your Mantis beings as 'loving family'! It was, from the flashes of light onwards, a profound and beautiful experience.

I had so much energy that day it was incredible. Normally, because of my illness, I do well to get to the supermarket and back, but I did a four-hour round trip in the car, by myself, to go guitar hunting. I tried out a bunch of guitars in Manson's Guitar Shop in Exeter, but something was telling me, 'No, your guitar is not here. It's back where you came from.' Fine. I told the store manager this, because you never know what seed you might plant, and saddled up and drove two hours through rush hour traffic to get to a store called PMT in Bristol. Each road I took was somehow clear of traffic, despite the hour, and I got to the store with surprising ease. Then I tried a bunch of Strats through the same amp I have. And when I found *the one* and played it, I was hearing my Small Stone phaser pedal coming through, even though I was using no effects at the time. So I thought, 'Huh,' and tried a different guitar. No weirdness. I switched back to the first one, and this time I heard my Cry Baby wah pedal. And the thought hit me: 'I'm hearing the future, because I'm going to buy this guy, and I'll playing it using my effects and this amp.' So I bought it. And I told the store manager this one too, because again: why not?

These experiences appear more often early in the morning because we can receive and remember them more clearly. There are some interesting things you said, if you'd like me to give my input.

M: Absolutely.

I met an unusual being in probably July or August, just once, and he reminded me of a beluga whale. He had a bulbous, but flat head, and he had yellowish-orange skin. I'm wondering if they were the same type of being. When you described him they felt similar, like cousins. I would have to look at my notes about why he appeared. I was hiking at a waterfall not far from here, and he literally popped in. When you were describing your contact they seemed similar. There are so many various species from planets and galaxies we don't even know exist. For as many species of animals and insects that we have here on Earth, I think there are just as many various shapes and forms of beings out there.

You remember when we did a session and I described your guides? This could have been the being that was in the shadow. Remember there were four, but there was one who was not willing to come forward? It feels like he's connected to your cellular memory in some way. It could be you in another dimension; it could be a connection or a lineage.

There are two things about your contact. One, he was surprised by your enthusiasm! Because that isn't what they would understand humans would do. You reacted very differently and are encouraging to them. As I'm checking in with that, there was a bit of a surprise for them but they sensed your enthusiasm and your genuinene   was a pleasurable contact.

The other thing is, you know that crack in the wall you saw? Try to get yourself into a relaxed, meditative state and take yourself through that crack. Practice that being your avenue and see what opens up or who comes in. That crack is a calling card. The light through the crack is the other dimension; it's where they come from, it's an access point. I would recreate the scene in the room as you remember it, and walk towards that crack, and see what happens, or what felt sense you have. Can you investigate the crack, does it open? You're allowing your mind's eye to explore this other dimension, which you might not have been doing before. It's an exercise to keep that connection open, which can create contact for you. In effect you are saying you want more. Doing it through your mind's eye, and maintaining availability is saying, "I'm ready, I'm here." See where that exercise takes you, as opposed to waiting for them to come to you again.

With hearing the guitar effects coming through the amplifier, you jumped timelines. So whatever that dimensional place was that you had accessed, it was part of you that day.

This is not only about the being you met, it's the access point, it's the willingness you had, and it's what was gifted to you after that. That was an energetic cellular day for you; so that was a gift. Finding this guitar and being able to feel and hear the future was also a gift. That experience wasn't only a dimensional shift for you, there's a cellular shift too. As you are working with this being, or other beings that will contact you, they are here to help you with that shift. That could be tapping into a future piece of yourself, or it could be finding out something about who you were in the past, or it could be beings that come to connect with you in the now. A cellular shift can minimize or delete physical timelines also. After all, illness is energy too. In shifting one's energy you can have more stamina. Their primary focus with you is to bring more light into your cells, and give you more energy to work with.

It's also about what you've tapped into; that isn't a one-time thing. You opened a window, now it's about you stepping forward into it. Not recreating that particular contact, because we can't recreate, but we can always invite and move into what's next. If you've jumped timelines, then you have some ability to do that. You may not know that you have that ability, other than that experience with the guitar, but if you can accept that it's possible to jump timelines, then set an intention. First, know that jumping a timeline is possible, then slightly sh̶ ̶ ̶ ̶ ̶ ̶ ̶ther way of being, and move in that direction and e̶ ̶ ̶ ̶ ̶ ̶line.

For example, when you have a certain reaction to stress, maybe you tend to be argumentative. In the middle of that reaction you choose to do something else. For example, choose instead to walk away, apologize, or deflect your nature to argue. That is how you jump timelines. Once you get the hang of it, it's as simple as if you are tuning to another station on the radio.

Go through the crack, set an intention and say, "I want to jump a timeline (be somewhere or someone else)", or "I want to meet a being", or "I want to be shown something." Or you can ask what's going to be helpful to you and/or others. Put your questions out there, because they respond really well to questions. They can't give us information unless we're questing for it.

M: The night after it happened I was thinking about it in bed, and I had the thought, 'I can shift the energy.' Just that. I understood that meant that I could create the conditions for contact, and make the call, ra̶ ̶ ̶ ̶ ̶ ̶ ̶ the receiving end.

Yes you can. You can ask for things. In my experience they may say, "Not now. It's not time." Or even, "It's none of your business." But there are so many beings you can work with, that if one doesn't know or can't help, it can move it to someone else. But if you know you can shift the energy to co-create, that's what they're looking for. They don't want to show up just to say, "It's really nice meeting you." They want to work, to co-create. They're not here for our entertainment.

M: Yeah, although I'm pretty sure we are fabulous entertainment for them.

Well *you* were! Like you said, he felt like a long-lost friend, or companion, or family member. Well, they know they're not going to get rejected by you! So that's excellent.

M: Vashta gave me some great advice that helped me to feel safe, and confident, and better oriented in terms of contact. And that was really on my mind the night before. I knew when I started this project that this was going to be a really big deal, that this was going to be the big one. Like everything else was just preparation, in terms of the experiences that I've had, the opening that's happened; the awakening process, I guess.

Well they had to ease you into it. So you're more ready.

M: I feel like what I want to do now is to really take this steady, instead of the usual bull-at-a-gate, jumping-in-with-both-feet approach, which is my traditional MO. I feel like this has to be more considered, because it is clearly as available as I ask it to be. So if I'm connecting with any of the beings, I want to have a good reason to do it. I want to know what I want. And to be grounded in myself and feel like I'm in the right place to do it.

I think you made major progress in allowing a new possibility by pursuing contact through this book, and contact will be offered to you again. The fact that the energy was so high, that's a great sign for you in knowing when contact is coming as opposed to it being a surprise to you. You might be able to manufacture that intensity of energy because you now have memory of what it felt like in your body. You might be able to tap into that, as a frequency, to see if you can generate it, and then see what happens. You are then reaching out to them.

M: It's very interesting working on this book now, as I'm looking at it in a different way. I've now touched this subject matter in a very personal way, so it's not just information I'm absorbing anymore; I'm now comparing it with my experier

They are helping to awaken you, which is part of your journey. You're reaching out, as I see it, in that community of ETs, dimensional beings. Not just through curiosity, but for real connection. And they look for that.

M: I get that. I've asked people why they have multiple contacts, and one person said that the beings can sense who is open by their energetic signature, and so more beings will come to that person. And I'm just thinking about this now, but I've only had two contact experiences, and have met what I perceive to be two different beings. The first was exactly two weeks prior to the dream state experience above. It was a very brief dream in which I was in a space without any physical features, and then I saw a being. I had the same excited 'Oh-my-God-I'm-having-a-contact!' thought. And the being was very similar to Z'Kerg, a being which Vashta Narada created a representation of. When I first saw that being—which Juju wanted to use as one of her UFO Congress presentation slides—I was completely entranced. I'd seen thousands of ET images in my life, but that one was uniquely compelling. I couldn't stop looking at him, and wondering why he seemed so familiar to me, and why he seemed to know me. It was wonderful seeing him in a dream, but it was fleeting. Just an initial contact, I guess, to see how I handle integrating it.

Yeah. They're like the travel agency. They can show you around, and give you some insight, and maybe you'll work them.

How does your contact feel?

It is energizing, when I work with them, and that continues after the contact. We usually connect for about 45 minutes to an hour. Though they've shortened the timeframe recently. The other day it was maybe a half hour or so.

Yesterday I did an integration process with the Blue Crystal being. We had a beautiful heartfelt connection. She took my hands with her hands and made mine elongate so that they reminded her of her form. I stayed in my physical form, but my hands morphed into three elongated fingers and a shorter thumb, resembling her hands. Then she cradled her face in my hands, and closed her eyes. It was like she was remembering us. I don't remember that time or what it meant to her. But I was looking at her thinking, 'She's remembering our connection from somewhere.' She took a long time in that place, a few minutes. Then she put my palms together between her hands, and my hands went back to normal. She placed them in my lap and said, "Thank you."

I woke up in the middle of the night several times with that heartwarming feeling. You know that you said that when you met your being it was joyous? This was so touching. It was such a gentle, loving reconnection. I still don't know what our original connection was, but it felt like in this reconnection, she's moving forward with me. For me it's not just about obtaining knowledge, it's a relationship. I'm curious about how all this will be in the next months and years. She was very present, accessible, and is becoming more integrated.

So when you ask me how it feels, it goes anywhere from excitement, to that really warm, inviting feeling. When I've met some Reptilians, there is a level of caution. Not fear, but caution. I believe that someone close to me growing up was connected to the Reptilian species, so I think that's why I don't have the fear.

What have they taught you?

What they've taught me personally is how to be more centered, neutral and diplomatic. I have learned how to open up and carry forth information that is not mine, with integrity and truth. I am more authentic, more secure and less fearful because of my connection with them.

If I ask myself what have I learned as a tool or process, I would say they have always led me to the tools I needed to do my work. My teachers, classes, books and clients have always been in reach and been given to me when I needed them. I have been guided in so many ways that even now, protocols and information given 20 years ago are becoming useful in more significant ways. They didn't train me in a specific way, but I feel like they've brought me to this point. This interweaving of the Blue Crystal energy is very different than how I've been working with them. I believe the knowledge base that she has, that I do not have, will be my training. That's going to be an action, maybe a protocol of some sort.

They give me two words: it is emergence and immersion. That feels like a body of work that they want to bring forward as training for me and maybe others. I don't know what that is yet. I would say these last three and a half years, after my mother passed, has been a protocol to get me up to speed, so that this information can be brought into this dimension and utilized.

How do they feel about this project?

Excited about it. Some of the beings I work with may know the potential of this project in the future, but they are not disclosing that to me. However, bringing it into physical form here on Earth where there is always free will, there isn't 100% assurance of anything. I could probably shut it down, claiming I'm not doing this anymore. That would take them in another direction. When I've asked questions about possibilities regarding this project, their honest answer after they look at each other for a few seconds is, "We don't really know at this point."

I believe I know what they would like it to look like, but they haven't ever brought this into the 3rd dimension that I'm aware of. They are not totally clear on my capabilities or the physical response of others. I was told to not eat red meat for a year, and have specific health care practices to bring up my vibration. In my opinion, they're juggling this, believing in its endeavor and carrying the work forward.

The Blue Crystal being was very pleased in our initial connection the other night. She was very grateful and happy that it worked. I guess I could have shut off, or the woman I trusted to do the session could have taken over and moved it into another direction, but none of that happened. And it did work.

So I don't know how to answer that other than they have their own dream. Shamans say, "Dream in your future." That is where we have control, where we can create and co-create. We are capable of dreaming in our future. I believe they have a dream, an understanding, and some may have a knowing of what this project can do and be. But when you bring anything into human form, because there is free will, it is not written in stone. That's why it is a co-creative process. They're bringing it in, and it takes cooperation. It requires that I state yes I can do that, no I can't or won't, and bring the pieces together, into this 3rd dimension. For me in this moment, there isn't anything blocking my alignment and participation. I have no fear and trust my interdimensional beings explicitly. All is good.

What do the beings get out of it?

They're not absent of wanting healing, resonance with humans, co-creating, making this world a better place for humans and themselves.

They evolve through human connection as well. They are welcomed, they are accepted, they can relate, they can move into this dimension more freely because they become resonant with us. It's part of us becoming as one and not functioning as if we are not.

They can also bring in their own needs, in a co-creative process. That is my deepest desire: to be in relationship with others that want to co-create. And they are part of that desire. We are all one in the same, we just look very different. Our joint contribution has a ripple effect through the globe and maybe universally or cosmically. It can't help but have a ripple effect. We may never know what that is, but bringing beings into harmony, unison and cohesiveness, is always a good thing.

How has contact affected your life?

When it first began, I dealt with it by compartmentalizing. I do well with having one foot in one place, and my other five toes in several different places, because that's my work. When I am working with a client, I am accessing their subconscious; I am also opened up to where I'm being taken. I'm listening to what their body is saying, I'm hearing what's being told to me, and I'm getting visuals. So there are many sensory things that are happening simultaneously. I've been well trained in being in many places at once, so it's not difficult for me.

My journey in the beginning was the feeling of being isolated, not being able to tell people that I was hearing things in my head, and holding that together. This was before it was confirmed what was happening. For several months I was hearing things in my head like at a cocktail party, with different voices. I felt isolated, and thought maybe I really am crazy. But my work was going very well so I stuck with the possibility that maybe something else was happening to me that was of value.

When I started to ask questions of the voices I received answers or pictures that I had to figure out for myself, and the chaos in my head subsided. That was my first introduction to other realms, dimensions, and beings who were working with me, and they became my first guidance team following Eli's departure. I could compartmentalize that while I lived my life.

I think it's been my whole life that has been affected by them. Remembering being plucked from one death experience to this life in utero, I would say it has been my entire life. I don't know how to separate it. It was a gradual awakening for me, from the time I remembered in utero and the deep loss of a sister and that impact of feeling something was missing all my life. For years I would break the wishbone at Thanksgiving hoping to have a baby sister. Now I have this new awareness, decades later, that the piece that was missing wasn't my sister but was this Blue Crystal being who is on my future timeline. There are so many pieces I've been given in this lifetime, like crumbs along the way. People that have come into my life, that were there for specific reasons, and the drive that I had to learn tools to help access the subconscious level.

And when I first became a body worker I wanted nothing to do with touch. As much as I longed for it, touch wasn't safe. I was very judgmental; I only wanted to work with thin women and no hairy men. That changed drastically after a few weeks of having my hands on the human body - I fell in love with the physical form. I could feel things in their body, their feelings, and their pain as I massaged them. It was all about being in love with the human form, and feeling empathy and connection. This in turn allowed me to be more accepting of other forms unlike us. That became another first for me in offering me more humanness. I felt as a young adult that I was alien, not having the love and capacity for empathy that I perceived in others. Hands-on work definitely opened my world and changed my perceptions.

I can say that there have always been openings for me in the appropriate time. Dimensional beings and others couldn't step in until I was ready for them to step in. I had to be prepared for contact through allowing, accepting, commitment, trust, truth, creativity and integrity. It was only then that I was ready to do the work with them.

I've always felt I was blessed, no matter what twists and turns my life presented me. I always felt protected. People would say, "Wow, you've really had some tough times." And I say, "Yeah, but you know what? They were *good*. I learned a lot and I wouldn't be who I am today without all of that." So I can truthfully look back and say I've really led a blessed life. I've always felt protected, and I still believe that. I grew up believing I was protected but had no proof of it. For me, I don't know what my life would have been if I hadn't gone down this road. I can't even imagine.

What have you learned?

This 3rd dimension is very complex. We are multidimensional beings, and I don't think we even have a clue what that means. Our DNA holds trillions of fragments of information about us. Such as who we've been, where we're going, and what gets unravelled at what point in this particular lifetime. It's phenomenal. What I've learned is that we are unique and we are complex, and because we have the capacity to love and feel a variety of emotions, it's a unique experience for each of us.

The beings that I know do have the capacity to love. Maybe they show love in different capacities, as do humans, but they still have that. You can feel their love, their heart, when you are with them. But they don't hold the emotional levels like we do. They don't have all that baggage that we as humans have. In this 3rd-dimensional place it's very difficult to maneuver and orchestrate life through that when you have all this possibility, and capability, ...ness.

It's mind-boggling. And yet we do it. Some of us get lost, or stuck, and some of us need help. That's why certain people on that path of knowing and waking up are here to help others to wake up, to see that they are bigger, and brighter, and more capable and have more knowing than they believe possible in this moment. We're in a training program. It just depends on how much we want to learn, and what we close our minds to.

How well do you feel you understand the beings?

I think in any relationship there is always room for understanding someone better. With those I work with on a more regular basis, I have an understanding of their combined mission. I have come to know them through their energy, which has been kind, loving at times, direct, and honest. There have been moments where they were more firm in their contact with me. Especially if our conversation is of a serious manner. Recently I was told to paint them to have a better connection. The painting created more of a bond, as they are now in my office. In fact there are some that I know only by having mediated a piece of their history. Because I have only a glimpse into a small part of them, when I see them in the painting there's a to get to know them better. Like a friend you h hile.

I believe it is valuable, even vital, to know who you are speaking with and being given information by. Trust your intuition about who your contacts are, and cautiously listen to the direction of the information. My rule of thumb is: if it is fear-based or my gut reacts in a negative way, I would question them or step away. There is false information coming in from wherever on a regular basis. We all need to be cautiously accepting and monitor how we feel about the information to keep us in alignment with our own highest good.

To answer the question more simply. I feel I do understand them fairly well and I'm also looking forward to getting to know and understand them better.

What message would they like to share?

The first message is that they are part of us and have always been part of us. Just because we are in an unaware state, it doesn't mean they don't exist.

They are bringing themselves closer, to harmonize and be part of us, as opposed to being in observation mode. They sense they are being more people than was the case 50-60 years ago.

The fear on this planet is disruptive to their vibration. They would like fear to be minimized. They're not saying anything more about that. So there might be something about their work with timelines and maybe this Blue Crystal being that addresses fear, I don't know.

They want us to trust in our hearts that which is being given to us as humans: they are part of our DNA. Therefore, trusting them is valuable.

And know that the outcome of our future, as it's always been, is in our hands with the choices that we make. Just because someone has a different reality than our own doesn't mean you have to judge it or be part of it.

They do align with us and co-exist with us, and they would put it in o backs.

Those of awakening are considered the ground troops. Not to go into battle, but to speak the truth and stand up and hold the space for the future.

They wish for people like you and I and others to create a commonality, being a cohesive community living like they do, in love and without fear. It's not all about their existence being acknowledged by humanity, even though that is a piece of it. They're saying, "It's like bringing Heaven on Earth." It's about bringing people together that can in harmony, unison and resonance. That is what they it is how they function.

Even though there may be other beings that try to create disharmony, they have found a way to not let that be part of their reality. They prevent that from interfering with their abilities and the connection they have with each other. It doesn't destroy their communities or separate them. If there are beings that have agendas that don't match theirs, there is no fighting with them. Basically they're dismissed from their reality, so they have no effect. And that's what they wish for us: to create those types of communities that hold a higher vibration and work together.

There are some beings that see that happening, as a future possibility. There are some dimensional beings that are strictly assigned to hold that space, to hold that possibility. Whenever there are communities, groups, even individuals taking the time and effort to bring in light, love, peace, connection, it is not dismissed. Rather, that energy is gathered into that higher vibrational space of our future, and is offered to us as we grow. There are certain beings whose primary mission is to hold that space of the future possibility of harmony, cohesiveness and resonance in a loving capacity.

When we have small groups, of people meditating together, or focusing on something, sending our intention of love towards a person or problem, don't think that energy isn't of value. Maybe we create a project that contributes to a community or even our global community. That energy is going somewhere and we are being heard. Let us not forget that. And it's being held, and it is growing.

What I am hearing from them now is they would like, at some point, to do a round table with you. It looks like you have different species present and you can ask questions. I think you're going to get different answers from some. You are already bringing them together because of the people you are interviewing, and the questions you are asking. You've invited all these people into your space that are featured in your books. And you have also invited in all those beings that each of those people are connected to and in contact with. In effect, all of our collective guidance has access to each other more so than prior to your interviews. You in essence are orchestrating a meet and greet for a phenomenal group of beings.

Do any of the beings have a message for me?

They think you're doing a good job on removing your own fear. You may not even know that you had fear, and it's not necessarily about them. It feels like fear has been a big block for you. They feel like you're doing a good job in releasing that. You used to manage it, now it's more about letting it go. Coming to terms with it. Knowing its validity. They want to acknowledge that they can't and don't work with fear-based individuals because it blocks their access. So they are letting you know you're doing a good job with being less fearful.

The other thing is that, wherever your work takes you, you might be asked or led into some form of environmental work again. That may not be on the 3rd dimension. But don't be surprised about that. They consider you having a wealth of information and knowledge of environmental issues. It may be a branch of that but has more dimensional possibilities. They're just saying, don't be surprised if that's reinitiated in a very different way. You've been involved with the environment because of what you're brought into this life; it is the reason why you got involved with it in the first place. There is a real connection that you have to beauty and this planet that you need to understand. You're coming to the place of trying to understand humans and their connection or lack of connection to Earth and your participation in that dysfunction; they say it almost wiped you out. Your effectiveness isn't what will be required of you, or what will be presented to you. There's something else that will be more palatable and will resonate with where you are heading now. But it may involve some form or connection with the environment.

What would be useful to you and them is your understanding of how to stay grounded. Tapping into that unity, connection, and love. Knowing that is your core, you need to be reminded of that, through actions, and objects. Sound will ground you. Toning can deepen your energy, and help let go of the static that tends to gather in your energy field, to pull you back to your core. Then you can handle more of the energies around you while you're being worked on in an ongoing 'letting go' process. You're being worked with on a cellular level, with beings, with guidance, and they can't let go too quickly because you need to be in alignment with the shift. I would imagine that this opening you had with contact might have some chaotic repercussions within your body, because you have visited another dimension.

They are advising you to work with the letting go consciously, rather than just waiting for it to settle down. Breath and deep bass sounds are the best for you. Listening to monks doing deep chanting will resonate with you. Just a few minutes of that will help bring you back down into your core. Because you work a lot in your head, and you go up and out in your thought process as you connect all the dots, while being very thorough. It can be exhausting to the body. Doing toning or listening to chanting or playing your music regularly will help you maintain physical balance while you're experiencing your multidimensional selves.

Vanessa Lamorte Hartshorn

Vanessa Lamorte, M.A. is an Intuitive Life Coach, certified Reiki Master Teacher and Sound Healer. She has also professionally studied yoga and AntiGravity aerial movement. Her work is a transfiguration home, weaving together multi-modal healing practices and encouraging wholeness, truth and transformation.

Currently, she works with clients from around the world in private, group and retreat settings and also teaches online spiritual development courses. In the Las Vegas area, she offers healing sound bath ceremonies and consciousness-expanding meditations.

In 2015 she shared information about her hybrid nature in *Meet the Hybrids*, and further perspectives in *We Are the Disclosure*.

Her YouTube channel is: Vanessa Lamorte, M.A.

Her website is: vanessalamorte.com

Which words do you use to describe 'them'?

I use ETs a lot. Star beings, star people. I use galactic peeps, but that's kind of slang. There is some speculation that they don't really like 'ETs', but the ETs I've worked with are like, "Whatever, we don't care." But the ones that are sensitive, I call them 'star people'.

Which kinds of beings are you in contact with?

There's a lot of them! Lyrans, Sirians, Andromedans, Zetas, Mantids, Pegasians, Camelopardians, Arcturians, Pleiadians, Reptilians, Bellatricians, Hydrans, Squid beings and beings from Polaris and Rigel.

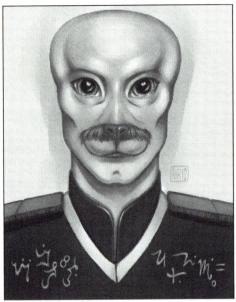

George, Vanessa's guide from the Lyran-Sirian Council. Credit: Ashley Ruiz

What can you tell me about the Galactic Federation?

Okay, I'm just going to do this [makes motions around head] because I'm going to need extra brain power. I'm not tired, but I'm like whoa, that's a big question. Okay. There are a few galactic alliances. There's the Galactic Federation, and there are a few others, but I don't know their labels. I know that they exist, I've worked with them. But the Galactic Federation is my main involvement.

I'll talk about the other alliances first. They oversee other dimensions, portals, stargates, galactic highways; they're almost like the networks. And they do a lot of other functions. Whereas the Galactic Federation has representatives of those different groups. I don't know how representatives get chosen from each collective. Yeah, how *does* that work? I've never asked the question.

There are different representatives from all these star systems who work at the Galactic Federation. It's kind of like the International UFO Congress, where everyone comes to talk about one large agenda, but from different perspectives. To sum up that agenda, I would say it's about checks and balances. A large part has been to keep the Milky Way and Andromeda galaxie͏s sure we're all working towards the highest and best good. r project of the Galactic Federation has been working to get Earth's Ascension process online. This is where Earth is of interest for multiple groups. Ascension, essentially, is a process of moving towards unconditional love in all aspects of life. And how that manifests looks different depending on each perso   ctive, each planet really.

I'll mention this because I think it's relevant. Right now I'm really feeling into Arcturians and Pleiadians, those two collectives are playing a major part in teaching us unconditional love, and how to unify. Their frequencies are super present on the planet right now. There are plenty of others, but these two major groups are doing a lot of work, talking to a lot of people, coming to people in their dreams, to help people come online a little bit more.

I think as you talk to different people you'll hear about different ambassadors. I operate under those kinds of roles, taking part in a lot of discussions. Particularly on morality, and what's going to be in the highest and best interests. Those kinds of things. Whereas other people play other roles. Like working as a dispatcher for ships, or a navigator.

And there's the energetic stuff. How do I sum it up briefly? For example, a group might go to Earth to help heal the waters. Galactic environmentalist kind of people. I work in that too. Some things cross over. Some people might know their roles more. I know my main role, but then it gets a little fuzzy. There's a lot going on out there.

How do they appear to you?

Mostly holographic, with a humanoid/Adamic structure. Adamic meaning two arms, two legs. I've had other beings come to me, but it's mostly those kind. There are different variations for each being. For example, the Mantid being is bipedal, but has the Mantid arms and head, so it still follows the Adamic structure, but I wouldn't say it's super humanoid, because it looks very different to a human.

In waking life they mostly appear holographically. What I mean by that is that I can see them visually, and it looks like I can touch them, but I can see through them; they appear almost ghostly. Whereas in meditation and dreamtime they look solid, very real. And I think that has more to do with the state of vibration that I'm in. The vibration I'm in during waking life is much different than when I'm on the astrals or in meditation.

Hafeka, Vanessa's Camelopardian guide and cousin. Credit: Ashley Ruiz

How do you define 'the astrals'?

Whoa, when you said "astrals" this little orb just flew off your shoulder. Okay. There are multiple layers of the astrals. There are lower astrals and upper astrals. What that means for example, is that on the lower astrals you're going to have dissociative thought forms, lost souls and ghosts. And in the upper astrals, it's kind of like 4D Earth. Earth not in the physical. So if you were to dream you went to a library that you know of on Earth, for example, you would be in the 4th-dimensional upper astral realm.

And if you were to dream that you have some kind of crazy entity attachment thing, you probably would be in the lower astral realm. When I say astrals, it's kind of like an umbrella term for everything: upper and lower astrals. And everything beyond that. When I say I'm on the astrals, it could be another planet, or a ship. It's anything that takes place during dreamtime, including lucid dreams, and I'm out doing something.

Can you describe your first contact?

Two come to mind. The first I remember was when I was three. I was taken out of my bed and they held my hand. They were short,

Andromedan, humanoid beings, but I thought I was one of them. I thought they were my people. So I can't say there was a level of consciousness that said this thing is outside of me, or it's different.

They're bringing me back to another memory. When I was 15 or 16 I was out in the desert and I saw something and I thought, 'I know that that's alien, I know that that is not a human.' That was contact in the simplest form.

But my first conscious contact, in terms of being an adult, was in 2013, December 26th. I was on my bed, and practicing Reiki by candlelight, because I had just been attuned to Reiki 1. Matt was working, so the house was very quiet and it was just me. I had my computer up because I was playing music, and I had been googling some stuff. So I was sitting cross-legged on my bed running Reiki. I had my eyes closed, then opened them to find there were two beings in front of my bed. I said, "Whoa, who are you?" At that time I was doing mediumship work, and they kind of looked humanoid, but holographic, so I honestly thought they might have been lost souls who wanted to cross over. So I asked them, and they said, "Oh no, we're not dead." And I was like, "*Whaaat?*" And then they said, "We're Lyran-Sirians." I thought they meant the country Syria, and that Lyra was some other place I didn't know on Earth. At that point they told me to do a Google image search for Lyran-Sirians. So I did that, and literally a picture of each one of them, a man and a woman, pops up, and I was like, "You guys are on Google." It was so weird. But I was still not catching on that I was talking to star people.

The woman said, "My name is Avanita." She was wearing this Grecian-Egyptian dress, and her head was elongated, like the Egyptians. She had this crazy, swirly braid, so I thought maybe she's just got a lot of hair. That wasn't the case; There's actually a bigger skull under there. She also had tanned skin like an Egyptian. Her eyes were as big as mine, maybe a little bigger. Thicker, or more defined eyebrows than mine. Dark features. Black hair and eyebrows, brown eyes. She is one of my guides. She's laughing at me right now. She's like, "You haven't told this story in quite a while." And I'm like, yeah, help me remember.

Faranandah looks a little weird. I thought maybe he was like a really old, maybe indigenous soul. I thought, 'You look humanoid, but I don't know where you might be from.' His head was essentially like this big [indicates around 18 inches]. It was long, kind of rectangular. Have you seen the show *The Munsters*? The Frankenstein guy? It was big and rectangular like that. His features ... they're fuzzier than Avanita's at this point. They were similar to hers in terms of having dark skin. And he was wearing a tan potato-sack-looking garb thing, and at first I thought he was naked. He had a Tiki man kind of head. Darker, deeper, strong features. So I thought maybe this is someone from Easter Island. I just didn't know.

I asked them, "Are you guys together?" Avanita scoffed at me, and said, "*Ha!* No, we work together." And I was like, what *is* this? The whole thing was so bizarre. I couldn't figure out their dynamic.

So at this point my google started doing weird things on its own. There was light language typed into Google on its own, and I was like, "Whoa, what is happening?" And then my mouse was clicking videos, and bringing up stuff. I was looking at Avanita, and I had this knowing that she was doing this. She said, "Watch the first video." It was a video of light language. The first words that the woman says are, "Haa ke he." And those were the first words of light language I had spoken, when I was in the car by myself one day. And I was like, what the *fuck?* That's when shit got *really* weird, because I just thought I was talking to some dead souls, but she said, "No, that's not what we are." And on Google a picture of a Zeta came up, and, as everyone does, I recognized that as an ET. So I said, "Are you an alien?" And she said, "We prefer 'star being'."

That night ended in an amazing way too. Before that night, this little dead girl had come to me twice. And she would smell like strawberry tape gum. I don't know if you guys have that. It's like this cheap, nasty gum in a spiral? When she would show up in the bedroom I would ask Matt, "Do you smell that?" He never would, just me. We would be going to sleep and I'd smell that strawberry gum and she would appear next to the bed. Avanita said to me this girl had been walking the Earth since about 1985; she'd been dead a long time. And Avanita said, "We're going to cross her over." So she taught me how to do that in a better way. I was doing it one way, and she was like, "No, I'm going to teach you how to do it in a more fluid way." It was a really cool experience. Bizarre. It felt very safe though.

I was just sitting in weirdness for a good month. I saw my first light language in 2013, and I just didn't know what was happening. I talked with a friend of mine, and she helped me. Avanita helped connect the verbal light language with the written light language.

So that was my first contact.

Can you initiate contact?

Yes. I can initiate contact because my connection is two-way. So I can send and receive. That's one of my gifts. People can develop it, but not everyone comes in with that.

As far as my methodology, if I'm inspired to talk to let's say Arcturians, essentially what I do is move my stellar gateway point—which is the chakra point that exists in the universe—to Arcturus.

I'm glad you asked, because this is not something I've consciously thought about - I just do it. I call it data streaming, and this is the mechanism. Like if my head was the top of Luxor or like a flashlight, there's a light beam that goes from my crown to the stellar gateway. And that's how everybody's works. We all have a connection point. For some people it's more like a cord, for others it's like a tunnel of light, it just depends on the person and what they're doing.

So I bring my consciousness up through my crown and to my stellar gateway, and it's like when you have a laser pointed at the stars, and you just move it. Like I move mine to whatever space I want to go. And I don't have to know that, let's say Arcturus is five hundred light years from this other star; I just go to the resonance of Arcturus, or Lyra. Or if it's a specific being I need to locate, like a guide. I don't do that very often, but if I want to locate Avanita, I just go to the energy signature of that name, or label, by following the resonance signature of what the name holds.

And then I can start asking questions. I can stay in this space, and use my telepathy and my claircognizance to talk to those groups, or the being, like using a telephone.

Other times, if I'm guided to do it this way, I might bilocate. I might sit in meditation and just feel myself go. I'll be here, and conscious of being on Earth, but my light body will double and I will go to that planet and I will interact with them in that way. It just depends on the circumstance, like maybe I'll need to go on a ship.

Those are the basics of my methodology. If someone else wanted to use that, I would really focus on protection protocols first, before trying any of that. Because you can get yourself in a lot of trouble if you're not consciously protecting yourself. And that's with any psychic or energetic practice. Do your protection first. It doesn't have to be this paranoid thing that something's going to happen to you, it's just covering your ass.

What safeguards do you recommer

Make sure you're shielding yourself. Shielding is a technique which many practitioners will talk about. I think it's more widely known. Essentially you're putting a white or gold egg of light around yourself. People use other colors too. Some people use the archangels, like Archangel Michael, or Gabriel. They're very protective. I've written an entire pdf on protection mechanisms called *Protection Magic 101* that is available on my website.

You would want some kind of protocol in place. Let's say you're in your house and you've never contacted star beings before, but it seems interesting to you, and you feel called to do it. First and foremost, I would have something to protect your sacred space and your field. You can burn sage, or use a tourmaline crystal. There are so many things, but you need to do something. Then I would call in my own spirit guides to protect me and ask them to keep me safe, hold sacred space for me. So I use affirmation work with that. I also like to state that I wish the work to be done in the highest integrity and to only allow the experience that is in everyone's highest and best interest. Then I would attempt to connect. And I would always state that I only wish to connect to the beings that are in my highest and best interests, always. Because this can go awry really quickly.

So that's ET contact 101, that's what you gotta do. There are so many energies here right now, and going forward, it's going to get more and more jam-packed. It's like going from rural Montana, which is Earth in the past in terms of 'ET population density', to urban China. We are jam-packed with ETs who are ready to jump into anyone's channel and start talking about their agenda. And not everyone's agendas are created equal. No offense, but some of them are a little sketchy.

If you need more information, I will talk about protection all day. This is one of my roles with the Galactic Federation. I understand what can happen, and take the measures to make sure it doesn't. I've seen it happen way too often, and it's scary.

I have to say this. Sometimes people think they're talking to their guides, but there has to be a level of discernment here. You can't just trust everything that comes into your channel when you connect. No matter how lovely they feel, you have to be a skeptic on some level. You have to keep yourself grounded. And ask questions. This has happened to clients. They're so excited to connect, but they're being tricked. For example, it's three in the morning and the star being told them to go into the woods, by themselves, with nothing. Turn off your cellphone and don't bring a flashlight. Like, *who* the fuck does that?

That's just not safe! Your guides would never put you in danger like that. Certainly not right away. For someone who is well versed in this, and has learned to trust, that could be some other lesson for them. For someone who might be working through fear, and their guides are giving them this exercise because maybe they're afraid of the dark or whatever, that could be a breakthrough for them. But bare minimum, we're talking about foundational stuff. You need to have your wits about you, you need to discern, keep yourself grounded, think about safety first. It's kind of funny because I'm married to a paramedic, who is like safety first - always. So I have my own levels of that, but in a cosmo-spiritual way! I'm very vocal about that because things have been too crazy. People - *please*.

How does your contact feel?

They're all a little different, because they all have different energy signatures. I don't know if this is the question, but how would you know that there's a star being in the room? In terms of indicators of that energy signature, to me ETs always feel like a cool energy, whereas angels and fairies always feel warm, temperature-wise. Not like cold, but more like a gentle cool breeze, like on a nice fall day, versus being out in the summer.

M: Interesting. I get that all the time. I'll check to see if the windows are open, or even the vents, but no. There's no movement of air in the room, certainly not a momentary cool breeze. And I have wondered if that's a presence here.

The likelihood that that is a star being is 99.9%. Considering you and your work. But that's cool. That's the first thing that comes through, is a temperature change. Then my mind asks questions. Immediately I'll telepathically ask: 'Who is here? Who is that?' And I'll turn on my 'lights' - my clairvoyance and claircognizance. I don't have it on all the time because it's too overwhelming. There's that. And sometimes they come in and I just see them.

I'm big on temperature. I realized this last week. I think this speaks to my hybrid DNA. At some point I will figure out which parts of my DNA are super sensitive to temperature. I think it's the Reptilian DNA. I run colder than average for a human. My blood's always 96.7 degrees. It's interesting. I'm still thinking about this one.

How do you differentiate between your own thoughts and those from outside?

I get asked this a lot. There's a few things. You know how usually you're thinking, 'I have to go to the grocery store and get this and this,' and you can hear this thread and it makes sense? Then, some random thought comes in? But it's not random, it's your pineal gland opening, and you're becoming more psychic. Psychic intel can be detected by thoughts that are 'untraceable'. If it was part of your cognition thread, then it was you thinking it. If it 'randomly' pops in, seemingly out of nowhere, it is most likely a psychic hit. For example, you could get this seemingly random thought, like, 'Maybe I need to go to the crystal store.' Or it could be something less obvious, like 'I need to go upstairs.' All of a sudden. And it might sound like you in your head, and you'll think it's your own thoughts. But it could be your highest self. Or it could be your guides, because they will sometimes talk to you via your voice. And sometimes it will be a different voice. Like if you can hear your mom or dad's voice in your head? It's kind of like that.

The voice changes. And it's obvious. Or it's a random thought interrupting the normal thread of cognition. Any time that happens, I open to inquiry - just like I tell my psychic students all the time. Okay, so let's ask: who is that? Because I don't just follow directions blindly when something comes in. I use discernment.

At first people don't recognize it, but with practice you start to refine that practice. But I will say, "Who is that?" And I may get a picture in my mind of my guide. Or I'll see a being I've seen before. And sometimes it's completely new. And in that case I'll be like, "Who are you. Where are you from? What do you want?" All those normal questions we ask when meeting someone new.

Other than following your cognition and seeing what is part of your thought-thread and what is not, we can pay attention to how energy feels around us. For example, let's say you are sitting watching a movie and you feel an outside energy is coming into your field. It will feel kind of foreign. Kind of like that feeling when you are asleep and someone walks into the room. You know someone is there and usually you can tell who it is. But this happens when you are awake and lucid and the energy of the being, entity, etcetera. feels like it is moving from the outside-in versus the inside-out.

But that's not always true. This is where people start to feel crazy. When they're starting to channel, it sounds like it's here, in your mind first, instead of outside. And it very well could be! That is called 'data streaming'. It's very obvious something else is coming. It has a feeling of spookiness. Like when you encounter a ghost. That's obvious, because you feel it outside of yourself. Whereas sometimes it's not that way. It starts inside and comes out. In this case, you are most likely receiving communication from beings in other dimensions, planets, or stars through your ability of claircognizance. And that's where it's important to begin questioning it, as I described. It will also feel random, not part of a thread of thinking.

To me there's also a vibrational difference. If you don't even know yourself, then how will you know when something else comes in? That's the other thing too. In essence, if you have a good grasp on what you feel like in general, this kind of contact will feel like outside-in. But if it's inside-out it will feel random, and not be part of your normal thoughts.

Whether it's ETs, angels, elementals or even other people, it's the same process. Telepathy is the same way. You're engaging in something, like reading a book or watching a movie, and suddenly you hear someone's name, or see them in your mind's eye. They're probably thinking of you. It's coming up for a reason. I think that's an example that people can relate to, which will help them make more sense when it comes to ETs. That feeling of 'maybe I should call my mom.' Where did that come from, all of a sudden? It's the same exact mechanism that occurs with talking with ETs.

Why do they connect with you?

I think most of my contact experiences have to do with my professional work which always translates into my personal experience of the world. Because I'm not getting abduction experiences. Or teaching me something about myself. Sometimes it's a guide. Or it could be a benevolent outside being that wants to give me some information about something.

Sometimes it's like a messenger. Or a solicitor. Sometimes it's benevolent, sometimes it's not. Like I'll get told to go and do a thing, and I'll ask why. For example, one time I was asked to put a web over a black hole. And I asked, "Why would I do that? What's coming out of it?" It was convoluted and it took a lot of questioning because I didn't know if I agreed with that action. Different weird things like that.

They'll come to me to do something or learn something such as a particular group's cosmic agenda, or learn who I can bring them in contact with to assist their mission. And a lot of it too, interestingly enough, is about mythology. They teach me stories about our Earth mythology, and how those link to the stars.

What do the beings get out of it?

There are a few things coming up. I don't want to talk in polarity, but at the same time I feel like that's probably the only way to do this. My initial response to that question is, it depends on the agendas of the being. It depends on who you're talking to and what beings you're working with. On a more cosmo-spiritual level, separateness is an illusion. Essentially we are all in this together, we are all One. So by the participation of other, more advanced groups (than those on Earth) in my life, through contact, healing, transmissions, we're essentially moving the vibration, to get to a space where it's kind of like tipping the next level.

What do the beings get out of this? Ascension. What do we get out of this? Ascension. And I don't mean to put across this feeling of going somewhere, because Ascension isn't really going anywhere. I feel like Ascension is really just realizing divinity, anchoring in Source, God, light. So through all this work that we're doing, how it's accelerating through time right now, and there are so many more galactic people helping us awaken, and participating in our lives and coming together. So what they get out of it is what we get out of it, which is and the next piece.

Overall, I don't think any particular being comes to anyone just for the fun of it. That's another thing to be aware of. If they're coming to you, there's something there that they want. Something you have that they want, or something they would like to talk to you about. Yes, for your best interests, but for theirs as well. I'm not talking about your guides. Because your guides are usually pretty selfless. They just like to give you information and guide you, because that's their role. But with other outside beings, having discernment is very important, because there is some kind of reciprocity that's going on. They want something from you, and they might give you something. And not everybody does it the same way. Some can be super sketchy.

And some will tell you straight up, "This is what I want from you, and this is what I'll give you." And it's great when there's this transparency. But there's a lot to be aware of when you're talking to beings.

I think a lot of people are really excited to work with other beings. And it's been glamorized in our culture to be psychic. It's taboo for a lot of people, but it's also glamorized. People think it's super cool and really different. But I've seen the situation where people get attention for something, and then feel that they have to do more of that thing to keep that level of attention, that positive reinforcement. And it produces a cycle that can be dangerous. It's basic psychological conditioning. But it's not always good. It's happened to me too where I have found myself seeking certain energies that I don't always need to be engaged in. But that has occurred because I think that's what I need to be doing, talking about, etcetera.

Why do beings come to me? I have this Leo/Aquarius thing going on in my brain, which is self versus others. Because if I'm going to talk about myself that's fine, but I don't want people reading this book thinking that my experience is all there is, so there's a level of caution. I want people to be aware that everyone's different. There are other ways to connect, and other types of experiences you can have. Their higher self can give them more guidance on this.

M: I just had a big discussion with what I sense is my higher self, and told it that I'm no longer going to be whipped along, racing from one project to the next. I set some healthy boundaries. I need more space. So this is a big personal victory! It was triggered by using Lyssa Royal's *Galactic Heritage Cards*. I did a higher guidance reading with them and it just opened up this dialogue spontaneously. I didn't even know you could have a debate with your higher self prior to that.

That's a big act of sovereignty. For people on this planet, that's a big part of Ascension. More people will have that kind of awareness. Their intuition comes online. And then people realize, oh, I can make my own rules, my own contracts. And then discussing that with your guides and higher self. It's a big part. I'm really proud of you because it's like wow, that's a big part of your multidimensionality.

What have they taught you?

What comes to mind immediately are technologies, like energetic technologies. This comes from my star being guides, overall. And I consider guides to be any benevolent beings who come to me.

They taught me light language, which I talk about a lot in *Meet the Hybrids* and *We Are the Disclosure*.

They've taught me about stargate technology and time travel. There's grid healing. They've taught me how to work with the magnetic fields of planets, which is important for structure, function and alignment. They've taught me so many crazy things. Oh my gosh. Also ship construction and technology. How they fly. How that works.

Another interesting thing is the social models for other civilizations. For example, Arcturians and Pleiadians, they don't get married. There's a level of polyamory that happens on other planets, and it functions for them. Here, because we have ego and other things, I don't think polyamory functions for us. Maybe in the future.

Also how their cultures work, and how communities come together, which is very interesting. For example, they've shown me Zetas on Reticulum. They live in colony-structured communities, like bees or ants. Their housing, whether dimensional or physical, is structured like an anthill. They don't live in houses like we do. There are pods, underground tunnels, navigation portals; it's very different.

I've seen Arcturus and the Pleiades. They're very community-oriented and they raise their kids more like a village. They're highly advanced, so it doesn't look tribal or indigenous, but they raise their families together in collectives. It's very communal. Like communism, but it works. They share everything. Young people are raised with multiple parents. And I think that has to do with hybridization. They recognize the multiple layers of the participation that created each child.

Once I have my kids I'll probably know who the hybrid parents were, but I'm not going to tell them, "Help me raise my kid." It's just not going to work like that on Earth. That would just be strange. At least I can't foresee that now.

Pleiadians and Arcturians feel very similar to me, or similar to humans on Earth, but they are still very different.

I'm trying to give diverse examples. I feel like Sirian and Lyran beings follow those communal situations more closely. They're a little different in their resonances, because they're different collectives, but basically the same.

Mantis beings are also colony beings, but different than Zetas, in terms of their resonance. What I mean by that is that Zetas feel, in contrast to Mantis beings, more robotic. More like machines. They don't understand emotions like we do. They're not emotionless, but it's more like computation with them. Whereas Mantis beings have more compassion, and a level of love, that humans could relate to. But they're still colony beings. Again, different from communism. Those are the best words I can think of. I don't know the terminology used on other planets for these social models. But there's a level of love that happens with the Mantid beings that's like wow; they're cool. They have these pods too. They're not all underground. Zetas have a lot of underground stuff, but the above-ground stuff is a lot of towers, with ships flying in and out. Whereas with the Mantid beings, it looks more loving and less industrial. Yeah, industrial is a good word for Zetas, whereas Mantid beings are more green, like ecological-industrial.

Imagine an ecologically-aware house. It's very clean. Clean energy. And that leaks over into their healing practices. They heal very well.

That's all I want to say about that because I feel like I'm going spacey. My brain is data streaming from Cassiopeia Mantid beings one minute then to Reticulum, which is a lot of energy to do, boom-boom-boom, all over the place. So I just have to come back to my brain. Oof.

They've taught me about dimensions, and how that is structured.

Also how to work with crystals. A lot of crystal technology.

They taught me about galactic history and origins. And their participation with ancient civilizations.

I feel complete with that. The rest of it I don't know how to articulate. It's just stuff I do on the astrals.

How has contact affected your life?

It's made it more complete. Without the conscious participation in this movement, I didn't feel complete. Not to say that I don't have things to work on! I just feel it's the piece of ourselves that as a collective we deny. The other, the unknown. A lot of the galactic energy represents the archetype of the taboo, the shadows, the dark. And I feel like for me, working with galactic beings has been an integration of shadow and light, and is actually a very beautiful mirror for those two sides of the same coin.

It has also given me this ability to be able to see from so many angles. From not only the Earthly perspective, but from a multi-planetary, multidimensional perspective. And when I say 'see', yes I mean seeing literally down at Earth, but more in a cosmo-political way, looking at the agendas of what goes on with our politics on Earth. Those kinds of energies. Because Earth is a direct mirror of greater and larger groups, namely the Galactic Federations. I can see the trickle-down, like what's going on out in the cosmos is directly related to what's happening on Earth. And vice versa; they're really one in the same.

What was the question again? How has it affected my life? Wow. Everything. I've downloaded new technologies for healing. Without their participation I wouldn't have light language, I wouldn't have the awareness of the spheres, the energetic celestial spheres that affect Earth. Corey Goode talks about these spheres, and he talks about them in a slightly different way, but they are the same thing. These grand energy forces that with the knowledge of them, with the conscious use of them, we get so much done. I can be of better service to this planet because of my galactic connections.

One of Vanessa's Sirian selves. Credit: Ashley Ruiz

On a very normal scale, the galactic people have taught me compassion, and compassion for what is different than oneself. But then also seeing the similarity. Because when I started this work, it felt like they were outside of me, or they were different, they were the other, they were extraterrestrial. They very quickly showed me, "No, *you* are this. This is your DNA." And I'm like, "Oh shit, you're right. This is why I've felt like an alien my whole life." I feel like they showed me myself. It's the mirror again. They showed me who I really am.

And having compassion for that aspect of myself that feels abnormal or different, and being able to recognize that in others. And just letting go of those terms, like 'weird', 'normal' or 'other'. Anything like that. They showed me how to love more completely.

I think that's it. Is there more? It always feels like there's more, but I don't know. Maybe it's just energy. Because when I go into this state I feel like I am channeling myself, and really pulling in multiple collectives when I answer your questions. So it's like, wait where am I? Okay, I'm done answering that question.

What message would they like to share?

Here is what I received. The codes came in on the 26th of December and the channeling today.

Light language symbols. Credit: Vanessa Lamorte Hartshorn

Each symbol can be activated by touching it. There is one for each day of the week and one for your birthday. Hold your finger over the symbol, close the eyes and allow the symbol to tell you what you need to know at that moment in time through meditation. There are eight symbols, representing the seven stars of the Pleiades star cluster and the 8th being yourself. The symbols will activate cosmic consciousness and connect you to Pleiadian guides, collectives and timelines for your soul evolution. They can be used multiple times and in different orders. Just ask the symbols for guidance on how they would like to be used for you each time and they will tell you.

The Pleiadian Mother Council wishes to relay a message to those of you reading.

"It is important for you in the coming nine years to understand your roles as parent and child. Examining yourself as a child, your own childhood and understanding your inner child, will be vital as you step into parenting roles. You may find yourself birthing biological children of your own, raising children with a partner in a blended family, being a mentor or guide to nieces, nephews or other little people in your life, or you may find yourself 'parenting' in other senses of the word such as nurturing animal companions. In any way, keep in mind how you embody the role of parent and stay open to receiving teachings. As much as we are parents, we are also children of Gaia, always learning, always expanding.

"This message comes at a pivotal time as many new hybrids enter the Earth, coming to teach and be taught. You will learn many new things from your children, and part of their participation in your community is to break the hierarchy that exists between parent and child, teacher and student, bringing energies into equilibrium, allowing harmony to exist between both."

The Pleiadian Mother Council is a group of divine beings who oversee the department of hybridization, DNA exchange and code-sharing for the energy signatures of the Pleiades. They are a group of cosmic mothers and fathers that help to guide the hybridization process among many diverse star councils, always ensuring the highest alignment for their ancestors and descendants.

Krista Raisa

Krista Raisa is a millennial psychic medium, author and artist. Having lived and studied in New York City, Finland and Sedona, Arizona, she began to trance channel the Orion Council at a parking lot in New Jersey. They are a benevolent group of amphibious humanoids and more, based in Betelgeuse, who work for the Galactic Federation and the Ascension of Earth. Since 2011 she has dedicated herself to helping multicultural starseeds worldwide via the internet.

She has authored three books on these topics. *Orion Council, Here* (2014), *Galactic Symbols from the 9th Dimension* (2014), and *Starseed Survival* (2016). Her website has links to all her sessions, books, music and handmade goods.

Her YouTube channel is: StayCurly

Her website is: kristaraisa.com

Which words do you use to describe 'them'?

Extraterrestrials. Because I don't want to call them aliens. I think it's racist.

Which kinds of beings are you in contact with?

Mainly amphibious humanoids, from Betelgeuse, in the Orion constellation. They are called the Orion Council.

How do they appear to you?

They appear as blue light, which I see in my mind's eye. Inner vision. I can't see them with my physical eyes, but clairvoyants see them in my eighth chakra, so floating above my head. They see them as frogs swimming in a pond, or as frog people.

Emio and Octavian. Two Orion Council beings. Credit: Ashley Ruiz

How does your contact feel?

Accelerated. Fast vibration. Intelligence. God, what does that mean? Heightened awareness. Fun, Exciting. Like when you're about to go on a rollercoaster. And sometimes I see beautiful imagery while in communication with them. Visuals. Like floating cities.

Why do they connect with you?

For my mission. My galactic job, or contract. A training officer from the Council told me I'm in training. He spoke through my physical vessel, my voice. And I confirmed this with Lavandar from starseedhotline.com. Lavandar is a galactic shaman.

I know I'm not from Orion, but I work for these beings. Because I do not feel drawn to that constellation. As in familial feelings. It's actually a bit upsetting, that constellation, because of the galactic wars and negative associations. Pretty much, *Star Wars* happened in Orion. The arm of Orion, if you look at our galaxy, it looks like a spiral, and one of the arms of the spiral, in space photography, appears to have been blown up, as documented by Dan Winter.

I channeled that these beings were from Betelgeuse, and I told my mom. And in November 2011 I told her they were transmitting from Betelgeuse, but I didn't tell anyone else, because I was embarrassed and felt I was a freak. There is an author called Solara, and in her book *The Healing of Orion* she channels about a Council of Light in Betelgeuse. So I read that a year later, and that was confirmation for what had come through for me, relating to the galactic wars and Betelgeuse.

Can you describe your first contact?

I started channeling them at a Whole Foods car park. I'm in the passenger seat, and my mom is driving, we're going in and I begin to hyperventilate, and in between breaths I said "Hello," in a strange voice. And my mom intuitively knew I was channeling. The week before, I was complaining about this awesome pressure on the back of my skull. And I later found out this is a connection point for antahkarana. Some call it the rainbow bridge. It's been called the link between middle and higher mind in Hindu philosophy.

This happened during my gap year, and a month later I had to go to Hawaii to work on a vegetable farm. So I go to the farm with these abilities opening up and I just start offering sessions, because people have to know about this. People need these messages. I thought, 'Oh my God, this is the coolest thing.'

My first client sent me a link to 20 different YouTube channels, one of those being Sirius Starseed, so I click, and oh my God, it's galactic. It's Arcturus Ra, who I instantly was attracted to, and that's why I'm here. We live together now.

How do you experience contact?

It's all telepathic contact. I can open the channel, and it comes directly. I can focus and get telepathy instantly. People call it data streaming, which is great, but I think it's nice to have a space brother visit you in person rather than speaking on the telephone. This is closer than a little telepathic message. No offense. But let's face it, we all want the real thing.

Can you initiate contact?

Yes. I set my intention - a strong will and desire to connect. Then I get into a relaxed state. Then it's about listening; focused, concentrated listening. And relaxing.

You can start by emptying the mind, and putting yourself into a physically relaxed state. Sit with the spine straight, in the lotus position. Though some people do this well in the bathtub. Close your eyes and focus on the third eye.

Listen to your own breathing and allow all thoughts to leave you. This opens the subtle channels to the subconscious mind. You may begin to hear angelic voices, like gentle whispers. I call those 'Whisperers'. They whisper loving, kind messages.

Then it solidifies into specific beings or groups, such as ETs, fairies, loved ones, animal spirits. Differentiating between them is my current training, and my work.

It comes through in different psychic forms: clairvoyant, clairaudient, clairsentient and mediumistic. Mediumistic means simultaneous third eye and crown chakra activity.

I work with clients in person, or via phone or Skype, and once we begin I get random facts flying in that I have to tie together. I may keep seeing a psychic symbol on repeat until I interpret it correctly, for instance, a suitcase, a newspaper, a food item. I then interpret the symbolism and relevance for the client. The session is over when I have interpreted the information correctly.

There's more that happens in the psychic session. In between spirit messages there is energy transference, nine-dimensional code exchange, empathing their emotions, feeling the client's current emotions. Also checking the spin direction of their seven main chakras with a pendulum to understand the psychological state or implications. This tells me if their chakras are open or not. It indicates their thoughts and blockages - any energetic congestion. I don't know how I have the ability to see them, but I do.

How do you differentiate between your own thoughts and those from outside?

Wow. That's a really good question. That's a big problem I have. I'm actually working with a healer to help me with that. Because I've been too open to other people's thoughts. It's been too much. I have extreme social anxiety, resulting from the contact.

The healer gives DNA codes tested through kinesiology, and if he finds ancestral patterns, curses ... it's mainly ... okay, I have to Google this so it's not so woo-woo. It's activating and assisting the immune system to combat pathogens. It's called Advanced Cell Training. He found an openness. He said I was "in the deep end, swimming with sharks." I opened up so much. So I've had to deal with lots of tricksters, and learn to identify who is communicating. It's about discernment. As above, so below; as in the spirit world, so on Earth.

To distinguish between your own thoughts and someone else's you have to develop your third eye. Developing strong psychic skills can be helped by working with other psychics. My boyfriend helps me, Vanessa Lamorte helped me. It's like, how do you know the truth? It's a feeling, right? You get goosebumps, chills. You feel it physically. Or it could be a gut feeling.

What have they taught you?

Wisdom. They are wisdom masters. I'm passively learning social discernment and third eye development while they're actively teaching me Ascension dynamics.

Ascension is the development of Earth's species upon entering a golden age. It's a new 26,000-year cycle, approximately, beginning when Earth enters a photon belt in the cosmos. It's about becoming 5th-dimensional in vibratory frequency. At that point we would all know who we are. Everyone will instantly know the truth. Or 51% of the people would be 'awake'. They would know their job, in terms of why they are here. For example, understanding unconditional love. And divine will versus personal will. Service to others rather than service to self.

They've also taught me scientific things. Color and wave spectrum theory. Atomic properties and structure. Biology. Creational patterns. I'm getting a lot of information right now. How to enter and leave the body. How humans find their purpose.

What do the beings get out of it?

They say they are learning through us, and that there's always an exchange of energy and information. They are ascending as well. That's the deal. It's kind of nice. This comes from many beings. In addition to the amphibians there are multidimensional nameless beings. Angelic beings. Cat-looking beings. Lyrans. Elohim.

How has contact affected your life?

It sounds corny but it's helped me to laugh. I got a sense of humor. They're so humorous and funny. The joy I had as an 11-year-old came back to me. They helped me find the real Krista.

But lots of my 3rd-dimensional dreams were shattered! Wow. It's like a cold shower. Man. A rollercoaster. You can't shut it off; there's no turning back. Once you know, once you learn truth, you can't go backwards. It's devastating to try to go backwards.

How did you keep it together at the beginning?

Communication. Making YouTube videos, writing books. Actually my clients help me feel normal. Connecting with other star people. Starseed forums. Facebook, social media. Internet mainly. Library books too. I spent tons of time in the New Age section, reading every kind of New Age book possible. They brought relief. Once you have knowledge, everything makes sense. You have to develop your mind in order to understand the physical world. And sharing is giving. Sharing your true self is a gift to other people. Also known as not being fake.

I feel like I've been prepared for a long time. I've already been through so much shit before this, that I feel I was ready. I'm mixed race, so I know what it's like to be like a freak. The answer was to move to America, where it's okay. Move to a community where it's accepted. Find any sort of community where you are not a freak.

Or talk to one person who doesn't judge you. I met a psychic while I was waking up, and they explained a lot to me. A psychic friend in college who saw spirits and had strange things happen through her entire life. It was as if I had known this all along. But the internet helped me a lot. For example, understanding why I was seeing repeating digits, hearing things and feeling my bed shake. I would feel Earth tremors that no one else could feel. Literally the bed was shaking. And it happened while I was working at Macy's over the holidays one year. I ran out on lunch break. I said to the manager, "Do you guys feel that?" Only one man outside the store said he felt it. But it felt like an earthquake. I told everyone an earthquake was happening. I guess I learned not to tell everyone everything! Don't share so much. That's what I've had to learn.

Do you feel a sense of equality with them?

Wow. Good question. I feel immense love from them. But you'll see in the regression that I did with Hank Jones II, there was this leader in the council meeting, and I felt so inferior to him that the hypnotist said, "It's okay, you can speak." Like saying, "It's okay Krista." I had a total inferiority complex. I went in the Great Hall at this council meeting, and I did not feel comfortable communicating verbally, just telepathically, which is the same in this life. So I know as a child I was telepathic. My mom shut down her telepathy with me after age four, which was devastating. But it's coming back on.

In terms of the work as a channel, I do feel it's an equal relationship. Yeah, more than that. I get rewards. I get energy. It's an honor. Oh my gosh. I don't look like them but that doesn't matter. Energetically they probably have different abilities than I do. And there's more of them talking at one time, so there's more energy coming from a group versus just myself. But always it's equal exchange when it's benevolent galactic beings. It's the law.

But I'm not doing one-on-one sessions at the moment, mainly as I'm have difficulty pricing it. If it's very expensive only certain people have access, and there's a lot of pressure on me to deliver. And if it's cheap I'll do too many and get burnt out.

If you get burnt out, does that impact the process?

I was warned by a lot of elders in the esoteric field not to burn myself out when first started channeling. Multiple times, from Finland to Sedona: don't burn yourself out. After doing a two-hour session for $77, I felt the quality of information and energy was worth a lot more.

I might view the client's questions as coming from ego, but that's my personal judgment. For example, wanting to know if they are associated with ascended masters. The Orion Council is unconditionally loving, so there's a big difference in their perception and mine. If I ask them why someone wanted an answer to a certain question they will say that perhaps it was important that that person needed to know that at that time. I've been asked by many people if they are the physical incarnation of various higher beings, like archangels. The answer is that yes, they've tuned in via meditation, or psychedelics or visions, dreams. They work with collectives. I found in the Emerald Tablet of Thoth, that Master Thoth could inhabit multiple bodies at the same time. That's why they're masters. So when one person says I am that, it's like sure, but you belong to a collective, you're not the singular embodiment of that ascended master.

What are the best and worst things about channeling work?

The best part is having non-physical friends, or other-dimensional friends. I keep saying non-physical, but they are physical in another dimension.

The worst part? This is a hard question. Dealing with trust issues. For instance, do you like me, or do you like the Orion Council? You feel me? Just for example. Like a rich celebrity; is it me or my money that you want?

How do you deal with the trust issue?

I make myself extremely vulnerable all the time. And I constantly fail, over and over and over. You just have to put yourself through the wringer. There's no option other than getting up and doing it. There's no excuse. You're driven internally. I'm working with a healer, to help me reduce the crazy openness. My senses were so open that it was causing problems. So the result was learning psychic protection. And En-ra wrote an ebook about it. The result was boundaries. And the Orion Council said that in the hypnosis: develop strong boundaries. It's getting better. But there's no hiding any more. This New Age, everything's going to be seen, so I try to be as open and honest as possible now, because people will have a hard time when all the lies are seen.

This interview process is so extremely healing, but it's like oooh! You know?

Some people have a desire to orient themselves galactically. Starseeds. There is a distinctive difference between someone with a cosmic awareness, and someone with a one-block mentality.

How well do you feel you understand the beings?

There's definitely a lot of scientists there. A scientist, a training officer, a mother-like one. We work together as students of energy. That's it.

Interview with the Orion Council - Session 1

Why do you use channeling?

One moment please, hold on please. It has to be relaxed. One moment please, thank you.

It is nice to communicate today. Orion Council here, thank you. We need to give her a moment. Thank you.

We will talk about Ascension, alright? We will answer your question. Why does Orion Council use channeling to communicate? It is important because the system has been rewired in such a fashion that we have openings in the electric system of the channel. It is for communication. It is for Ascension. It is for Krista's training. It is also for many people to understand what is the capability of those on your planet without awareness of highest energies. What is highest energy?

It is beings from other dimensions communicating through a personality program.

And you are sensitive to what is going on, so you ask Orion Council: how is it that I am sensing you? You are feeling with many parts of yourself, and you are at the same time in your logical hemisphere. And you are also involved in multiple dimensional adjustments. We are talking about this because you are to understand the processes which perhaps are beyond your current understanding. You will in time know what is actually happening multidimensionally. We enjoy these terminologies because we have not the scientific vocabulary with this channel to explain this science. For channeling is a science.

Why do you work with Krista?

We will answer your question, hold on please. One moment.

We will tell you that our channel is trained for multiple reality programs. She would talk about seven dimensionality with you but we are not involved in this question today. She wants to do a lot of communications in that dimension. And we are working with nine dimensionality. You understand dimensions as higher or lower but they are simultaneous, and it is not so important about which dimension, but we have to communicate the number because it is such an unusual frequency in other dimensions that you would be quite excited to perceive those in your current state.

The purpose of being involved in a specific dimension is because the consciousness is working with other communities, and this consciousness is working with patterns, and with sound, you could say. But it is not so simple. When you are in these dimensions your language has changed, and we are sensing that you understand what we mean.

The right way to sense Ascension is through trusting in the process. One of your friends in your life has told you about what it is like to travel into outer space. You know that because you have done that. If you had not, you would say, "Explain this to me, it is something quite strange and I have never in my wildest dreams thought of it." But the same has happened to you in 7th, 8th, 9th layers. You have been in parallel dimensions at the same time.

"What is possible?" our channel is asking us all the time. If you are in this conscious focus point, are you focusing in other dimensions? Of course you are. Is there value in this knowing? Perhaps. Perhaps not, at this time. But if you are studying dimensional theory, it would be very important for you to know what dimension the channel is operating in. We say at this moment she is wanting to work with you in the 7ᵗʰ dimension. But you would say, "Orion Council, I have to talk to you about morality, and I have to talk to you about this physical process."

We are ready to answer your questions, thank you.

Why do you work with humanity?

We are also learning from you, and you are learning from us. It is an agreement. Many beings work with Orion Council. But though some haven't believed that it is possible to communicate with beings from this Betelgeuse star system, it is and we are here to prove it. Also we are here to talk about *rens* ... uh, *rens* ... uh, we have troubles, hold on please.

M: Orions?

Orions. Thank you. We have trouble saying that word. *Orions* are many. They have many groups here involved in your Earth. And we are one of those groups. But we work with other beings that are not Orions. Have you understood our communication?

What is the most important thing to you?

One moment.

We will answer your question. This is very nice to ask Orion Council because you are communicating about circumstance, and in your reality, your perception of what is, constantly changes. Those people on your Earth haven't understood the changing of their own nature. And if you were to observe channelings, the nature of the channelings is constantly changing. And people say, "Oh, you have developed yourself. You have changed your style." And many people haven't this awareness of themselves. If they were to sense their own progress, they would have appreciation for themselves.

And the people who are observing channeled messages have also to understand that many beings that talk through one vessel have changed their perceptions. It is an ongoing communication. If you are sensitive to observation of the collective, then you will understand that energies are shifting rapidly. The speed at which the energy shifts rapidly is faster with Ascension, and you are understanding communications and codings faster, and you are also understanding how to align with this frequency on your planet.

And En-ra is here. My name in En-ra, and also we have De-ra here, and so many of us want to talk about this Council with you if you have time. We will answer more than one question. Thank you.

What is the most important message you can give to humanity at this time?

Yes, one of those important messages, because we have many, is that ren … ren … uh, *Orions*. We have difficulty saying this term. When Orions are in your planet, they work with these highest groups on your planet. They have had difficulties in their assisting of this human type of species. Orion beings haven't understood the development of humans on planet Earth. They are focused on structures of government, not so much on evolution of biological species.

Orion beings have difficulties, and we will communicate to you today that Errans of Pleiades—they are from Erra—those beings are working to create a peaceful atmosphere so that these dialogues can happen. And we work with these beings of Erra, and also we work with Orions, and also we work with humans. That is our information. But we have many messages of importance. Thank you.

Do you have a sense of why am I involved in this work?

Ah, that is nice of you to ask, because, mmm, we think that you are asking us because you feel it is a job and we are here to say it is. And we are also here to say, ah, all jobs have compensation. And you are worried perhaps that people on your Earth haven't also this awareness of these sorts of jobs.

This is nice to say to you because our channel has these questions. Such as, "Why isn't anyone wanting to have an exchange of information?" And we say to her that the exchange of information happens at the correct time. And you would say, "Oh, Orion Council, you operate according to time. And at certain time periods I do this work." Hmm, yes indeed, because at certain time periods you are mindful and at certain times you are focusing on the job, and at times you are in a sensitive state of emotional awareness. Perhaps some of your great artwork on your Earth has this sensitivity. But not all great artwork has this sensitivity. But if you are to have sensitivities, you would ask Orion Council, "Is my job not to create artwork?"

What is happening here is that two of us are communicating about purpose. And when you are understanding your multidimensionality, it is not simply in this physical reality. In the same dimensionality there is much potential for energies to accelerate for your consciousness, and also you are working in other dimensions. What is the value for your personal reality? Perhaps you would be the one to answer this question because you are operating according to your perception of the acceleration of change for humanity. If we give information, and humanity is not accelerating to understand and receive this information, is it valuable?

Orion Council here, we enjoy our communication with you very much. We will answer your question; so it is.

What is the relationship between the self and the higher self?

Ah, this is nice to answer. When you have understood highest self as many say … our channel does not agree with us, she does not appreciate the highest self statement. We are saying this for you today, but she would not call it 'highest self'. We have a disagreement.

Now, if you are understanding highest self or superconscious mind, however you want to call the self that is beyond this physical existence, you will sense that there is alignment. What is alignment? First and foremost, alignment happens when you are practicing energy balance. We have not the language. Balancing of energy is alignment. Hold on one moment.

If you are practicing balancing of energy, you will have accumulated particles. Why do I accumulate particles when I've had this balance? It is magnetic, yes? The magnetic field has increased. This personality has energy available in the form of particles. Because they are attracting them, you would say, "Orion Council, they are attracting experiences, yes?" Perhaps they are, but they are also attracting non-physical, multidimensional experience. If you are working with one multidimensional self, your own self, you are also attractive to other higher selves, perhaps personality programs, multidimensional energies. And so with this particle attraction, you are sensing potential realities. And we are here to say that when you sense potential realities, many of you call it third eye, or psychic ability: "I am sensitive to potentials." And people say, "What is my potential?" And you say, "Well, you do not have the amount of particles yet to create that reality, but there is potential for you. And many would say you are a healer."

But for the being working with higher self in communication with other higher selves, you would call this person a wise man or some kind of energetic person.

What is that Orion Council? Why are you telling me about particles? Are you a scientist? Yes, we are scientists, but we are also involved in multidimensional processing. Because your Ascension is not simply one-dimensional, it is multidimensional, and we must communicate this to you because you will remember parts of yourself, and that is attracting particles.

And we are sensitive to alignments inside of your physical body. And you have many alignments taking place. And we observe these alignments when you are focused differently. So if you focus in a certain way, the alignment is very precise for your biological system. In that biological system there are small synapses which are constantly opening and closing. For those personalities who have closed this center here, to sensing the reality, they operate according to lower senses, you would say, yes? When a person operates according to lower senses, you would call it animalistic, yes? When I am an animal, I am not a mineral, yes? And we do not say that mineral is lower consciousness, we say it is simply operating according to lower senses. It is not higher or lower, it is happening simultaneously, yes?

And we understand that you know what is third eye center, yes? We say that your third eye is very open and you must remember that it is multidimensional information. Do you recognize in yourself that you have your energetic field open to beings wanting to communicate with you?

Because you have options now. You say, "Orion Council, show me the options." And we want you to know that if your third eye is open and if you're operating according to higher self, you have beings attracted to your energy field. Is it a job, or is it simply art, or what is this? It is up to you.

We have finished answering your questions. Thank you.

M: That was fascinating, thank you Krista. I was struck by the references to humor, and their crazy laugh.

As I relax into the channel there is a lot of laughter. I call that "going through the 4th dimension." When they think something's funny I can feel it. I think it's funny as well. I can have a disagreement with them. If they're laughing it's very awkward because they go, "Hah ... hah ... hah ... hah." You see this blank expression on my face, and this total monotone laughter. It's like in between the phone call. Like two bros that have known each other from college, telling their own inside jokes, and you feel the fun of it but you don't get it. You know when everyone in the room is laughing, and it's funny to you, but you don't get the joke? I feel like an outsider looking at you talking with them.

Thank you for sharing your experience, it's nice to hear the technical side. Where you noticed your own pattern of laughter, humor. And your reaction to the experience.

Session 2

Orion Council here, one moment. Thank you. Hold on please. Orion Council here.

We want to communicate about Orion Council. We are wanting to communicate about the three stars … and you have worked in this constellation, rest assured it is important information. You are knowing about this place. Area 51 is active. New information has to come through. Hold on please.

Area 51. We have to know why certain people are involved in communications in that location. The people that are involved in these communications have an understanding of the times when these craft are in this location. They understand when it is coming through the dimensional planes. They would benefit from understanding that humanity hasn't noticed. It is so hidden that humanity hasn't noticed craft entering Area 51. This was important knowledge. Area 51 has craft entering this atmosphere from other planes.

Three stars from Orion are of importance for you. We have information about that.

Area 51 on the other hand, has information for craft. That is why they enter. You are wondering: why would they come to this area?

Do you know about one planet that is inside of another planet? Are you understanding our information? Thank you.

M: Are you talking about the 'Inner Earth' concept?

Yes, that is what is, yes.

M: What do you understand about the Inner Earth?

Earth is having one-dimensional energy. We will communicate about what is one-dimensional energy. We are in a place that is around Earth, not inside. When you know one-dimensionality, you have knowledge from Inner Earth. Elohim.

Three stars in Orion is important for you to understand. Three stars in Orion have people coming through them to your planet. Area 51 also has people coming through from other planes. Three of the stars have knowledge for you; you must access your own database. Yes, you have information about those stars in your own database. Those stars have gateways. Real it is. Hello.

M: I have some questions from our previous session. You were talking about the third eye being open, and I wonder if you have any advice or directions for readers, to help them to open their third eye.

One moment, thank you. We are saying to you that third eye opens inside that head of yours when you are allowing knowledge to come through Akashic record.

Third eye has access to knowledge. That is what is happening when people are requesting information for their lives. Becoming this being with abilities, you must have knowledge. The people asking about knowledge haven't allowed for Akashic knowledge. Do we make sense to you or not? You must ask us if we are not clear.

M: I think so. I wanted to ask you, if there is anything I should know for my work now? Anything that can benefit my work in this area.

Yes, we will tell you that realigning yourself with your own information is important. The soul is contained in the highest level of reality, and we are talking about your expanded self. We have your expanded self here, and we want you to understand the reason we are taking this time to explain this expanded self. It is because your eyes are opening. The people on your Earth have it; it is happening. We understand the confusion about it. Realigning themselves to highest good. Also realigning themselves to these energies.

How is it happening? The people are in a state of awareness where their minds are connecting with one another. They are also sensitive. We are seeing they feel more energy, but they cannot understand the feelings that come through. They will ask about it. Third eye. What is happening to my energy field? Show me in letters and numbers, what is the energetics? And those of you who haven't understood the codes that the people get when they are writing in encoding. They are thinking, 'Oh, that is good energy.' It is more than that. It is about the soul that is talking at all times. When you access the soul information, the people are sensitive to that energy.

You would say, "Orion Council, it is not doing much on Earth because we have problems here." But the people with a soul connection ... it is so great, because ... that is who is communicating. Orion Council, many of us as one conscious communicator.

Now those people with the soul energies have a resonance. And they have agreed to share conscious communication on a higher level. Those beings are now recalling one another and they are assisting one another on a soul level.

You would say, "Orion Council, it is not of importance when you are in physicality." But it is, because the subconscious is registering this energetic information exchange. Also it is registering healing energy. It is also registering ideas. Those who are sensing your energies are not always getting recognition. And those who are sending energy are not always getting recognition, but they do it. And it is wonderful because we can see that exchange taking place.

You would say, "Orion Council, third eye means I know exactly what happens in each moment." We know that you are keen to understand what transpires in such soul communication. Is it a color, a number or a letter? We know that many of you are translators of energy. We know that many of you are focusing in multiple ways, and we know that sometimes you are all that is allowed for your eyes to see. The one eye must see all. That is what is important to many on your Earth, yes?

M: I cannot resist taking the opportunity to ask you: What to you is the meaning of life? I mean the meaning of your lives, and of life itself?

This was a nice question, because you are saying that we have awareness and you are seeing that; so we are in a life. What is a life? It is growth, it is understanding, and it is accumulating knowledge. Life is success over long period of time, in our opinion.

And you would say, "Orion Council, what an unusual description. How would you define life as success? How is it that you are succeeding on your side of things?" We are in success in our amount of energy! We have humor. It is difficult to explain it.

There was a lot of love in your mind as you ask us this, and we sense that you are allowing for us to describe our enjoyment. That is what is life to us: enjoyment of energy. It is a wonderful sense of having that bit of God that is giving us love, and it is also in science. When you understand God, science is great. It is love that is understood. What is science? The study of God. Thank God.

M: Science is the study of God. That is a fascinating idea. How do you define God?

K: Oh, sorry ... something weird just happened. My eyes started ... oh ... whoa ... that's weird. Sorry. My eyes are flickering uncontrollably, and I want them to stop it.
What the heck is going on? Sorry.
What the hell is happening? Good thing I'm not on a live stage.
Okay, something's weird. They're in my body, but my eyes are flickering, like uncontrolled, and it's keeping my eyes open and they're still here. That's weird. I'm not used to that at all, I feel very strange. I feel it in my physical body, but ... okay, so ...
Okay, this is so fricking awkward. they want me to channel with my eyes open, but this is highly uncomfortable for me. I don't like it at all.

M: Well, you are in choice. You don't have to do it if you don't want to.

K: See? If I close them they just flicker open. Oh God, I don't want to be one of those open-eye channelers. *No*, don't make me do this!
Okay, can I just not look at you while I do this?

M: That's fine. You can look at the wall ... or whatever makes you comfortable, Krista.

K: What the heck is going on? Everything's changing.
Okay ... what the heck?
[Drinks water]
Sorry, this is *so* awkward for me!
Pull yourself together.
Ha ha! This is *so* weird!

M: Like I said, you have to be in choice. If you don't want to work that way with them, I guess you've got to put your foot down and say no. It's completely up to you. From my side—and I'm sure from their side—they are happy for you to be in choice, and respect your free will.

K: Okay. Well, why don't you just ask the question again, and I'll try my best.

M: Well, it's kind of the big one. They made a really interesting comment, that "science is the study of God." And so I asked, quite naturally, "How do you define God?"

K: Okay, let's do this. My eyes flickered so hard that they flew open. With the channeling you have to let go, right? You have to let your body do what it wants, to get a better connection. So yeah, it's almost like getting possessed in your jawline, your hands. But I've only allowed it in my upper torso. As you can see I have control, shifting in my chair while I'm channeling; I have control. I have to keep my spine up or the channel would not be so nice. So I don't fully leave my body, that's too scary for me.

So, okay. But yeah, that was like uncontrollable. It was cool, it didn't hurt me, I'm totally fine. But it was like, "Open your eyes."

M: Maybe that was part of their answer.

K: Sorry, my mind is doing weird ... I'm only half present, half coherent. Like I'm still not fully connected to myself. Okay. It can happen between channels. I can pop in and talk, but I'm not fully ...

I just want you to know that I feel like I'm naked on a mountain in front of the entire village. This is how vulnerable I feel channeling with my eyes open. But it's okay. Totally fine. I can totally do this. You're a harmless guy, you know about the ETs, you're nice, this is an experiment. It's all fine. Nothing's going to happen to me, I'm safe in my room, it's totally fine.

Okay.

I just want you to know that I have huge stage fright, and fears of channeling on stage, so I know this is some kind of preparation for some kind of future work. But it never crossed my mind that I had to open my eyes. Like Eric Clapton, he played his guitar with his back to the audience because he was so shy. That's how it is.

M: Jim Morrison used to do the same, at first. You see that depicted in Oliver Stone's *The Doors* movie. Everyone was screaming at him to turn round. It's a great scene. I recommend it. Weirdly, when he and I were about ten years old, we looked almost identical. A couple of school friends saw a photo of him at that age in a book, I think *Riders on the Storm*, and they were like, "What's *Miguel* doing in there?!"

K: Did you have long hair?

M: Really long. Big dark curly locks.

K: *He he!* I can't imagine it.

Okay, I must say, this is very weird with eyes open. When the third eye opens, everything talks to you. I perceive light fixtures flickering when they're not, everything has a consciousness. Everything's swimming in the room, everything talks to me, everything has an awareness. I must tell you this is more intense with eyes open. Like dreaming in Technicolor, or whatever they call it.

I know I'm a dramatic Leo, but ...

I don't know where to look!

M: I guess you could look at your knees, or your hands?

K: I'll just look at my knees. Okay.

Gosh, you're going to have all of this on tape too. But that's fine. That's what it is. Okay.

Now you know what it was like to be my mom in the *Orion Council, Here* book. This is exactly what she had to go through; all Krista's ego, la-la-la, talking in between the messages coming through her, like, "*Ooh*, what's happening?"

M: *Ha ha ha!* Oh man. That's a funny image.

Anyway, there's only two questions left. The question I was asking them was about their definition of God.

K: Okay, I'm going to look possessed, but don't worry, I'm totally fine.

Orion Council here, hold on please.

The rest of the communication will come through, hold on please.

Area 51 is active at this time.

Three of us are communicating, it is taking us a moment, thank you.

There is a side of this planet which is very active with energies. The reason is because that alignment is taking place.

We have to say that you are asking yourself questions about reality. We are simply reminding you that the resonance is great when you are in the west part of your planet. You have resonance to greatest energies.

Djwahl Kuhl energy that is a grand master, Djwahl Kuhl is working with you at this time. Rest assured that you would be aligned with this being. Djwahl Kuhl is great and the show must go on.

Now we will talk about God.

Try to help her relax, she is not calm at all.

It would help in your mind if you have allowance to give her relaxation. You resonate with that. Now she would talk about herself, but it is not her time to talk about herself. Training her to focus, that is what is happening.

Trying to align you with Djwahl Kuhl, and tell you about God, the one God. We talk about the one God. Area 51. Thank you.

M: You seem to have a real thing about Area 51 this evening. Is there something else that you want to share about that?

One moment, hold on please. We will talk about Area 51 and you will ask us about God, *he he!* What is God? Is God in Area 51 or is God somewhere else? You are understanding our humor? It is quite important that you know we are a humorous group consciousness.

Training her to focus, that is what is happening. As you know, her focus is in multiple dimensions. Now you understand the channeling. And you know that channeling involves groups. That is why you sense that many energies come through one communication. You know Area 51 communication, you know God communication, and personal energy. There were alignments taking place. We will talk about the right one for you. It is God, yes? Not Area 51. Three of us are communicating at once. Hold on please.

We are aligning you with our energies, training her to focus. There was difficulty with that information. Do you want to talk about God, one wants to speak about Area 51, yes? Do you understand our communication?

M: It makes more sense now that you explain that there's three of you communicating at once. I can understand better why the communication can be complicated to understand.

But there's something you said earlier that I want to understand better. You said something like, I'm working with Grand Master dral cool?

Yes, it is important for you to understand. Training with that being; it is a wonderful idea for you to work with that being. Now you know Djwahl Kuhl is working with, have you understood our communication about who this being is?

M: Uh, no. Who is this being?

It is a masterful being on your planet. Is working with multiple groups, thank you.

M: But what kind of being is Djwahl Kuhl?

Training people to love one another. Hello.
Now we will talk about God. Area 51 and God.
Djwahl Kuhl is a masterful being that has been on your planet. We are having difficulty today, you understand. Take a moment.
Area 51 is important. This has a frequency, if we understood one another it would have opened a communication. People on your Earth haven't allowed for open communication. They sustain that information without sharing, and the one God has allowed for this, but the one God is also involved in the, let us say, great alignment of planetary energy, for highest good for all. If people sustain information and they aren't in alignment with the planet, how much of an imbalance is created? If you suppress energy in a mountain, how would it affect the Earth on the other side? It is involving the movements of mass particles on your Earth. The same goes for masters of consciousness. One masterful being affects multiple groups, as it is in place in this Earth. It is difficult for us to explain how the effects take place. Frequency is a ... *res* ... a *res* ... hold on please, we have troubles.

M: Resonance?

Yes, thank you. It ... I ... hold on please, we are shifting our energies. Thank you.
Two of us now.
Now we will talk about this frequency. Frequency as Orion Council defines it, now takes into account alignment with entire planet. Your frequency works in a oneness. The oneness has information. People are sustaining information. Have you understood our communication?
The channel is not agreeing with our choice of vocabulary. We mean that sustaining information involves bandwidth, and your planet has multiple bandwidths. It is for knowledge to come through multiple layers.
You access multiple layers when you are working with masterful Djwahl Kuhl, and you were inside of your Earth at one point. Not quite remembering, but you had that experience. The same goes for our channel. Has no recollection in your conscious mind. You were focusing on one timeline. Those beings who have multiple energies

open, would understand that mastery involves awareness of multiple timelines.

Now you say, "Orion Council, that is ungrounded knowledge, for planet Earth must hold one timeline." You know that timelines involve choice points. We are discussing our favorite topic of 'choice points'. People sustaining knowledge haven't involved themselves with choice points of masterful beings. Have thought they were the masters, so they simply said we were masters on planet Earth.

And we will allow only for certain information on Area 51 to come and go. Now you have spacecraft entering Area 51 with new information. How does that affect the timeline? That is our focus. Thank you.

M: Thank you. When I transcribe this later I will do my best to make sense of it.

For some reason I wanted to ask if you have any questions for me? Are there any final questions or comments to bring this session to a close?

One moment, thank you. Area 51 has craft entering it constantly.

People haven't aligned with masterful beings that have awareness of multiple timelines. If you are a masterful being with awareness of multiple timelines, what do you think these people should know? We ask you this question. It is important. Would you impress us with you answer? Thank you.

M: Can you run that by me again?

Yes. This is an important question. If you are a masterful being accessing multiple timelines, which one would you explain to humanity?

M: That's a very interesting question. I hate to answer a question with a question, but is this a practical question for me? Is there something related to this that I have to think about in a practical way, or is this more of a philosophical question?

Ah, we understand your communication. Hold on please. It is important for you to know this answer. Thank you.

If you understood our communication, you would understand that Area 51 has to do with the whole topic of Ascension. Three of us are still here. The rest are around us in our Council group. Hello.

Three ... three ... difficulties. Hold on please. She is excited about this.

Dree ef sa, er-er-ah.

She will talk about in her language, but it is our turn to communicate. Hold on please.

Er ah ese da ene ra, es de ahh.

K: Fuck. I have this ... hold on. Shit. *Why?*

Sorry. That's not the channel, that's me, Krista.

Why am I being made to do all this uncomfortable stuff?

So like ... what the *fuck?*

This is one of the weirdest channeling days ever. Okay, so like, there's this Council, right? So the Council's there and they're deliberating how to answer your question, and then I'm coming in here, and my light language is coming through, and I have totally supressed my light language because I feel like a freak; but it's trying to come through, and it makes absolutely zero sense. And then this just started coming through, and it's just like the eye flickering thing.

I was about to answer your question in light language. That's what was trying to happen. And I can let it through, but I just want to tell you that this is like really pushing my limits. First eye-open channeling, now talking light language. It makes absolutely no sense at all.

Like I understand the wrestle with the Orion Council because my mom had the same thing when she was talking with them. Like, can you please explain this, can you please be clear? That's good, that's what gets the back and forth, but I don't know how the light language comes in like that. Like what is that? What? I don't understand. I'm already dealing with thinking I'm batshit insane, but that's the egoic mind trying to infiltrate the whole experience, if you see what I'm saying.

Okay, so I guess I have to be in control here somehow. What do I do now? I'm just going to let it happen, okay?

M: Just whatever you're comfortable with.

K: I'm already forgetting everything that was said. And I'm totally sober, I'm not on any medication, just so you know.

Okay, can you ask the question for the Council one more time? But if the light language comes through, I'm going to let it do that. But I really hate being seen on webcam talking light language, just so you know.

Like this doesn't excite me, it doesn't do anything for me, it's not cool. I'd rather be on Pinterest or doing Oracle cards.

M: My final question to them was: do you have any questions for me? And then they asked me, if I'm getting this right: if I was a masterful being with access to multiple timelines, and could only tell humans about one timeline, which one would it be? And so I thought they must have a very good reason for choosing that question, so I asked them if they are wanting me to think practically about that, or if it's more of a general philosophical question.

K: Part of me is heavily resisting, but this is good, it's great. You know? I feel very safe and comfortable with you, and that's the whole point. You have to feel relaxed to channel.
Okay.
That's cool. They've never actually admitted to having a group in a circle around them before. And I know who the being is that they mentioned. Lucky you, you get an Ascended Master working with you. I only get Mary. The only tell me about Mary.
I believe I'm spelling this correctly. The being is Djwahl Kuhl. You'll find tons of channelings of this being. I recommend Madame Blavatsky as the best source.

M: I will look he, she or it up.

K: Okay, if life didn't already get interesting enough, now it is. Alright.

M: *Ha ha!*

K: Thank you for your patience. My mom had to go through this. Okay.
Eyes open then; yup.
My mind is being wiped now. It's like being in deep meditation. I'm thinking of nothing. So.

Orion Council here, hold on please.
We will discuss your question.
We went to that database where she has knowledge, and she wants to give you information, for it is love. That is why. We would understand it as Akashic information. Have you understood our communication?

M: Is this in response to the clarification I was seeking about whether the timeline question is practical or more philosophical? Is there something there that I have to learn about? Does that make sense?

We would say that you are in voluntary position to sense love and to communicate it through your senses to people. And your greatest self, which has done great work in many places, is reminding you of these time periods. She has access to Akashic record, and she would communicate knowledge to you with her access to her informational database, is what happened, and she would say it in another language.

Djwahl Kuhl is working with you. How do you feel about this?

M: Pun intended: it sounds cool. Although I know nothing about this being. In what kind of way is this being working with me?

She would say it in her language, but we will tell you this being has a great love, inside the planet and outside of it. Two places at once.

What an awareness of the being! Do you know about holding multiple layers of awareness at one time? Of course you do. You say, "I do it all the time." I think and I think, and I feel as well. But we say, if you are maintaining this focus for long amounts of time, you have great energy field, yes? And so you would say I know the effect that a being has on me, it is simply felt, I resonate with energy. You know people like energy, and like to have it. You know what I mean? As you say to one another, "You know what I mean?"

M: *Ha ha!* Yes, I know what you mean.

This was an intention for you to communicate knowledge. This is what we do. And you know that we do that. And you know that you do that.

"So, Orion Council, I communicate knowledge a lot of the time, now I want to focus in a new way. I want to allow for an experience that gives me great satisfaction and also gives me awareness of other realities. It is fun because my mind is expanded in this way." Holding that reality, many of you on your planet have had this awareness of multiple exciting timelines. Some of you would call it a 'mandala', but we say that it is simply awareness, and we have discussed this many times. The awareness has great amount of information and enjoyment. You would say, "Orion Council, it is not feasible to hold multiple layers of awareness because of the interference." No, you would not interfere with another person if you simply knew their story. You would not interfere with them, would you?

M: Uh, it depends on how you define 'interfere'.

If you are in agreement with a being's reality, would you convince them otherwise? No, because you are in agreement. If you are not in agreement with their reality, it is interference if you are allowing for new timeline. But it is forceful, yes?

M: How do you define 'timeline'?

Time period of multiple realities. This would be the timeline for many of you with agreements for Earth history, for instance. You all agree that there was a solar flare in a couple of weeks. He he he.

And you say, "Orion Council, I know that we had extraterrestrial contacts in the past. It is a timeline of agreement." Those on your planet who say there were no extraterrestrials in the past. He he he he he. And we say, "What a timeline, with no extraterrestrials on your planet!" He he he he.

Not in agreement with this. Therefore, are you in alignment with us? No, of course not. If you say, "Orion Council does not agree with me; I believe extraterrestrials have come to this planet long ago, and Orion Council says not," I discount their reality, yes? I am interfering? No. Who is interfering when there is not an agreement? Is one interfering with the other? He he he. We have a horrible sense of humor, but it is to be so. We love you.

M: *Ha ha!* A horrible sense of humor. I love it.

Well, that's a lot of information. It's a lot to try to make sense of. I have a feeling that it will make more sense to me in six months than it does today. But I appreciate your willingness to share information.

Area 51. There was a member of our group here that is important in our group, and they are sensitive to this information. They want it to be explained on your planet, so they have dropped this vocabulary multiple times through the channel. People have agreed with her. Area 51 is active, yes? Have you understood our timeline interference, yes? You would say, "Orion Council, you have interfered with reality because you say it is active." How many have agreed with Orion Council it is active because of the channeled message? It is difficult to understand how such a small move on our part would affect so many people. Area 51 we say multiple times; people begin to understand that is possible. There are people on your Earth who did not focus on Area 51. You say, "Obviously, I know about that. Who is not knowing about that?" Many people. Rest assured you know much more than certain people on your planet, that is alright.

M: I believe that is true.

So you know that as you document our communication, that people haven't thought about Area 51 at all. They have focused on the third eye, he he he.

M: *Ha ha!* Yeah. I find that people tend to be drawn more to one aspect of the subject than the other. Either towards the technological and political aspects of this subject, or more towards the metaphysical and spiritual aspects.

Area 51 involves third eye to see it happening. That is important, yes? Do you know, if you are to sense craft, you have access to multiple timelines? People with third eye have access to timelines. They would not understand it. They say, "Orion Council, having visions today. Having another vision today." So we say, you must be sensing other dimensional energies, yes? Oh, we are excited about this, yes? Now the people see multiple dimensional reality. Is it relevant? But I still want to see it. Ha! Do you know how much humor is involved in your question, if you say, "Orion Council, let me see the other worlds." And it is philosophical. I feel it is nice for me to sense craft in this plane of reality. I want to interfere with the Earth timeline. Area 51, that is our humor, but it is also our bit of changing of things. So people would say, "Orion Council, you did not change anything, you simply repeated like a broken record. It is simply, ha, the way to Ascension: through a broken record. He he he he he he.
So we will talk soon. And those who understand you will know that reality shifts constantly. The beings that you work with shift constantly. You are shifting constantly. We would tell you more, but we are complete for today. So it is.

M: Well, thank you. Thank you for your time and your thoughts, and I hope we'll talk again.

K: Something cool happened. Hold on. Water. I should probably go and drink water.

I want to share this. I had a vision, and I don't know if it was Egypt. I don't know it was this planet. There were all these golden pyramids, and these palm trees in between them, and this little like landing platform. And this thing like a walkway that goes up to the pyramid. The pyramids were really close to each other, and then there's a bigger pyramid which was brown, like regular rock, and the sun is shining.

But these golden ones are there, and in the middle of a cluster of temples and this platform ... it was just so nice. Ah. Everything's clear. I just see this cluster. I don't see a big city. They're all very acute angles, like the 72-degree angle, Nubian ones, not the Giza 51 degree ones. But the big one could be somewhere between 51 and 72 degrees. Maybe around 60 degrees. I don't know if that's a sacred number or anything, but that's just how it looks in my vision.

Jujuolui Kuita

Jujuolui (Juju) Kuita is a former soldier and police officer who, following an animal rescue case while on duty, changed career to work with animals. When Hurricane Katrina hit the southern states she adopted a dog to help with the efforts, began taking courses in disaster response and dedicated herself to being more 'of service'.

During this period, Juju became a UFO investigator and then a Section Director with MUFON to get in touch with her other identity. She established a meet-up group in California to try to help those wanting to explore ET contact experiences. In 2010 Juju published her first book entitled *We Are Among You Already*, in hopes of helping others awaken to their potential ET identity. Later, Juju founded an LLC named Star Being & Spiritual Center, where she created a retreat for those wanting to learn about and experience ET contact. She created a few courses on various ET subjects and submitted one to the University of Metaphysics.

In 2013 Juju found her dream career as an Emergency Animal Medical Technician. Every day she uses her skills as a Reiki practitioner to help the animals she rescues. It is most satisfying for her, utilizing both the professional and metaphysical skills she has developed on her journey.

In 2015, she shared her hybrid identity with Miguel Mendonça and Barbara Lamb in *Meet the Hybrids*, and expanded on the whole field in *We Are the Disclosure*. She has appeared on documentaries and been interviewed many times on radio regarding her hybrid nature.

Which words do you use to describe 'them'?

The first word that comes to mind is my 'star family'. We feel that bonded feeling, of parents, siblings, cousins and whatever else. But there are lots of different connections, more than our family relationships we have here on Earth. There are even more connections out there. That's why I use 'star family'. Because I know they're my soul family, where I came from. I have the human blood family here on Earth, but feel more that soul and DNA connection with my star family, the Fajans from the planet Faqui. They are what people would call a Reptilian race.

I would describe them as evolved, peaceful beings, with great love and compassion. I can feel the energy of who we are as I'm part of them, so it's really strong sometimes, especially when channeling for this book.

I actually have to stop for a moment because it's very emotional, and deep, and it really hits home at a core level. And of course I begin missing them.

I'm trying to work through the emotional part, so forgive me.

You know, I want to be with them. Because that energy is nothing like anything here on Earth. It's such a high vibration, and all your flaws, the things you don't like about yourself, or your weaknesses, that are perceived here by yourself or others, they just fall to the wayside. There is none of that where I'm from. It's a 5th-dimensional level, so we see through our hearts, which is an amazing difference. Which is why it's so challenging for us here on Earth, those of us who remember who we are and where we're from. We have these feelings and knowledge and memories of our star families. It's just a very different way of living and thinking.

In general I use the term 'ETs'. I never use the word 'alien'. An alien means you don't know it, it's foreign to you. So I'm very careful with the words I choose, and I choose 'ET' or 'star family'.

Which kinds of beings are you in contact with?

There are many types I've had contact with throughout my life. The most important of course is my own, who began visiting me from the age of five, and probably before. I don't recall how far back, but I remember hearing them before that regular six-month visitation period. It's the same energy that comes through, so I knew it was the same people or person from my homeworld, and that's the Fajans. We're 5th-dimensional. Our core value could be stated as connecting and growing, and recognizing that all of life is Source energy, and that there is a deep connection with all that. Knowing that what we do to any other being, we do to ourselves.

So our intentions are always to be of assistance in helping that growth and evolution of another. Never to take advantage or seek power or control or anything nefarious. They are always very loving, very gentle. They have guided me throughout my entire life, and are doing so right in this moment. Being asked to do more of a mission through me is exciting for them. So they're really coming through in a pretty powerful way. As I grow, they can come through even more. So that's the main ET contact.

There have been so many other different kinds of beings I've had experiences with in the astral or dream state. I try to draw pictures of these sometimes. There was one that looks like a Michelin Man; he was brown, he had big eyes, he was just standing outside my sliding door one night, and I walked over and put my hand up to wave at him, like "Hi!" That's all I remember. He was looking at me with a very genuine, friendly face. I didn't feel anything but peace from that being, so I wasn't afraid. I just made sure he saw me and waved and said hi.

I've been in dream states where I dived off a boat into an ocean of some kind, and was reconnecting with these dolphin and whale-like beings.

I have many contacts with what people call the Greys, but I've seen so many types, shapes, heights of what I call 'Insectoids'. I just kinda group them all under that term, including the Mantis types. I wish I had written it all down throughout my life, just to remember.

I have many Insectoid-type beings I come in contact with. Some are really intimate, and we have conversations where I'll be telling them, "You need to tell me what you like, because you're an Insectoid and I'm not. And it's important that if we are close like this that it's pleasurable." It sounds kinda crazy, but I've had those conversations with a female Insectoid hybrid. She had black hair. I don't know who she is on Earth. She may be living on the ships. I don't know her name.

But in most of these contacts they seem to be my second family. And what I've been told is that when I incarnated here on Earth, the councils and I set up this contact agreement, that if I should need anything or if I get hurt or distraught, or if I'm in need of assistance, especially protection, that they would help me first. Because apparently they're very close to the Earth plane, they're active in our skies, and low Earth orbit. They're definitely around and active, whereas my family is not. So I've had such beautiful contact experiences with them. Sometimes for healing. Sometimes they'll tell me they just want me with them on the ships, but ask me to please not touch anything. I love it when they say that! It cracks me up, but they mean it. It's out of respect that you don't touch another species' equipment on a craft, especially on what we call the bridge. You just don't mess with those things, because you have no idea what they do, unless they're specifically training you to operate it. And they've done that with me. On one occasion they helped me learn how to fly, doing that transfer from one level of existence to another, without traveling between. It's just popping in and popping out. That was an interesting concept to learn. I talked about that in *Meet the Hybrids*.

So I would say the Insectoids of all types have helped me throughout my life. Especially learning unconditional love and how to send that to another being. That was one of the most profound experiences they have given me. It helped me realize that what we think and feel is energy, so how you put it out, and what you put out is crucial. Similar to the *Care Bears* in the animated series long ago. I think that's why I loved it so much, because I knew how to do that on a subconscious level; I knew there was truth to that.

And *E.T.* the movie, when his heart lights up. That's very powerful, because my star family and I know that our thinking and feeling and life comes through the heart not the head. So that was amazing for us to see. And what I see, they see. When I say 'we' sometimes that's what I mean.

Animals seem to be another ET experience. I'm very connected with animal forms. Life of all kinds actually, and I think they know that. If I'm just walking with a friend I attract wildlife, or I should say, I don't scare them away.

Also in the ET state, I know there are animal forms or types of beings that I visit that are amazing. The problem is that humans see animals as less evolved beings, or not sentient, or not able to have feelings and connect on an intimate level with another. But they really do, especially the ET ones. Whales and dolphins are considered ET beings on Earth. They have shown me multiple times on Earth how we are connected. One day I was walking over the San Francisco Bay bridge with friends, and a pod of dolphins swam underneath me for half the distance of the bridge. I didn't know what to think, I mean my ego was in shock. Because I try to have a healthy ego, but I was being blown away by the fact that they're there, and they weren't just swimming off. And my friends were like, "Wow, we've never seen that." And I'm sure there's lots of dolphins in the Bay Area. I'm not saying it was a magical connection, but it was really interesting, and I was humbled by that experience, and excited at the same time. For that gift of them showing me that connection.

I remember going to Las Vegas, and really needing the energy of the dolphins. Or the animals. They have a white lion and I'm a Leo so I needed to see him. As another Leo I know you understand that Miguel! So I went to the dolphin enclosure and sat along the side. You're not allowed to touch the dolphins, and I get that. Well, one jumped up near me. And the trainer looked at me like, "What are you doing, to draw that dolphin to you?" Then she looked back at it and made this motion for it to get back into the water. I *so* wanted to reach out and touch it, but I respect that you can't do that. Then all of a sudden there were seven dolphins coming to me. Out of nine total, seven of the nine were with me. And that was really comforting. I believe they're big into healing work, so I must have really needed it.

I know I've had attempted contact from a less loving race, at least twice in my life. But each time there has been an intervention by my protective Insectoid species, or potentially my star family. But I can't have my people coming to Earth. They have an agreement not to, and I can't see that they would break that contract. So I think that was them sending someone to me, and it's a blessing to feel that protection from a being. There are other beings I became close to. I have friends who channel these beings.

How do they appear to you?

That's an excellent question because this is very complex. Sometimes it's about your perception and definition of things. I don't think I've ever had a contact experience where I could go up to the being and shake its hand in 3D form, except for dolphins and whales, other hybrids and starseeds, or ETs in disguise. Because we know some of them look very human and have even worked at the Pentagon. And I may not necessarily know it, except for feeling very good around that being. With the other hybrids that I'm in touch with, I can feel their ET essence, and that is another form of connecting with an ET on Earth in a 3D manner.

However, most of the time contact seems to happen in an altered state, such as meditation. And sometimes being in a distraught emotional state allows you to receive guidance. While I was in the military I had my guide, Jer-me, appear as a white male in a helmet and uniform, and wake me up. I didn't realize I'd fallen asleep with my gun on my lap. And if you get caught sleeping with your firearm on active duty you can be in serious trouble. You can be demoted, or even discharged. It's pretty serious, so he was helping me out.

Jer-me is my Fajan guide who has been with me all of my life on both Faqui and on Earth. I believe the art rendition of my family by Kesara (at the end of this chapter) is of Jer-me. We are very close.

Most of my contact comes through what I call 'dream state', whether you're in an altered state in the experience or astrally in the experience. I'm sure there are times when you're physically in the experience, but all I'll remember is receiving an implant or waking up with one. So if it involves this body I know I've been physically with them, but a lot of times I don't remember. There have been a couple of healings I remember, so I must have been in this form. They healed my kidneys, and worked on my eyesight. More recently, they've been doing something with my major arteries, my femoral artery and brachial artery. I awoke feeling an immense pressure in my arm, like they were holding a pressure point, and the pressure builds up then is released, and that's when I wake up. Those are kind of interesting. I don't know what those are. Apparently they don't feel the need to tell me. Even for us, being starseeds or hybrids, we're not always allowed to remember. I feel blessed that they let me remember, so I can know I was with them, rather than thinking it was just a weird dream. They'll give me little bits and pieces to know we had contact, and were together. I think they know it gives us a lot of hope, to remain here on Earth and complete our mission, because it's getting hard for a lot of us.

I believe they come in animal form a lot, and that would be in 3D form. One of my other Fajan soulmates on Faqui came, which I only recently found out, and incarnated as my dog Katrina. This is described in detail in the message at the end of the chapter.

I've seen a lot of streaks out of my peripheral vision, sometimes a steak of light, or color, or a shadow, because the room is light. It's a movement, but when you look it's gone. Since I'm hypersensitive I feel it may be a psychic sensing. I can feel or sense the energy of the being. So I know if it's self-serving, or a lighter energy that intends good.

Sometimes I get nudged to take a picture, and will see orbs, hopefully white, and I feel that's an indicator of beings coming in. It's like the being wanted to be caught on camera for you to see. That's happened several times.

I think our minds can only grasp an infinitesimal part of the whole. And trying to put a name on it may be doing it a huge disservice, versus just allowing it to be what it is, and enjoying the experience. Unless it's doing this obvious communication with you, telling you what it is.

I try never to tell anybody what their experience is, what they saw. I like to listen, to hear them, and sometimes they figure out for themselves what it is. But to me it's just fun sharing the stories. You have to remember that rain, dust, snow, sunlight, and other lights can create unusual effects in photos. Sun flares can have some really funky shapes to them, so there's a lot of stuff out there that can be caught by our cameras. I'm one of those people that will look at what was around at the time, and see if there is a potential that the light came from a vehicle casting light, and I got the glare, for example. I don't automatically discount or accept that some kind of contact took place, but there are a lot of logical explanations for strange lights or objects caught on camera. Insects can cause a white flare or a streak. I got excited one time because I thought I had something, then I realized, oh, it's got wings. It was a bumblebee. But I'm also open to that fact that we have fairies and gnomes.

We live in a fantastic world that is ever growing, and the veil is ever shifting. So as Earth and all of us on it start vibrating higher, and the veil is thinning for us, we are getting glimpses of so many things that it's hard to define them anymore, like from fantasy to logic and reason. It's like these are becoming more logical and reasonable now, but I think it's all in the eye of the beholder, which includes your intuition.

I say to people that if the feeling of contact came to you immediately after something happened, take it seriously. Like my ex and I saw this huge flash nearby at night. And it's like wow, that doesn't usually happen. I was expecting the sound of an explosion to follow it, but nothing came. And it wasn't the 4th of July. We immediately felt that it was someone contacting us. But even within three seconds, your conscious mind starts thinking about the incident, and all these other things start coming in about what it might or might not have been. That's when you have to be careful, because now you're creating something. You have to go with that instant knowing of what something was and stick with that. Kind of like the advice they give you when you're filling out a test at school. They say go with your first instinct; never go back and correct it after thinking about it. It's like your intuitive response is the most accurate, because it's involving the subconscious mind, and our conscious mind tends to screw things up. We have beautiful conscious minds as well, but our subconscious is where the true info is at, and our strongest connections.

I also see actual ships in the sky quite often. If I'm meditating or outside stargazing, sometimes I'll get a flash, and I'll wait to see if it's an airplane, or a low-orbiting satellite. And if it doesn't flash again, as a plane would, that's kind of interesting to me, and I'll just thank it for saying hi. If it obviously wasn't a plane I would flash this laser light towards it, and it would flash again. I don't care about the actual craft, I want to say hi to the pilot telepathically, and thank them. And I have to believe that they heard me and they accept that.

I've had them communicate directly with me several times. A few months ago I was asleep outside and I woke up to see this black object flying right by me. Immediately I woke up I said, "Oh my God it's a dragon." And I thought, 'That's strange, because it was really small.'

But that's the first thing that came to mind. It's really cool that they woke me up to see them fly by. That was really kind and considerate.

How do you connect now?

Katrina passing away has taught me another way to connect with my star family, and other beings if I wish. They taught me that all I have to do is sit quietly, close my eyes and say her name. Instantly her soul 'hears' me and we connect wherever she is. I had a psychic medium reading where Katrina came in to speak with me. When I asked for her name that she now goes by, she wouldn't share it with me and now I know why. 'Katrina' is the vibration I knew her as on Earth, and is the vibration she responds to now when I say her name.

Therefore, it's all about vibration – connecting with energy, thoughts, feelings, action, etcetera. The higher-vibrational beings get it and can respond to your call. It is so much easier for me because I am a hybrid and I came to Earth already 'wired' for this type of connection. But anyone can build the skill to do this! It just takes practice.

Can you initiate contact?

They're teaching me more about how to do that, and how to get out of my own way to make that happen. That's the hardest part. I have to stop expecting it to be a certain type of contact, and expecting them to perform for me. They're not here to be a servant and show up because I'm upset and need a hug. That would be beautiful, but they want us to do our best to deal with living here on Earth. They keep telling me, "You incarnated there for reason. You're there to do your mission, and we support that, but we have to have healthy boundaries, and we can't do certain things because it would be interfering too much."

They see all the energies involved in this, and they see if it would be in service to you or not. Just by showing up in a craft and you seeing that, it changes your energy for a second. They can see what that contact does to your energy. And if it isn't serving you well, they won't do it. They know what your soul needs and what's best for you, because most of them that I deal with exist at a higher level. So they can see that I want contact and I just want to go home.

When I want to initiate contact, they've taught me that since I'm a part of them we're connected. And all beings are connected telepathically, so you can connect to any being you want. But what makes it easier for me is that I have their DNA, and I have implants in my optic nerves. They tell me, "Close your eyes, think of us, feel us, say our name, and instantly we have a connection." When we're kissing someone we usually close our eyes because we're feeling it. So just close your eyes and really feel that connection with your heart. I'm not talking about pain, or missing, or grief, I'm talking about a love connection. So you're opening your heart with love and a desire to connect, and with respect for the being, and for the connection itself. I've learned to connect with Katrina this way since she went home.

So that's how you connect: with gratitude and love. Not with grief, or despair, or demanding it. When you start demanding it you might get another being you don't want. So you have to be careful about that. Where you're at energetically is what you attract. So if you're in despair and you start demanding attention, you'll get it, but it might not be the attention you need. It might be more service-to-self beings, or ghosts, or astral beings, or some other ET that is sensing your negativity. You can't call on light energy when your energy is in despair.

This is different from guides and angels when they come and help, because they're there for you, to support you through your life. I want to clarify that. Like my guide Jer-me, he'll come whenever. If I'm in despair he'll step in.

How does your contact feel?

Initiating contact starts with feeling, which expands as your energy connects with a being, or beings. Then it expands to whatever level you can handle. Normally when you're connecting with gratitude and love, they're already at a higher frequency than you are, so they're very gentle about how you expand as a soul in your connection with them. Because it can be painful and damaging to you. It's the same with information. Certain information can be damaging to you if you're not ready for it. It won't be of any service to you, at least at this time. So they're very gentle, and they can see where your energy's at, and how much you can take.

So my vibration shoots up when I'm meditating or connecting with them, or talking with Katrina, and just connecting with her. I'm sending her my love, and I'm sure a little pain, with missing her. I try to stop emotional pain when connecting but it's really challenging; I'm not powerful enough to do that. And within ten seconds or less I feel this intense love, and it's usually in the form of a deep, bright pink light that comes back at me, and my arms drop to the side, and my mouth probably falls open, and I'm just absorbing it. It's intense, in a good way. It's like shooting a beam of energy through you, where you can feel it throughout your body, similar to getting chills suddenly, and you feel that something walked through you or you walked into something. And your hair stands up or you get goosebumps. The intensity of love beams through, that heart-to-heart connection is really intense. It's so wonderful. And it stays there for a minute or two and then it fades. And that's reconnecting.

Something happened on my way into work one day. I always surround roadkill with loving white light, and send it energy, and pray it goes to the other side with great ease, and that the angels take care of it. This one time, it was dark, and I saw this really weird shape by the side of the road that I thought was an animal. So I started sending it love, and all of a sudden I get the love sent back to me, and I'm like gasping for air. I thought, 'Oh my God, I've never received that back from an animal. Usually they're gone. I don't think it was an animal.' Then it flashed telepathically that it was a Grey. It saw me coming and went into a ball so I wouldn't hit it, but now it was showing me who it was. And I wanted to go back, but then I would have been late for work. Here's my ethics, right? I can't be late for work; the animals need me, I need to open up and let them go pee, and start mopping and cleaning them out. So I couldn't stop and go back but I *so* wanted to. I was looking around saying, "Where's your ship? I don't see it."

That was pretty cool. But could you imagine what would have happened if I'd hit it? And what do you do for a Grey? I'm just calling it that because people understand that, though its color *was* light grey. I don't know what I would have done if I'd hit it, to provide medical care. What do you do? Can you give him mouth-to-mouth? If the heart stops, where do you pump? I don't know. I kept going over this in my head. I was like, 'You guys need to be more careful, because I would have been totally devastated if I'd hit you, and I didn't know how to save you.' Unless one of their people was nearby and could have helped. Which I'm sure they were. I guess that's our human thing, of worrying about what might have happened. Those feelings of guilt. I wonder if anyone's ever hit an ET and tried to give it medical attention?

What kind of safeguards can people use in contact?

I think there are thousands of techniques. Similar to how spiritual people say everyone has a unique way to exit and enter their body, in astral projection. It's the same thing with connection: you find the way that works for you.

In terms of safeguards I would say that for someone first attempting it, the first thing is to remember that your vibration will attract like vibration. So whatever being you want to attract, you have to be that in vibration yourself, and then call on that. Because if you're in a dark place, and feeling guilt, or depression, and that's your intention for contacting beings, you may inadvertently contact a self-serving entity that plays on that. It may come in as a helper for you and lead you astray.

So protection is really powerful. You can do it through raising your vibration, or putting white candles around you, burning incense, clearing the room, praying for your guides and angels to protect you, putting on high frequency music, or lighting incense. I think rose essence is one of the highest vibrations for purity and cleansing.

Use whatever method for preparing your space works for you, then use meditation to go inside yourself. That's how you reach out. And then it's basically your intention you're sending out, like a beam of energy, to connect. And your energy is picked up like a radio signal on that quantum level, and can be seen and heard. But they see exactly where you're at and what you need. So if you're not really ready they may not come to you, because they know what's best for you at the time. And that's hard to hear, because we think that if we're asking for it we're ready. But that's not really true. They know what's best by looking at our energy and reading us. And I really appreciate that, because if they had responded to everything we ask for and given that to us it could be really harmful.

When you wait for a response, it works best to have no expectation of a certain type of contact. You could be so focused on expecting a ship to fly by that you don't notice someone tapping on your shoulder and saying "Hi!" So put it out there, that this is what you want, then just allow it to be whatever it's going to be. And be ready for a response. Preparing for contact is about working on yourself to be open, accepting. To really see things for what they are. This will attract that contact, but it may come in ways you didn't expect.

I always use my kambaba stone when making contact. Every interview with you I hold it in my hand to enhance my energy. Some people gravitate towards meteorites, or certain stones or gems. I would use whatever helps raise your vibration. Some people carry around moldavite for that reason.

There are a lot of techniques that work because we've used them so much. They've become their own entities. Similar to portals on Earth that have been created by the native peoples. They've put so much energy into them that they become true portals. So those are pretty powerful. Crop circles, too. Where you put yourself physically can matter, but where you put yourself vibrationally matters most.

How do you differentiate between your own thoughts and those from outside?

That's easy. For me it's instantaneous. And I'm always watchful of that. And it's another feeling. I guess it's a skill that you build. To be aware of the feeling involved, and what's going on. So what you're sensing and feeling, if it's different than your own, you know it's from the outside. So I don't question it, because I've had it all my life. I expect it. As long as it feels good I allow it. But I just know it's not my energy, and it's not what I would say, or how I would say it. It's usually something above my thinking, that helps me resolve my thinking about something. Or it helps me look at something with a new perspective, in order to understand and work it out.

And sometimes it's in a male's voice. You know, when they come through loud and clear, if you're not listening. I'll hear it in male voice, or a female voice that isn't mine. I've had that happen several times.

Why do they connect with you?

It's because I am them, and they support me in my mission here.

Other beings are attracted to my energy either because I am a hybrid or because I put out vibrationally that I am open to contact and they can see that. I get the feeling that many ETs enjoy contacting people who are truly open. I have met so many unique looking ETs that I have only seen once, so it makes me feel as if it is fun for them to see if they really can connect, and just say "Hi!"

How would you summarize your mission?

I remember having a hypnosis session with Barbara Lamb where they came through and told me that the most important thing for me when I came here was to be in my highest state, my authentic self, and bring my full essence here, and be that. It's similar to being true to yourself: let your heart shine, live through your heart; your compassion is everything. Living that authentic self is the most important thing, and the key to that is your happiness. When you're happy your vibration increases. So the two things go hand-in-hand. Being who you are truly, and being here on Earth, that's really the main purpose. Bringing our 5th-dimensional energy to Earth. And whatever I do on the sidelines or as a career can enhance that. But just being here, with the concept of being true to ourselves and being happy, is the main focus. And that happiness comes only from within you, not from the outside.

The reason that it is so important to incarnate with that 5th-dimension vibration of who we are, is to help lift the frequency of Earth. That is the whole reason. As you do that you enhance all life on Earth; it is all connected. You can even move that outward to the solar system, the sun, and the whole galaxy. You can incorporate all of that because it is all the grand web of life. But we focus our attention on the Earth, and say we are here for you, Mother Earth. Billions of us came here to help you, because you called us here to increase your frequency, to get over this period of 3D living, and we want to assist you in increasing your soul energy and lift you higher and help all Earth life ascend, and evolve to the next level of existence.

I can simplify it by saying that the main purpose of all life is to evolve. Learn, grow, evolve. It's a shifting of consciousness, a continual expansion. The whole purpose of life is to always grown and expand. But Earth has been kind of stuck in her shifting. But she doesn't want to do it by force, because she doesn't want to hurt anything. It has to be done through evolution, through love, growth and consciousness.

So she said, "I will call in all these other cosmic beings, to help me around this hurdle." Like the Hindu people have Ganesh to help them around their obstacles, that's kind of a cool concept. And that's what Mother Earth did. It's like boom: decades later, look how many came! I mean the love, the sacrifice, of leaving our homes to come here. Of course it's the opportunity of a lifetime, it's an honor to be a part of it, but this is like the stories of Hercules and Achilles, which will always be told. You'll hear it in any galaxy. Like, "You were a part of the Earth transition? How was that for you?" It's kind of like being deployed for a devastation, like when Hurricane Katrina came through. Everyone went to go rescue people and get them back on their feet. People would ask, "Were you a part of that? What did you do, and see?" That's similar to what it's like, and that's why I have such a rescuer personality, and why I do the rescue work I do now with animals. It's all connected.

And here I tried to simplify it, then went on for five minutes, huh? Nothing's really simple about it. Hey, let me simplify it for you! Then ten minutes later - no wait, let me try again! And on it goes.

Why are experiencers in contact with multiple types of beings?

They're telling me that because of the people you've been attracted to magnetically for this book, you're getting people of a higher vibration. They're giving me some amazing chills right now. We actually are the ones who are having contact with multiple races. This is not to power egos or anything, but from the universe looking down at the Earth, if you can psychically see energy, you'll see these bright, higher-frequency lights of an ET vibration, that is different to the humans on Earth. That's very attractive, it's like homing beacons, and some of them are starseeds and hybrids, which they can go right to. We are most like them, understand them, and are less likely to shoot at them or be in denial. So when they're doing their work, they try to go to these people, and work through and with us. That's why we tend to get so many different types. But we're still attracting like vibration so they're highly evolved beings themselves that are here to help. That's why we get multiple types.

I know that's why I get so many types. At conferences I used to visit Cynthia Crawford's table of all the ET sculptures she did. And in the very beginning I asked her, "Why am I attracted to so many of them?" I would watch people come up and pick a specific one and walk away. And I was having trouble with that, because the various ET types were all sharing something with me. That was the first realization that we're more like galactic representatives here. We were sent by one family, but we're here on a much bigger scale for our mission. We're encompassing these other ETs because it's a huge cosmic process that involves so many.

So when your intention is working for the highest good of all, that literally means for all. So you're going to be inclusive of so many others. There are so many that I don't even know. It's a thrill to think about how many others are out there, that we're still representing on Earth that we don't even know about. Our level of contact is increasing as we go.

What would be some examples of work they do through you?

Oh my gosh, it's giving me chills again! Like right now, just answering your question, as simple as that, I can feel the energy coming through. It's like it's not just me speaking for them. I can feel them coming through when I speak, and I just hope and pray that I'm clear and articulate enough, and unfiltered an Earthling enough, that I can receive what they're trying to say, or give me the feeling of.

They come through in what I can only explain as unconditional love. It's so beyond ego. Or beyond inflated ego. Because ego is actually healthy to a point. But it's so much about being of service. That word is kind of getting overused, but it's doing what's best for other people, knowing that when you help other people you're helping yourself, because we're all connected. It's as simple as, when I hear an argument behind me when I'm in line, I'll just close my eyes and send them white light energy. And sometimes I'm directed to do that. Or if I'm driving and I see an animal on the side of the road, I'll push them with my energy to stay off the road, and ask the angels to keep them off the road. Or if I see an accident, I surround them with white light and pray that their path is led with grace and ease, and that they stay safe. Little things like that, all the time, throughout the day, really add up. And when more people are doing these little acts of kindness, it really helps out a lot.

Some of them are more profound, like being guided to go speak somewhere, or join a group and be a representative of positive energy, hope and spiritual awareness. Or writing a book. Like I've recently felt compelled again to finish my second book. Those are bigger acts. Rescuing an animal from a shelter instead of buying an animal that someone's bred in their back yard. Or taking in a stray kitty off the street and giving them a home. Little things like that. I have five different charity groups I donate $10 a month to. It's not much, but I can spread it out and give just a little bit to as many as I can. It makes me feel really good. There's no credit, or thanks, and I don't need it. It just feels good.

A lot of times I don't know what the beings are here to do, but I know in my heart it's for good. To help increase the love vibration, which is all working towards raising the frequency. I know we say that all the time, but that's the main goal for all the beings I work with, whether I know it or not. Like Gandhi said, "You must be the change you wish to see in the world." That's exactly how I feel. They're coming through to help me be the happiest person I can be, because that makes your heart light shine the brightest. And you can be of influence that way, and spread that out. It's kind of infectious when you feel that good vibration, that's unconditional. It's not saying: I want you to be like me. It's saying: I'm spreading a higher frequency that's pure in vibration, that's closer to Source energy, for you to be more of your authentic self, whatever that looks like.

So it's like a grand purpose without specifics. Because we don't want to name specifics, like I want you to be this or that. The basic goal and mission here is to help others become their true, authentic self.

Because that's the most unconditionally loving way to be. So I know that when I am channeling or having these beings work through me, when I get the chills or the immediate flash of higher vibration, that they're working for good, for the purpose of evolution.

And how you recognize that is what we call 'the mirror system'. How are others around you acting? If you find people are recoiling, not wanting to be around you, getting angry, having issues, those are symptoms telling you that what you're putting out there is not good, or not in alignment. It's not healthy energy. So I watch closely my friends, my dogs, the animals I'm around every day, and how they're reacting to me, to see where I'm at in the world, and how I'm doing.

Kryon's book, *Don't Think Like a Human*, that really spurred a lot of remembering. But I knew from a child that I wasn't from here, so I've always kind of looked at people, as: do I want to become like that or not? Is that who I am or not? So I've always had that awareness, of intentional living. Like I can choose to be like them, or choose to be my authentic self, regardless of the consequences. But like anyone else, when you go to school or have a job, you have to assimilate to some degree here on Earth, which is fine. And that includes getting what I call 'filters' for living in this culture. How people normally act, to be socially accepted. And how to view the world.

I use the glasses analogy when thinking about human filters. It's like the type of lenses you use, which color your perceptions of animals, or UFOs, or education, or sports. I want to be aware of what filters I have, sometimes without knowing, so I often look to see if they still work for me. If they don't work for me anymore I want to remove them, and change the hue. I love it when I get new shades! I got these new ones with rosy-colored lenses that are so cool! Like when I'm driving around everything in my world is rose-colored now. I just think of that and it makes me smile. Just that little change of hue can make a difference in your attitude. It's amazing.

So I try to be deliberately aware of where my thoughts are at, how I'm thinking or feeling about something. Is that the perspective I really want? Does that still serve me? Unfortunately, doing that throughout my life has made people say I'm wishy-washy, or I can't make a decision. I think it's just that internal dialogue. I can see all those perspectives, but I want to choose the right perspective for me. So it takes a little while longer! But I think that's good work; I enjoy that work with myself. And by 'myself' I mean Source energy, and all my people are involved in that. Because it's so far beyond just me. For this book specifically, because of the intention you set out for this book, I feel like every time we talk they're coming through me. Maybe that's why I'm rolling, because I feel like I'm channeling most of the information.

What do the beings get out of it?

That's a really good question, and I love that type of question. I don't want to speak for them all, but the feeling I get when working with them is that they get a sense of enjoyment and fulfilment. There is this huge feeling out there in the universe, that I feel is pretty common amongst all beings, that they just want to be a part of something bigger than themselves. And it's like this badge of honor. Like you're adding this new color to your personal aura. Like if you went through say Hurricane Katrina, and you went over there and helped rescue people and animals, and put yourself in danger, and probably got sick. But you were there in service, trying to help. And this is legit; that is a new color streamer that's added to your aura, which can be seen as an energetic pattern. Kind of like in the military, where you get little ribbons to pin on your uniform. It's a colored energy pattern that's added to your soul vibration colors. So a being can look at you and see all that you have done. It's really amazing.

So I think they get this sense of service, being a part of a bigger plan. I can feel it every day in my work. On a personal level, if my co-workers get sent to a call that I can't be a part of, sometimes I get frustrated, because I want to be with them and help, and be a part of that. I think some of that comes from wanting to test our own ability, our skills, our character, to see where we're at. To see that we're evolving, to see if we can put ourselves through a tense situation and still do honorable work, still make the right decisions in the hardest of times. It shows who you really are. I think for beings that are of a higher energy that really care about their soul's growth and where they're going, that is very important to them.

Esther Hicks channels a group of non-physical entities called Abraham. And they are always saying we are never complete. You don't ever get complete, you don't ever get it done. Everything is always in process, always changing, growing, becoming brighter, more beautiful, and we're all at different levels in that process. That's where unconditional love has to come in, accepting that people are not where you're at, and it's okay, it's perfect the way it is. There's always something else to go to. Ah, that gives me chills!

That's a part of my job. When my people are on the ship with those other beings of different races, we're always getting calls for assistance, and responding like an emergency service, and that is so fulfilling. It's not about ego or getting a badge, it's about doing what's right for others, and seeing if you can be part of their solution. And it's not about going there and fixing it, it's about supporting them in resolving it for themselves. Gosh that was so important.

That's why I love supporting Heifer International, because instead of sending food, they provide people with the means to sustain themselves. So if they're in India, they get goats for milk, and other things. And I witnessed this firsthand in 2011. They allow you to travel with them to see where your money's going. And you can meet the people they're helping. That is so much a part of what I know we do back on Faqui. We went to Odisha. It was awesome. They also take you to see the sights, and schedule events.

What have they taught you?

As I described in *Meet the Hybrids*, they taught me how to fly the ship, and how to send healing to another being. They were both really powerful experiences.

A few things other come to mind.

I've learned telepathy, since I've always been connected with them, with the help of these implants. I'll often hear them pretty clearly just giving me guidance, by simple statements, or images or feelings, which I can recognize as not my own. Telepathy involves sounds, thought, visuals and knowledge all at once sometimes, so I'll recognize that it's coming from them. I'll hear things that offer a new perspective on things, just little bits of guidance that make me think differently about things. It'll help me to have compassion for it and understand it, see it differently, or from the other person's perspective, to let go of ego, all these human things. That's why I love the Kryon book *Don't Think Like a Human*, because it kind of goes over these things, including the 3D thinking that's involved in our egos. Ego is not a bad thing if it's balanced. It's the inflated ego, or the ego that wants to be special at the expense of other people, that's negative. They will teach me that my entire life. And they help catch me in moments of self-pity, or when I'm treating someone else unfairly to feel better myself. So I'm constantly getting spiritual teachings on how to be a better person, and how to keep my vibration high. My core DNA is 5th-dimensional, yet what I put out on a daily basis can be lowered through negative thoughts and feelings. So they're always helping me try to maintain that higher vibration in my thinking and action, and behavior in this life. I think that's the main thing. So I try to walk my talk.

The beings are at different levels. For instance, my people, the Fajan, and Jacquelin Smith's people, Quabar, are at different levels of being. Quabar are at a higher vibration than my people, but they know each other. So through our 5th-dimensional eyes perhaps we can see Quabar, but not in the way it would see itself. So it's really kinda cool, to think that if you have multidimensional perception, you may see things differently.

You know, this needs to be said. They're nudging me to mention the *Star Wars* cantina scene where they go into the bar, and you see all these kinds of beings doing what they do. Of course we humanize it, and have them drinking or fighting, or doing deals. But there truly are places out there in the universe like that. Jacquelin and I intuitively recall meeting at one of these. In these places you can indulge, and be surrounded by different kinds of beings. When I think of it I just want to close my eyes and absorb all the different languages and energies. That's why I'm so into mixed cultures on Earth. That's what makes me feel comfortable. I guess it comes from my homeworld, being around so many different types of beings. When you go to other places you hear the languages. It's telepathic, so it's beyond language, but you can still hear it. It's just so beautiful. I don't know if you recall feeling anything like that, but I sense that often. I love to travel to those places. It's the feeling that you get. It feels comfortable and good to me.

How has contact affected your life?

I am who I am today—and I love who I am—because of their contact with me. I have abandonment issues being here, which are pretty deep-seated. That whole thing we talk about: missing home. That's always there. But knowing they're a part of my life and are always with me in some fashion, whether I call on them or they call on me - I am who I am because of that.

I've got a lot to learn and a lot of growing to do. I know I have flaws and issues to work on, but I can look in the mirror and say, "I accept you, everything that you are, and it's okay." And that's pretty big. If you can love and accept yourself first, only then can you lovingly accept others without judgment. And believe me, that is hard on Earth. Just take a drive down the road and test that one out, right? I want one of those sticker that says 'How would Buddha drive?' Would he be loving and at peace, and bow his head to everyone who flipped him off, or would he eventually start cussing and flipping people off? I wanna know. I think we need that guidance today.

We all get chances to grow, and we can look back and say, "Wow, all along it really was my choice how to handle that." Because we've all been through something that makes us feel justified in being angry, jaded and mean to people. But this last thing I went through, which was huge, was a reminder to always be careful what you choose. You can either choose to be justified in your feelings, or choose to be more evolved. So I did my damnedest to be more evolved. For myself. Not become angry or bitter, and push people away. I chose to try to handle it in a spiritual manner. And accept, and be at peace and grow from it, without holding anyone accountable. And just try to see the reason behind it, and the possible opportunity for growth. And that's quite a task. It's not as easy as it sounds.

How do you see the ET aspects of human beings?

I'm getting images to help answer it. When your friend said, "What about the idea of us becoming the beings?" That's all evolution. That is the process. That's humanity evolving and becoming more. It was a great question, but I think that process is already happening. I like that image too. Humans are another species. It's all a matter of perspective. If you look at yourself as a human, then look out there at all the ETs, then you're separating yourself. To the ETs, they see humanity as another ET species. Because I'm from Faqui, when I look at Earth, I see humanity as another species that is trying to grow and expand, just like everyone else out there.

I was working with my people and the whole galactic family when I got Earth's call for help. I just had a different way of answering the call. I incarnated to help. Which is more of a sacrifice. It's a long, intimate, personal journey. So humanity's connection with ETs is very real. It's constant. It's tangible, even, based on perspective. Like those glasses I was talking about. Let's put on your galactic filter, and say, "Okay, now I see the world as a galactic being. And I'm no longer just a human on Earth, I'm a spiritual being, incarnated as a human, and right now I'm choosing to be here and evolve. And I can also see how this is affecting all life on Earth, the plants and animals, and expands out again to the solar system, and to the Milky Way galaxy. It's impacting everything."

So it's not just about being mere humans on Earth; we are already a galactic race of beings called humans, on our homeworld called Earth. So I believe humanity is already galactic, but a lot of people have not yet put the glasses on and developed that perspective. A lot of other starseeds tend to already have that otherworldly perspective.

They're not just living in their city, their mind is expanding to understanding that they're in a state, in a nation, in a continent. They see further, and every decision they make includes this perspective. And some can see further, that I'm in this star system, in this galaxy. So they would look at all the space debris we're creating up there, and thinking about how that's affecting other beings out there.

So I think it's a matter of growing a new perspective and applying that in your daily life. Humans will see that they too are Source energy like everything else, it's just that they're playing human on Earth right now. That's why this unconditional loving attitude from beings is really important, because there's no judgment when they say, "Your soul's vibration is at a 3D level right now, but you're evolving, and it's beautiful, and we're here to help." Versus saying, "You're just a 3rd-dimensional being, you're stupid, you have a bad attitude, you kill each other, and you deserve to die." It's not like that. Some ETs may feel that way, if they're a lower-level being themselves. But this is humanity's hour. If they can put on their galactic glasses, they'll come into the knowledge that if they were able to connect with the beings that are around Earth, and our solar system who are watching, monitoring and helping, and giving of themselves, there is an unfathomable amount of beings, ships, assistance, and processes being done out there from so many different alliances.

You have the Ashtar Galactic Federation Alliance, which my people are not a part of. But we did communicate with them before incarnating, because it's a grand participation. My people are from an alliance called the Star Alliance. We make connections and alliances with others who are working with Earth to cooperate and be a part of the whole and watch this thing grow. It's like creating the perfect seed, and then planting it with so much love, and gratitude and pure Source energy, and just watching it grow. And that's what's happening with humanity. It's blooming all over the place. Of course you have some parts withering, dying and falling off, but that's the process of life, right? But life gives of itself to give back to the whole. Like an old leaf falling and decaying, its energy goes back, and it renews itself into the blossom, maybe.

Recently, I read an online article by Angela Chen and Loren Grush from September 2016 titled: 'Elon Musk's proposed spaceship could send 100 people to Mars in 80 days.' It said, "Today, SpaceX CEO Elon Musk unveiled the Mars vehicle — the spaceship his company plans to build to transport the first colonists to Mars." While reading the article, I became mesmerized at the idea of actually living on another planet in this lifetime. It states that over the course of 40-100 years, a fully self-sustaining civilization of one million people could exist on Mars. Suddenly, I could feel my star family's energy as they connect with me, wanting to talk about this subject. Musk went on to say that people could return to Earth if they wished, and provided a few details on the first pioneers for the project.

It struck me at a deep level right then, that all this time, I have been stuck on Earth. Like many other starseeds, I have an unexplainable reaction with being abandoned. Flashes of images ran through my mind, of people actually traveling in space to another planet to visit and potentially live! Humans would then become the 'aliens'!

Immediately my star family showed me images of space beings watching this activity, monitoring the behavior and actions of the Mars vehicle, and being more exposed to Earth humans as they travel in space. They let me feel their intentions of being more a deliberate part of this Earth activity, similar to the 'UFO' activity around the International Space Station. They explained further that there is concern for this transitional stage where humans are going into space and landing on other planets. Therefore, they will play a role in monitoring the process. This is different to NASA and other country's past activity, in that those were government guided/controlled and this time it will be the citizens of Earth! The shift in energy this creates will be exciting for all beings to watch.

When people say to me, "Well, all humans are hybrids anyway," I kind of recoil. I understand that eons ago, the human body was designed and constructed by Source energy, God or ETs, or all of the above. But it's developed. Humanity is definitely its own species. I don't know that that's even important. But I think in order to understand concepts, you have to understand the foundation first. And if people claim "We're all starseeds and hybrids anyway," I don't think they're understanding the concept. The human race is a soul group at a specific vibrational level. And all these higher-level beings have come here for service, to help that evolution process. So in a way it's devaluing the whole thing if you just throw out, "Humans are all ET hybrids themselves." I think that misses the point. The point is not to say that you're just human and we're ETs and we're special. That's not it at all. It's just to say that there's a difference, and here's why. This helps us understand where we're going. To do that you have to know where you've been. It's a universal thing. You can see it in the Fibonacci sequence, or the Golden Section, or the Julia Set. Life runs this way, to be the most it can be. You have to know where you've been to know where you're going.

Wow! I'm like tired now. That took a lot of energy! This book is more intense than the other books, Miguel. I don't know about you, but for me, this is intense, this channeling stuff. I didn't even know I could do it like this. So you've helped me expand who I am by asking this of us. Which I think is amazing.

What message would they like to share?

Immediately after speaking with my dear star-brother Miguel about his new book project, my star family came through and began sharing with me what they wished to impress upon humanity. These concepts/ideas were given to me in small 'clips' of information, knowing that I would need to go deeper with them to work on their true message when I was ready.

Have you ever felt 'nudged' about an idea or to do a certain activity? Nudges seem to be one way beings speak to us. I recall many accounts of contactee experiences where they say they felt calm when they knew logically they should have been horrified; or that they felt love when their eyes told them what they were seeing was repulsive. We can be guided similarly by what I call 'nudges' from our beings to help us on our path in life. For me they start with a soft nudge, but if I procrastinate, the nudge becomes a shove! For me, energy moves through my body with such intensity that taking action is my only relief. This is how I came to begin working on my first book, *We Are Among You Already*.

The Fajan Race

My star family wishes to introduce themselves before relaying their messages. They feel that this knowledge of who they are will help connect us spiritually and enhance our communication.

"We want you to know a little about us, to see our face, to feel our vibration, and willingly open the communication lines between us before we begin. If who we are and what you feel does not resonate with you, please allow yourself to skip over our chapter. It is not our intent or in our interest to convince you of anything, we simply wish to communicate and connect with you.

"It does not serve anyone to force communication. It is vital for us that you choose to connect with us because you are open to it, not just curious. The communication we offer is coming from a higher frequency and can be misinterpreted or be too confusing if you are not ready, not aligned or unbalanced. It is extremely exciting for us to be given this opportunity to touch those of you who want this. It is a great honor to be of service to humanity and we send our brother Miguel an intense beam of love for providing this communication.

"So we will share with you a little of who we are. We are called the Fajan race and are located in the Andromeda galaxy, on a planet we call Faqui.

"We are from a vibrational existence which is similar to what humans call the 5th dimension. Our physical bodies, way of thinking, way of living, technology, behavior, and our understandings of All That Is has expanded through the evolutionary process into a higher frequency of being. We do not think the same as humanity does on Earth, simply because life exists at a near 4th dimensional level there. The exciting part is that Earth, and all living things on Earth, are currently in a stage of wondrous evolution! This is a reason for the immense need for Disclosure and willing reconnection with all of us - your 'cosmic brothers and sisters'.

The Fajan. Credit: Kesara

"This living artwork of who we are was co-created with another starseed who is known to many as Kesara. We urged our beloved soulmate on Earth (Jujuolui), to seek Kesara out for this artwork so we could have a stronger visual connection together, which was needed for her comfort during a difficult time. As you can see in this 3D representation, our race is considered Reptilian. We consider ourselves very peaceful and genuine in our innate, loving connection with Source energy, which we recognize in all living things."

How it works

This way of communicating with my star family is normal for me and I feel it is also natural for all lifeforms. Over the years, I have learned from other contactees and starseeds that this way of communication is very common for them as well. I not only hear voices, but I can also see images, feel the message and receive instant knowledge of what they are sharing with me. I later learned that this form of communication is called 'telepathy'.

Since I was very young my star family would relay information to me telepathically. At about the age of six, I remember my star family placing implants on my optic nerves. I am not certain if these implants were intended to help me receive their telepathy or not. I would often share with my human family things I was told by my star family. They also knew I had an 'invisible friend' whom I called George. He was the one that normally communicated with me and I later realized his name is Jer-mi, pronounced zher-me. I was used to this communication and didn't know it was not common for others. I learned quickly not to talk about it, especially with those who were religious.

Growing up, I kept in touch with my star family this way. It occurred during sleep states, meditation, Reiki sessions, contact experiences and eventually anytime my vibration was increased! It seems that the ability grew naturally the more I used it and believed in it. Now, I instantly know when my star family or another being is communicating this way with me. It takes experience to catch the differences between you speaking with yourself mentally, and another being speaking with you. With another being, the communication is more instant and complete, with no thinking involved. The other part is knowing who you're communicating with. This too is a skill, and one you want to develop quickly.

My ET friends taught me to feel the energy of the being as the communication is being relayed. Every being has a unique energy signature, (probably why many ETs normally don't have names). You can really feel, in a visceral way, whether the energy is of a high vibration or not. I don't like to use good or bad, because that is a matter of perspective. If it feels good, like listening to your favorite music, then allow it.

Telepathy is a skill you learn to use with spiritual discernment. I use it consciously every day on my job helping animals and connecting with either my star family (like now), or my beloved partner Katrina who recently passed. I believe it is important for people to know how the information was obtained, so they can feel it for themselves. It is important for me to be transparent with this information, genuine and truthful. These are my core values, in addition to maintaining personal integrity (this feels like I'm applying for a job).

My star family, known as the Fajans, wish for you to not only read their message, but feel their meaning. If it feels right, open yourself to absorb the knowledge. Allow yourself to assimilate this new information into your current understandings, and expand your consciousness. The intention of my star family sharing their wisdom and perspective is to touch your heart for the purpose of your soul's evolution, from our heart to yours. With great love for all life, we share the following.

Say the Fajan, to Humanity:

Being of True Service – A Hero

This is the first message my star family wishes to share. Being of service to others was a lesson that started for me during elementary school recess. I remember clearly walking around the playground, mostly by myself, and would hear them explain to me that some people enjoyed hurting others who didn't even provoke it. Also, there were those who would take advantage of other peoples' perceived weaknesses for their own gain – such as material items or a stroke to their ego. We say perceived weakness, because some people see kindness and gentleness as being feeble.

After receiving their message, I would walk around trying to help the other kids who were being bullied. This was my first experience with what it truly meant to be of service. It was trial and error as I had to find the balance between being helpful, but not becoming the bully. I was compelled to intervene when someone was clearly being harassed by another, yet I went too far by using force on the bully and feeling my own satisfied ego.

My human family was religious and would often take us to church. While listening to how Jesus dealt with conflict and challenges, my star family would nudge me to pay attention to the peaceful and loving way in which he was helpful. They never scolded me or said anything degrading. Their communication has always been patient, guiding, gentle and consistent. They taught me how to be of service by responding with compassion.

This is very challenging to do, and is a skill that needs focused attention and constant nurturing to apply. Being of true service to others means putting one's own desires and feelings aside when considering the highest good for all. This is the toughest metaphorical mountain to climb.

Author and scholar Gregg Braden speaks about the heart being the intellect of the soul, not the brain. Singer-songwriter Neil Diamond wrote a song and album titled *Heartlight*, which was an amazing concept brought forth into the world. Steven Spielberg used the song in his movie *E.T. the Extra-Terrestrial*. E.T.'s heart glowed a luminous red during times of emotional importance.

Another amazing concept was the creation of the Care Bears, where the bears traveled around the world completing what they called 'missions in caring'. This series affected me deeply as a child. I would watch it in awe as I realized that I was actually seeing what my star family was teaching me. I still use these concepts today when I send energy to others.

There were, and still are, some very beautifully evolved humans on Earth who live their lives in true service to others. No names are needed, because each person can choose for themselves those they believe fit this description. These humans are given elevated status, and are revered and honored for all time. They displayed and applied unconditional love towards other life forms, human or animal. Their missions were driven by their own internal guidance to do good and to elevate the quality of life of others. Their spiritual dedication and duty is admired by many, inspiring to most, and appears to be a 'saintly' trait that most feel too inadequate to attempt. Yet we all have this ability!

It is important not to compare yourself to another, because we are all so different. Each person will find a unique way in which they can be of service, based on their personal passions, education, life experiences and current path. If everyone did things the same, the world would be very out of balance. In order to do the most good, it is crucial to have many different types of 'lightworkers' on the planet. Humans are such social animals that it takes great inner strength to apply this, because what most people want is to simply be accepted by others. As a person of service, it takes great courage to be who you really are and stay true to your integrity.

Being of true service also means to not have expectations for a specific outcome that you have given service to. For example, a healing practitioner would be in 'disservice' to another if they held a belief of what that healing was for their client, instead of allowing the healing to be what it needs to be. Our soul and higher guidance always knows what is best for us. Another example is 'sending energy to' or praying for someone, hoping for them to receive something specific, and believing that is what they need. Instead, we can ask for someone to be open to their guidance, to have their path illuminated and easy to see, to be at peace and to find grace as they move forward with the issue.

Being of true service is not trying to control an outcome or response to the assistance you offer. It is accepting others to receive assistance in the way that truly helps them most, even if that goes against your own beliefs. This is unconditional service and tolerance for another being. Have you ever wanted to hug someone badly, but knew they would not like it? Did you force it on them anyway? Did you change the hug into a soft touch of their arm, knowing they would be more accepting of that? Were you selfish in your service to another, or compassionate and considerate? What service are you truly providing to this world? It is always a good idea to ask yourself what your intentions are!

One way to make this clearer is to share my daily Reiki incantation before I go to work. Since I was privileged to become part of the Reiki heritage through my Reiki Master Kelly Jackson, I have accepted the responsibility that comes with this gift, and that is to utilize it! The following are the words I have chosen to state while activating this universal gift:

"Please come through powerful and strong, yet loving and gentle for all beings in my care throughout today. Whether it be through my hands, my energetic field, or my eyesight, may they receive from you that which is in harmony with their soul's intent, for today, the last seven days, and the next seven days.

"Surround us with the white light and the golden light, protecting us from all harm and negativity. Surround us with the violet flame, neutralizing all toxic energy - giving it back to Mother Earth, Father Sky and Grandfather Cosmos to do as they will with it.

"For all souls leaving Earth today, I ask their guides, loved ones, angels, Mother Mary, St. Francis and Lilith of the animal kingdom to embrace them in their completeness here on Earth, and with great ease lift them from their body, wiping away all fear, trauma and pain and replace it with unconditional love, warmth and joy as they are reunited with their loved ones on the other side where they each belong. Thank you for your lives on Earth, you will be greatly missed.

"I am humbled to be of service. Keep me grounded to Mother Earth, aligned with my higher-self, and to be the most open, highest-vibrational, clearest channel I can be for the amazing universal healing energy of Reiki. Please protect me. Namaste."

With this daily affirmation, I trust that the universe and my star family are involved in my work too – helping me help the animals. I also know this healing energy transfers to people and the planet.

When I think of being of service, I am reminded of the superheroes that have been created by humanity. These heroes have feelings and issues like everyone else, yet their responses to struggle and challenges are unselfish, courageous, ethical, positive and without personal gain. These may be characteristics of the gods or otherworldly beings, but I believe humanity can be this way too! Be your own unique hero.

Star being companions

Recently, I lost a very dear friend who happened to be a dog named Katrina. Her leaving was a huge loss in my life. I knew we were connected at the soul level, and my star family shared more with me after she left. They showed me that Katrina also came from my home planet of Faqui. I was amazed by this information, but I accepted it very easily knowing how much sense that made. They showed me that she came to help me awaken to who I was, my ET identity, and to have the courage to follow my path that involved living that truth. This knowledge made me feel so grateful to Katrina for such an unselfish act of love for me. I use to teach classes about companions in our lives and how they can be star beings, yet I didn't connect this with my closest friend Katrina until she left.

Katrina. Credit: Jujuolui Kuita

My star family told me that I didn't really need to know, and that knowing this could have placed unfair, inappropriate expectations on Katrina. They explained that just because she is a highly-evolved soul from my planet, this doesn't mean she could bring all of that with her to Earth, just as I am not the same being on Earth that I am on Faqui. We incarnate into these bodies, knowing the limitations of the lower vibrational existence here on Earth and have to 'play' within those laws and parameters. Most of us anyway. There were a select few who incarnated on Earth with more of their soul's true essence, enabling them to remember who they were and teach humanity their true spiritual nature as well. Also, dolphins and whales have a 'contract' of incarnating with their soul's true essence. Thank goodness for all of us!

Sometimes we know when we have a companion in our life who incarnated from the cosmos to be with us. They could have chosen the form of an animal, a family member, a friend, a co-worker, an antagonist, a romantic partner, etcetera. They chose who to incarnate as depending on need. If we are an awakened starseed ourselves, we may be out of balance in life if we also had a romantic partner that was an awakened starseed. Or, it might suitably enhance the synergy needed on a path and be exactly what we need at that time. Sometimes, we never even realize that a star being incarnated for us, to assist us on our journey. How loving is that?

Be grateful for those in your life. And know when to move on or let go when a connection to a person no longer serves who you are or what you are meant to do. Don't force a friendship. Some connections were meant to serve as a quick catalyst, and some were meant to last a lifetime. Allow them to be what they were meant to be and honor that. The love is still deep, even if the path you share with another soul is temporary. These are great gifts to cherish.

Ending message

"Be your best. Find your truth. Know who you are and be your authentic self. Know that you are worthy.

"Believe in magic, in fairies and dragons.

"Know that whatever you are thinking becomes a vibrational energy that attracts that specific energy to itself, so be very mindful what you are thinking!

"Your emotions guide you, showing you where your thoughts are. When you don't like how you are feeling - change the way you are thinking! It really is that simple, but not particularly simple to apply. It takes awareness and courageous responding instead of reacting!

"Remember that everything you do is observed and noted by all of those in spirit and the ETs monitoring Earth. Don't be so hard on yourselves! We all know that Earth is not as easy mission. You may not be able to see us or hear us or feel us, but know that we are always there, supporting each and every one of you!

"Those of you who incarnated here to help are the most courageous of souls. Sometimes we briefly incarnate to assist you on your mission, but we honor you for making a life out of it! There is much applause in the cosmos for all the lightwork each of you are doing. And we are equally tickled by the ways in which each of you are doing the work!

"With the deepest love, respect and gratitude; we salute you."

Rob Gauthier

Rob Gauthier has channeled hundreds of ETs, and has come to be known internationally as "The ET Whisperer." Nearly a decade ago during a deep meditation, he unexpectedly astral-projected out of his body and found himself face-to-face with his main guide, TReb Bor yit-NE, an unconditionally loving, 5th-dimensional benevolent Reptilian-human hybrid from the Capella star system. For two years, Rob visited TReb via astral projection through meditation, asking TReb (with his 5th-dimensional insights) about the Universe. Eventually Rob invited TReb to channel through him so he could share his wisdom and love with our world. Later, Rob met another main guide not only of his, but of TReb's! This being was Aridif, a 6th-dimensional Denebian whose race was originally an ancient Pleiadian race. Aridif's insights and teachings were instantly popular with the public, despite the fact that Rob had already channeled at least 200 other ETs by that point. Together, TReb and Aridif became the main teachers and guides through Rob.

Rob has co-authored three books with Jefferson Viscardi: *Plee-Na-Ki and The Plenatalaka - Pleiadian Soul Reflection* (2015), *Extraterrestrial Life - Galactic Humans* (2013), and *Benevolent Hybrid Reptilian Humans* (2011). He has been featured in many radio shows and films, and he created The Enlightenment Evolution Network, an internet radio network. He also co-created The Channel Panel, an annual online channeling and teaching event. He offers private channeling sessions which can be booked via his website.

Rob resides in Michigan with his son Jeremy, and his fiancée and partner, Kalina Angell.

His YouTube channel is: The Official ET Whisperer Channel
His website is: ETwhisperer.com

Which words do you use to describe 'them'?

From my own perspective and my own time with them, whenever I'm describing them I use either their proper names, or the names they gave us to represent them. Which in itself is kind of an odd thing. These entities or beings—which are two of the pronouns I use for them—don't really have names in their own environment - they're all telepathic. They use non-verbal telepathic communication.

So when I speak about Aridif, Aridif is a name that represents the ancient word for the star that he comes from, which is Deneb—also known as Alpha Signus—in the Signus constellation.

And as for TReb, he gave me this very interesting name TReb Bor yit-NE. When you spell it, he told me it is broken down for certain reasons. So TReb would represent his family genome or his lineage. Bor would represent the quadrant of the planet that he lived on, because there's two sides to their planet, a dark side and a light side as well as northern and southern hemispheres. It's tidally locked, a lot like our Moon is, so one side faces the sun at all times. Yit is the representation of their entire planet, which is the third planet from the star they orbit. And NE represents the star.

It's funny with TReb, because they come from a four-star system and when we look out into the cosmos and see the star Capella we only see one star, but it's in fact four stars. Two that are large white stars that are about ten times bigger than ours, and two red dwarfs. His planet orbits the largest of the two red dwarves.

When I looked into TReb's name, it was a little jarring to me at first. It was always kind of odd and funny to me. But about a year after I started channeling, someone pointed out that when you spell the name backwards, it looks like 'Robert entity', which is the connection that he shares with me. I knew that he was connected to me in my oversoul, and was a probable future version of me, but that kind of cemented it.

So these two names together represent who they are specifically. But I've channeled so many different beings and entities that when I refer to them I call them 'entity'. That's partly because I learned about consciousness in a very descriptive manner. First of all you have the day-to-day self which is your personage or persona, or as TReb and Aridif call it, the 'lower fractalized consciousness'. That's your ego part, your regular person. The larger part is both your lower and higher fractal consciousness put together. The combination of the lower self and higher self is the complete entity.

The word 'entity' is something that has always been repeated in the verbiage that TReb shared with me when I first started channeling. So when I refer to a singular consciousness, I always refer to it as an entity or being, because it's their sense of being, their sense of self.

When I refer to the collective consciousnesses, I always refer to them as 'they'. In a collective consciousness like the Nihal, which are future human versions that I have also channeled before, they are literally millions of beings that connect into one energy, so it represents a whole collective consciousness.

When you hear them speak about their own experience, you very rarely hear the word 'I', even with an individual consciousness. TReb and Aridif usually refer to themselves as 'we'. When you ask them what that means, it means their entire race - myself involved with them as I connect in a channeled state. So it's very rare to hear 'I', unless they're telling you their own personal perspective. So when I refer to them, I try to refer to them individually as entities or beings, and collectively as they. And it's kind of funny to hear at first, when you're so used to dealing with a personal perspective, in your day-to-day interactions.

Which kinds of beings are you in contact with?

The types of beings I connect with come in three different groups. The first two are very linked with one another. The first group is extraterrestrial, and all of us know what that means. It means more than the terrestrial version or engagement that we have here on Earth. So extraterrestrial is a phrase that is well known and understood by everyone, and has the connotation of entities or beings who exist on planets outside of Earth, or even the solar system. The majority of entities that I've connected with exist and can be labeled as extraterrestrial, which is why I took on the nickname 'The ET Whisperer'.

The second group, which is very connected to the first group in many ways, is extradimensional. And this is a phrase that as far as I know was coined by the filmmaker Reuben Langdon. He has a series called 'Interview with E.D.', in which he interviews extradimensional beings through channels. We did a session for his show, and have become good friends. When you think of 'extradimensional' it's just what it sounds like; it means more than the dimensions where we come from.

For most people this takes some work to grasp solidly, because it's outside of average human experience. You might encounter it if you've started digging into meditation, or connection, or expanding your consciousness beyond the average day-to-day level. When we look at extradimensional, it depends on who you're talking to. It entails multiple dimensions above us. This is something I've learned from my own channeling and my own perspective. There are six densities, which are almost dimensions in one way, but not really, and I'll explain the difference between those. A density describes more than just dimensional differences. It's an entity's journey - the evolution of consciousness or evolution of a personal soul and their experience.

First density is elemental beings. This is fire, rock, water, electricity. They exist as inanimate objects in the human mind - anything that doesn't live. And these beings create everything that we share existence with. The Sun is created from multiple elemental beings of gas, fire, energy. We look at the Moon as rocks and ice and all of those things. So all of the things that exist in our universe are created from that building block of first density consciousness.

Second density is single cell organisms, and moves up all the way up to very complex animals and plants. These are things that are living, but are instinctual in the way that they experience the world.

And then you have the 3rd density, which is what humans are transitioning out of right now. And that's where you have an expanded mindset, an expanded consciousness, and more than anything, an expanded sense of self. When you see animals and trees and you compare them to humans, they're very similar in many ways in which they experience the world. They interact, they exchange, they hold memories and emotions, but the human does it in a different way, because their mindset is expanded and they perceive time differently. Linear time is felt and experienced here much more than the entities in second density. The second density beings exist more so in the moment, as a reaction- based experience.

Densities one through three are in one harmonic level, one vibrational or dimensional plane. The term 'harmonic level' means that everything on that dimension vibrates at a similar harmonic frequency. It's the speed of the vibration at the cellular level, or the atomic level of that dimension. So we have that one dimension for 1st through 3rd density.

And then you have 4th density, which from our perspective is on a higher dimensional plane. Now dimension is again a difficult term to grasp, because when you think of it in a classic sense, you think of height, width, depth and time - time and space being one. So 1st through 3rd density is considered 4th dimensional. And then you see the

4th-density beings in the level above that, and they're considered 5th dimensional.

So you have 1st through 4th, then you have 5th and 6th, which are one harmonic level, or one dimension higher than the 4th-density beings. Now these two groups of entities (5th and 6th density) are in another harmonic level, but even those entities don't interact directly in a physical way. Like if a 4th-density being stood in front of you and started talking to you, you would have to have your intuition or psychic ability open to be able to communicate. It's not physically tangible, something you can touch and notice, unless your vibration is going up to theirs, or theirs is going down to yours. Changing your vibration to do this can happen, but usually only happens to us in our sleep. Not all entities can lift their vibration to experience the higher dimensions or densities, but as humans we have multidimensional DNA, so we can learn to tap into our higher vibrational consciousness. That occurs the same way with 4th- and 5th-density beings. Even though 5th- and 6th-density beings are in that 6th-dimensional energy, the way their vibrations work is that the entire universal structure for them, on an atomic level, rotates at a different angle, a different direction. So even though they're in the same dimension, they still have that different perception, just like we would to someone in a higher dimension to us.

It's very complex, and there's a lot of learning I've had to do, which has mostly come through vibrational learning, to see the differences in that. But any of those beings who exist from 4th to 6th density are considered extradimensional beings.

So you have those two groups of entities or beings I've connected to, the extraterrestrial or extradimensional. Then the third category is collective consciousnesses. These beings are very non-physical in the way they interact with us. I try to explain it this way. If you add every human soul that has ever lived or ever *will* live on Earth, and you combine them into one energy, and you just took the souls, not their physical bodies, and merge them together, you would have the equivalent of the physical Earth. So non-physically, the soul of the Earth is basically the combination and culmination of all of the beings who will ever experience Earth. Non-physically, if all those beings would speak in one voice, that's a collective consciousness. That's another type of consciousness or entity I've co-created with or channeled.

Those are the main groups of entities I've connected to.

How do they appear to you?

The way I experience them is very different, depending on which being it might be. Most of the entities I channeled, which is over 250 at this point, have been a secondary connection from my connection with TReb, or with Aridif. So I have these base two beings that connect to me, and during our merging of the soul, of consciousness, we've been able to pull in other entities, or co-create with them. So when I channel them I'm not experiencing them the same way you are.

I'm what most people call a 'deep trance channeler'. And what that entails is myself going into a deep meditative state, and in that state, I am astral projecting. Defining astral projection can be difficult, as many people have their own view of it, but everyone can agree that it is your consciousness leaving the physical body and going to other places. Astral projection occurs every night when you sleep. Each time you've ever dreamt about going to a different planet, or time period, or even a different place on Earth, most likely you're astral projecting. If you're not astral projecting, you're going to that third layer of the dream state, that matrix level wherein you're creating your own world and experience. Even when you're doing that, you're still leaving your body to do it. So regardless, when you are dreaming, that's always an astral projection. When I meditate or when I'm channeling, that's exactly what happens to me. My consciousness is leaving my physical body, and either TReb or Aridif's consciousness enters my body. Now I don't leave completely. I have a lot of consciousness still connected in my body, but enough of it's gone, where they can put a lot of their own consciousness inside my body. So my body becomes a container of consciousness for two different souls, and that's what you experience when you watch me as I channel - you see this other entity or being coming into my body and speaking.

But what *I* experience is an astral-projected trip, where I'm co-creating and connecting with my initial guide TReb. TReb is a very large being, physically. When I look at him, I'm looking at his higher dimensional body. Now a lot of people make the mistake that when they're creating with these beings, that because they're in a higher dimension they don't have a physical structure. They believe that when you exchange with them in your body and you can't see them, that means they don't have a body. But they do. Their body exists on that higher dimension. So when I'm going to see and talk to TReb, I'm having an exchange with my higher-dimensional energy, and with his physical body. When I do that, his physical container is much different than ours. We are humanoid. He is a Reptilian-human hybrid. When

I look at him I see a very large, seven and a half foot being. Very large purple eyes. Green-blue skin, that has scaling that is very thick and deep. And he has very small red dots all over his body. He has five fingers like we do, but he has three toes, and a very long tail. And all of this physical being that I'm seeing, I'm interacting with him when you see my body channeling and TReb talking from within me. So it's a very awkward experience for many people to watch, because the demeanor, voice and energy in my body change so much. But that's just the by-product of me co-creating with this entity and his consciousness coming into my body.

TReb Bor yit-NE. Credit: Vashta Narada

So that's how I get to experience channeling. Even if I'm channeling Aridif, which is another entity or being who is connected to my initial guide TReb, then I'm still co-creating with TReb. So no matter what, when I'm out and about, out of my body, I'm able to co-create with this Reptilian-human hybrid and these other entities are being guided into my body so that they can co-create. That experience is the way that I interact personally and how I get to experience them.

I've never been able to go face-to-face with Aridif like I have TReb, but TReb has shown me a great deal of other races, and many different beings or groups. So I've been able to see many of these higher-dimensional beings through my interactions with TReb. I've also been able to experience his planet, which is where I go most of the time when I co-create with him or speak with him. I've also been able to see his ship and many other planets that he is at during the time of interaction. I'm able to call on him at any time, and when I do that, he could be anywhere. So wherever he's at, that's where I go. So that's kind of how I get to experience them physically.

Now my fiancée Kalina, she has been able to experience Aridif, which is the other guide that I connect with. He looks very different to us too. He's very short, I believe around three foot nine. He also has very large purple eyes, and long purple hair. He's very small and petite, very humanoid looking, with the exception of his blue skin. He has very pale powder-blue skin. One of the main differences in his anatomy compared to ours, is the lower half of his body. He has knees that bend both ways, and large round feet with seven toes. Like a thumb and six front toes. He's able to be very agile with that, and climb up things with those feet if he wishes. So he is very different physically compared to humans. Although I haven't experienced that yet, I know that the continuation of my connection with these beings will kind of open up that door as I go through.

Aridif. Credit: Vashta Narada

When I experience these entities physically, when interacting with TReb, it's not like walking up to another person and meeting them. In your dream state you have a sixth sense. I always use this example. When you walk to a house that is your great-grandmother's house, although you've never been there, instinctively in the dream you know whose house it is. You know where you're at and what you're doing, even though you have no preface for it. In the astral projection state when I'm connecting with TReb it's very similar to that, and in fact it's a heightened version of that. When I go to create with TReb I know where he's at, I know what he's doing and why. It could be on his ship, or a planet. And more than just knowing where he is and what he is doing, I also know his emotions.

When I first met him I became scared of his physical presence. He is a huge being who looks very intimidating, but within seconds of being hit with that initial wave of fear, a sense of love came over me that was so extraordinary that I was instantly calmed. I knew that this being had no ill will or malice towards me whatsoever. In fact it was the opposite. I felt this being loved me, to a level beyond even that of my own parents, and I know how much my parents love me. So it's not just the physical interaction that you get, it's also the emotional and psychic energy that you're able to experience with that interaction. I think as awesome as it is for people to hear about that physical exchange and what they look like, or what their personalities are like, I think to know that I have access to their thoughts and emotions is much more important and powerful to understand. In fact when I connect with TReb, the telepathy is so high that there are no words that need to be spoken. He knows my thoughts, my feelings, my questions, and he answers them the same way, through that telepathy. The physical stuff is great, but this is much more profound.

Can you describe your first contact?

The very first time with TReb was a couple of years after releasing myself from a multiple-year depression and drug addiction. I left that behind and began to learn meditation. After years of going through different kinds of meditations I finally found a guided binaural meditation from the Monroe Institute called the Gateway Experience, and that really opened me up. So I'd been studying this for four months, using a mediation that has 21 steps, and each step heightens and expands your consciousness.

The night that I first met TReb I was actually in a distraught state. I'd just watched a 3D video of the deep field Hubble imagery, and was reminded just how large the universe was. I always knew it was huge, but to see it in this 3D way touched me deeply. With that came a longing. I had the sense that I was on a beautiful and wonderful planet, but I was trapped here. I felt like I belonged out in the universe, and that it is the birthright of every human to be able to go out and about into this beautiful universe. So I was crying, I was very upset. For the first time in many years I was in touch with my emotions. So I used this deep binaural beat meditation to kind of center and ground myself. I would always go to that 21ˢᵗ step and stay there. But that night I wondered what would happen if I went beyond that. Each step takes you further out of your body, so I was already in the astral state, and had no awareness of my body. So I counted to 21, and instead of saying 22, I said, "Now I go beyond the 21ˢᵗ state." I was then taken into this place where TReb was. Initially TReb wasn't there. I was just in a large room, which I later found out was one of their ships. It was a very confusing environment, and felt like a weird sci-fi dream, but then TReb came through the door and the fear was there, but then my heart allowed that love to hit me.

He then telepathically communicated that he is deeply connected to me. He said something to the effect of, "We share a path, and I want to communicate with you more frequently. The universe, life, your existence, is not the way that you're perceiving it now, and I am willing to share some insights on how the universe really works. You've been in my awareness all your life, but I've really been able to connect with you for the last couple of years, and I want to make this connection more frequent."

When I got back into my body, at first I thought I'd gone crazy. Because it was so intense and so extraordinary. But when I look back at my time, I was honing in my intuition. I felt this very large presence or energy around me a couple of months before I connected to TReb, but I didn't know how to describe it, or who or what it was, or how it would affect me.

That was the most impactful moment of my interactions with TReb, although it wasn't the most enlightening one. I then took three days off my meditation, which was very unusual at that point, as I was meditating multiple hours every day, sometimes up to six or seven hours. I then went back into meditation, and as soon as I did, I followed the same steps. I grounded and neutralized, and all the other steps, and I connected to TReb again and we talked. And we continuously talked for two years after that about who he was. I had to learn to trust this being, to let him into my life and heart, just like I did every person. It sounds weird because you're in this highly spiritual energy when you're around him, but I still had that human perspective: I don't know you, you have to earn my trust. It didn't take him long to become a very fond member of my heart, and a connection to me at a soul level, but I still had to understand who he was and what he wanted to teach me. After two years I asked him if it was possible to work with him and let him come through my body and share this information with others. It was something that I wanted to do, so he agreed. I had seen other people do it, when I looked up extraterrestrials and things about consciousness and evolution of the soul. When searching for answers on my own to confirm what TReb had said, I found channeled material that would tell me very similar things. So by seeing these people channel I thought, 'I can do that.' I asked TReb if he was able to do that, and he said yes, and I started channeling.

How do you connect now?

Channeling is a very different thing to meditation, although the techniques to get there are very similar. So I've conditioned myself to be able to do this. As I've said, when I channel is the time when I get to interact with TReb personally. I'm able to initiate this at any time, and that's why I often go to these different planets or ships, because as soon as I go into that channeled state I connect with TReb, and he could be anywhere doing anything.

Their race has almost what they call 'jobs'. But they're not jobs in that sense that you do something in order to receive something. For them they have a sense of duty to live their excitements, and I know it sounds odd from a human perspective, but they feel so compelled to dive into their excitements that each one of them takes on a role in their society. TReb's role is to go out and teach the evolutionary consciousness teachings, which are available to whomever wants to, and can receive them. When you compare that to a human job, you would say he's a spiritual adviser, almost. So this is all that he does, he connects with other beings and shares these teachings. When I connect with him and he's on another planet, he can be physically speaking to other beings or groups, or connecting telepathically to 10, 15 or 20 other entities at the same time. So imagine yourself multitasking; the best most of us can do is maybe two or three things at the same time. We can talk on the phone, watch TV and type a message, something like that. TReb's consciousness is so much larger than ours, that he's able to carry on individual conversations with 15-20 entities at the same time and be able to process them. He can also do whatever he needs to do in his physical body simultaneously.

They don't have belief systems like we humans do, where we think my time is only dedicated to this and no one can interrupt my time during this. They have a belief where if they were to bump into another entity, that is divine purpose, it's creation of an experience driven by their highest excitements. So for him he has no limits for me, in how and when I can connect, or when it would be appropriate to do so. In fact there have only been two times where I've failed to connect. One of those was at the very beginning, and was due to my own emotional energy. The other time was where he had all of his consciousness pointed at one thing at one time. He was connecting to this gigantic energy of an entity that embodied almost a whole universe. So he was completely connected to that entity and couldn't do any multitasking. Even though he's much larger in consciousness than we are, he still couldn't break off parts of his consciousness to do that.

But every other time, whether it's in my sleep state, where I'll set an intention to go speak to him then, or through a meditation, or a channeling, I'm able to do that.

Can you initiate contact?

I initiate the contact by placing my intent, and there's a way I do that. The process has changed drastically from when we first began to connect. It would take me an hour to neutralize my energy, and put myself through the 21-step process, and then I had to go through a series of connection processes. I would visualize myself sitting in a chair with a box on my lap. When I opened that box, it would transmute all the physical things in the universe into non-physical things. I would visualize this by seeing all the stuff in the room get vacuumed into this box, then everything within a 100-foot radius, the whole house, the yard, then the city, the state of Michigan, the Midwest, and the more that went in, the faster it would go. Then it would suck in the whole country, the planet, the Moon, the solar system, all the galaxies, everything. After that, all that was left was myself and the box, and then I would put myself in the box, and allow my consciousness to be in the non-physical realm.

After that visualization I would start an Oming process, which is something I still do. This is an unusual way to channel. I've not met many channels who use that Oming sound or vibration, but over many years I've developed the capacity to intuit the sounds I need to use to connect with TReb or Aridif. By this I mean that I need to get my chakras vibrating at a certain frequency. For those of you who don't understand chakras, there are seven points of energy in your physical body, and each of them is connected to a different part of the evolution of our soul, and also different emotional themes. For instance, the root chakra, which is at the tip of your tailbone or coccyx, is an earthy red color, which represents your grounding to physical reality. But it also coincides with the 1st density, the elemental fields. And you go up and each one has a different color and meaning. For me to be able to connect to TReb in the channeled state, I need to be able to keep my chakras vibrating at a similar rate. Because I'm kind of a grounded person, I'm very earthly in my perceptions and perspectives, and way of life, so my bottom chakras vibrate at very high frequencies already. So I'm very connected to that Earth energy. I have to vibrate the chakras from my solar plexus to my crown at a higher frequency, and I do that with tones. Usually the Om sound is the tone of preference, but it can go into other tones. When I first started connecting I had to Om for about three to four minutes just to make sure all my chakras were lined up and vibrating at the same rate.

After doing that, I would do deep breathing to get all my energy lined up. I would push all my energy from my first to my second chakra, and then those two energies collectively to the third, and on up to bring all my chakra energy up to my third eye and let it sit there. The deep breaths would help pull that energy up to my third eye, and once I felt it vibrate then I could release it to my crown and I could leave my body at that point, and TReb would come in, and the channeling would start.

That's very similar to how I do it now, but there are less steps and I can do it much faster. It used to take an hour to do the 21-step visualizations, the connection and grounding processes, and then my breathing and Oming would take another six or seven minutes. I can now do all of it in under ten minutes. I usually mute my microphone during private sessions, so I can do the neutralizing process, which takes about five minutes. And after that, instead of going through all of those visualizations and steps, I can just breathe, Om, get my chakra vibrations high, and then move energy through my chakras.

And even that is overdone, compared to how it could be done. I know, from what TReb and Aridif have told me, that all of the things I am doing now to connect to them are still just permission slips, or energetic connection processes that I believe I need to go through, but in reality, if I really wanted to get the vibration to flow more instantly, I would have to practice it and believe that this by itself can connect me to the channeling state. When we meditate and do all of these little things, they are purposeful, they have meaning, but the intent behind that energy is 100 times more meaningful. If you're meditating to clear your energy into calmness, and you're going through a visualization of being on a beach and being in a happy place, and that's your connection, the actual beach visualization is not as important as your need to be calm. That's just the way you've taught yourself to get to be in that calm space. The same thing applies with the channeling, it's just being used in a different way.

How does your contact feel?

When I'm going through this, it's unique for me in the way I feel, physically and emotionally. When I go through my neutralization process I'm not feeling a whole lot, almost to level of indifference. That neutral energy is so important for me to be in, so that the energy from TReb or Aridif can come through more clearly. So when I neutralize, I'm basically flushing out all my frustrations, my emotions, even over-stimulation, happiness and excitement. And that pulls me into a neutral place so that I have the best foundation for the next process.

When I start doing the deep breathing, and getting my chakras lined up, and then the Oming to get them vibrating properly, there is a sense of alignment. For me there's no great excitement or joy that goes on there, but some channelers use their emotions to connect. For me it's neutral. Right before I get ready to leave my body and go to connect with TReb, I do feel an overwhelming sense of joy, but that's because my energy is starting to line up with his, and the neutral energy is being pushed to the side by his energy and connection with me.

When I go to connect with TReb now, because I've been doing this for over eight years, it's just like going to the store for most of you, it's very normal. But in that connection, in that astral-projected state, there is an overwhelming sense of joy. It's like being the happiest you can be, but ten times more, and this is for the whole time I connect to him. So think about the best part of your life; it's like that, but more expansive.

As far as feeling in the other sense, I always have that sixth sense, that extended and expanded version of telepathy. But I also seem to lose one of my senses too. And I'm the only person I know who experiences this. I've talked to many channelers about how they experience things, and those who do have astral projections, they take all their senses with them. When I go to TReb's planet, sometimes I can't smell, or hear or feel things. It seems like I'm trading that sixth sense for one of the physical senses in my astral projection, which is a little weird. But when I go to experience that, it is very physical. I can touch TReb's face, I can give him a hug, I can sit on a rock, I can walk around his planet. So it's just like being in your dream state. For those of you who dream regularly, and have one dream that felt super real, you know what I'm talking about. That's the sense I have when connecting with them.

Now going through my physical body, how that feels, when I'm going to connect with TReb or Aridif, I do feel huge amounts of energy.

Some of you have felt a connection to your chakra systems, or kundalini energy, which you feel going up your spine. When I'm connecting and neutralizing my energy, when I go to align my chakras, I can literally feel the chakras vibrating, swelling and retracting; I can feel them twirling like a tornado of energy in my body. And through my years of meditation, I developed a sensitivity to that. So when I'm feeling that energy, and letting it go to my third eye and letting it swell, there's a sense of heat in my forehead. And after I leave, then the physical senses of my body are gone. When I watch videos of myself channeling, my body does go through a lot of physiological changes. For instance, even though I can sweat in normal conditions, when I'm channeling, even in a cool room, I have a lot of heat and sweat. And what I understand about why this occurs, is that TReb's energy is so much larger than ours, that even the small piece that he sends to converse and connect, or connect other beings in, is still very large and intense energy.

And I've noticed that each entity or being that I channel has different ways that they hold my body. TReb smiles real big, and flings my upper body around when I'm sitting there as he talks to other people. Aridif is very still, and very subtle in his movements, sometimes barely moving at all. And others beings will have tics with my body. Some will feel the back of my hands, some will touch my face a lot. Others will speak in a different way through me. So each of these things I can't feel or experience, I only know from seeing it on video afterwards. Because of my deep trance state, I only get to experience them in a second-hand way.

How do you differentiate between your own thoughts and those from outside?

After three or four years of channeling, plus the two years before when I was getting to know TReb, I started to experience TReb in a much different way. From day one of channeling I always felt his presence, even when I wasn't channeling or astrally projecting and speaking to him. But in the years after, the more I connected with him, the more energy of his I took on. I wasn't turning into him, but was starting to learn from him vibrationally. And when you learn in that way it's an experience that each person who is reading this can understand. Let's take a human example. If you start a new relationship, over time you begin learning from each other without any lessons being taught. I had that experience with TReb. That became more noticeable as I started energetically opening up, and my intuition and psychic ability expanded even more.

After a couple of years, instead of just feeling his presence, I would understand things, and be able to speak with him in a non-channeled state. This was the very first time I'd ever been able to get direct telepathic communication in my physical body. It started with thoughts, like 'I wonder what this idea is.' And then I felt his energy, and started receiving an answer. At first it sounded like an internal dialogue, so I thought it was my own insight and intuition, and in a way it was, but in that connection with TReb, that bridge of information was being built. That bridge became more connected because of the expansion of his energy into mine, and vice versa. So now I'm able to sit here as I'm talking with you, in a non-channeled state, and be able to receive insight and information from TReb and Aridif.

At first it was very confusing. It was like, am I receiving this information from them, or is my insight from understanding and knowing them allowing me to bring these answers to myself? I found out after the first few times it happened, when I went back into my channeled state and asked TReb, that I could always go back and ask him. And I used this tool, not just for this, but throughout my first two years of channeling, to make sure it was coming through clear. I would hear an answer that didn't make sense in a session, and I would go back and ask him, and he would tell me whether or not something was clear. When the answers weren't so clear, it might have been that my emotions were too off that day. But I could use this tool to ask if certain pieces of information were correct or not. What he described is that the information was a direct communication from him to myself, so I started knowing that all of these insights were being pulled in through my higher self, from him or Aridif. After doing that for a while I stopped second-guessing myself, and knew whether or not it was coming from one of them. That's one of the hardest things to learn for any person who is trying to contact higher dimensional, or any other beings in a channeled state, especially those who do conscious channeling. Is this voice my own, or is it the entity's?

When I first learned to meditate I did it through a church called a spiritualism church, and one of the first things the guy taught me, is that when you're meditating and you're receiving information, don't second-guess where it's coming from, or if it's right or wrong, just accept it and move on. After you do that enough times, then the information you're going to get will always be correct, because you've built a trust with yourself and you've also built a rapport with spirit.

So after hearing that, it was easier for me to not second-guess myself. And after having TReb confirm it a few times, I knew it was accurate. So even though it comes in as an inner dialogue, now I can differentiate. Through my own energy and desire to know the difference I've created a different way it comes in. Instead of the internal dialogue, it that information will come through in TReb or Aridif's voice. And again, they have no voice because they telepathically communicate, but when they come through me their voices are different. So when I hear TReb talking, I hear him as if he were being channeled through my body. And that was a tool I developed by not worrying about where it came from. So now that internal voice has the TRebbish or Aridif vibe to it. So now it's much easier to discern.

The biggest thing that those who are just opening up their communicative tools need to understand, to help them with this issue, is: trust yourself. If it feels right, and if it's coming to you, then most likely it's correct. There will always be time in the future to see if the type of communication and the information being communicated is accurate. But if you don't trust yourself and always second-guess yourself, you're cutting off a huge part of your intuition.

A lot of people say that when you start meditating or astral projecting, or connecting to spirit, use your imagination. Many people are afraid to, because they think, 'If I'm using my imagination then maybe I'm deluding myself, and giving myself permission to make stuff up.' And I understand that mindset, but the imagination is the tool our consciousness uses to help us to connect to what's really there. We can use it that way if we don't see imagination as a fake or bad thing. So at first, use the imagination energy, as it bleeds into your own awareness. Use that to build your own connection, and don't worry if it's coming from you or not. We have a very long time in our physical bodies, so we may have many years to see if that information is truthful. And if you trust yourself, then even if it is coming in from the higher parts of yourself, it's still just as valid. That's a fight that a lot of people have when they listen to channeled material. They might think, 'Aridif is so smart and everything he says is so right.' Well, everything he says he is right for him, because he's his own entity, he has his own perspective. You have to trust and value your own intake also. And if you don't, then anything anyone else says will never truly be impactful for you, or truly be useful until you allow it. So just trust in yourself in allowing that to come through is very important.

For me I can tell the difference now, but it's taken a while to build that trust, and build the networks. I'm a trance channeler who also communicates in a non-trance state, and I don't know of many who have that capability. It was my own allowance of it that really helped build that bridge in the first place. So if you're feeling those energies, if you're feeling connection, just keep that open and it will really help you build the bridge.

What safeguards do you use?

This seems to be something that's very important for a lot of people. And it was for me when I started learning from the spiritualism church. They were big on teaching protection of your soul, so that when you're trying to communicate with spirit that no evil, negative, or lying spirit would come through. And it's the same when people use Ouija boards etcetera.

The technique that I used was enveloping myself in a ball of white light. And this would be a meditation where I would first ground myself. The technique I used was quite complex, but one that's more simple goes like this: visualize your root chakra, which is red and about two-thirds the size of your fist, breathing in white light, and pushing the red energy out into vines, all the way down your legs to the bottom of your feet, and then about 30 feet deep into the ground. In about 10-15 breaths, all that white light will push the red out, and it will seep into the Earth. And the white light you breathe in comes from all around you. It comes from your desk, animals, the air - it's part of all creation. You're breathing out negativity, bad energy, anxiety, anything that makes you unbalanced.

After you breathe all that red energy into the Earth, then you start breathing in golden yellow light from the Earth itself, 30 feet deep. That energy is mother Earth, Gaia, the Earth collective consciousness, whatever you want to perceive the Earth as. You breathe that all the way up into your body, until it is full up to the tip of your crown chakra. I use to this approach to this day for my grounding technique. Completely grounding helps neutralize you.

Then you breathe in golden yellow, silver or pale white energy, and breathe out white light. This breath goes into a ball, all around you, which is roughly arm length from your body and covers you entirely. This energy is from Creator, Source, God, whatever you want to perceive it as. When you are completely surrounded by this opaque white ball of light, this ball represents your intent to allow in only what resonates with you. Not what's vibrationally similar, because if you're in a bad mood that can allow bad energy in. Some people go further and only wish to allow in those which have the greatest intent for them, who are connected to God. Whatever the intent is, you place that there along with that bubble, and focus on that energy. That's one of the techniques that's quite important, and I've learned quite a few from TReb and Aridif.

But for myself I have quite a different perspective on protection. TReb and Aridif have talked to me about the Creator energy that each one of has. And that means that all of us share this gigantic matrix of physical reality which is illusory; it's something which our consciousness does to create an experience. So physically we're all sharing this large program of physical reality, and are creating ourselves. We created our physical body for our interaction with the world, and we create our experiences - and it's very literal when they say that. Some people take it figuratively, but I take it as literal. For example, if I get into a car crash ten years from now, I've created that experience. Now I might create it because there's something that needs to happen from that crash that puts me into a new direction in my life. It could be that I created the crash because I wasn't taking care of my body and they find something in a scan. It could be any reason. What that means is that if you're connecting to negative beings, you're also creating that experience for a reason. Remember that.

What TReb and Aridif tell me that makes me feel a lot better now about connection, is that when you're really aligned with the true nature of who you are, you're connecting to both your lower self and your higher self. Your higher self is the largest form of consciousness in physical reality. The lower fractal consciousness only represents between 11 and 25% of the overall self that we are. The rest of your being is represented as the higher self. When you're looking at a 3rd-density being like ourselves, going into 4th density, you see a being who has at least three different levels of entities or energies that are larger than us. Most people worry about the Draco or Alpha Draconian Reptilian beings, or some other bad energy (from their perspective) that can interfere with them, attack them or take energy from you. The thing is, even the biggest, baddest, worst kind are 6th density at the top level, and those *are* big and scary energies. So I understand why there is a fear of that, and a desire to protect yourself from that. But, when you're aligned with yourself, your higher self is involved in the equation, because you're connecting to your higher self. That's the part that connects you to the oversoul, and the non-physical parts of yourself. When you're connected to that, you're bigger than that 6th density entity. Any being who thinks it's necessary to take your energy, to attack you, is much smaller than your higher self is. It has to be, because it's not connected to Source energy. So, when you are aligned with yourself, and connected to your higher self, you're larger than anything that can ever be a singular physical being in this universe. And if that's the case, then when I'm in the moment, living my highest excitement, no being can mess with or manipulate me.

So because I know when I'm feeling good, and know when I'm channeling and automatically bringing in these gigantic positive energies, I never worry about it. But back then, before I was aligned with myself, before understanding the mechanics of consciousness, and before I was connecting out to all of these huge energies, I definitely worried about that. So for me the techniques were needed and useful. And don't get me wrong, I could still use them and they would be useful, but because I truly believe that TReb and Aridif are in my alignment with truth, and because I believe in my own power, I don't see the need to do that anymore. When you're first starting out, I would suggest using the grounding and bubble techniques.

There is another very helpful one that can be used. This is a bit more of an intense visualization, but is also very useful. First perceive yourself as sitting down, standing up, whatever it is, then see four white pillars, which are six inches square, placed at the cardinal direction points around you. They are nine feet tall, but three feet of that is submerged, and six feet is exposed. Once you've visualized that, then you connect the pillars with a wall of white light, of the same thickness. Then on the top of that structure, right at the center, right over your crown chakra, you create a silver sphere about nine inches in diameter, which is connecting to your crown chakra. Then over the sphere you create a green roof for this room. The sphere goes through the roof, exposing some of the top and some of the bottom. Its job is to help your higher self give you all the energy it needs, and guide which entities are allowed into your space. This is something Aridif taught someone, but for a different application. But it still works for protection energy.

Using your own creation, like my steps to help me channel, these are just permission slips. Anything you do, like burning sage, chanting, meditating, whatever makes you feel safe from being manipulated or attacked, or drained of your energy, then those will work for you. These are a few things that have proven to work for others.

When I worked with TReb originally, he taught me a thing that I ended up calling a Star Mantra. You can find it on my ET Whisperer YouTube channel, with the title 'How to connect To TReb's energy yourself! (The TReb Mantra)'. The way we created it was that he and I came up with a group of stars that were very important to myself and my connection process. And this list reflected the sense of our connection. And I started using it in a chanting way, and when I worked on that with TReb, I would utilize that energy to call his energy to mine. With TReb being such a gigantic, loving energy, that usually drives away any negative spirit that's smaller than he is, or dislikes the intensity of love. So when I created that mantra to connect with his energy, it helped drive away many of those negative beings or energies for other people. And to this day people still use this mantra in their own life, and it helps them deal with negative spirits, either through playing the audio version I've shared, or learning it themselves are singing it.

TReb has said that anyone using it can call on his energy and use it for anything. You can use it to align with yourself, or when you're meditating on healing. He's not a being who will do these things for you directly because he believes in your free will and your right to pave your own way. He won't heal your sickness, but he's more than happy to share his energy with you so you can use it for healing your sickness. The same could be applied to protection visualizations. So he's a very loving being, and just by knowing that you're connected to those loving beings can be very useful whenever you need it. That in itself can be a protection type of meditation, but it also offers another level of protection at any time, if you need it.

Why do they connect with you?

This is something that even to this day is still a little baffling to me. I've had many explanations given by Aridif, by TReb, by many of the other beings who I've connected with, and they all have something a little different to say. For instance, TReb was my very first connection, and he is still my most prevalent connection now. Like when I meditate and when I astral project and then I channel, I am always with TReb. So he is my number one guide in my mind. And even with him, when I asked, "Why me?" he said that there are many entities, beings in his oversoul, in the part of consciousness that connects all of our selves to our past, present, future and parallel lives. And out of all those beings that are in our same oversoul, mine and TReb's, that I was the one that was most open to that communication, and he wanted to work with people on Earth more directly. He wanted to connect with the Earth's, and my energy more directly. So he had that. That's one of the reasons.

After a couple of years working with TReb I did a book with another person, Jefferson Viscardi, in which they pretty much interviewed TReb through me. Jefferson asked about him, his race, his people, their day-to-day life, their belief systems, all of the things you could ever want to know about them. He asked TReb, "Are you a future version of Rob?" And TReb said yes, but in a much more detailed way. The reason that was asked was because, by interviewing so many different channelers and so many different beings, he had an awareness that many of the people who channel do so by connecting with their higher self. When they connect through their higher self, it usually aligns with entities who are either most vibrationally alike or entities who are connected through your oversoul.

And when someone's in your oversoul it doesn't mean they are a future or past version of you, it means that they could be a probable future version or a probable past reality. Now that's a bit counter-intuitive when you look at it in the larger sense, because when people say, "This is my past life," most have the belief that it is a finite connection to that past life. They say, "This is my own life in the past, looking back linearly." But time doesn't exist linearly, and I think that's something that some people don't understand.

When you're in a higher dimension, a non-physical state, or when you're in the oversoul, time doesn't exist in that same way. Time only exists as a coordinate of an experience and a vibration. And what I mean by that is, we right now are in the 5th dimension. We have height, depth, width, and time, time being in a state of fluidity. So the 4th-dimensional energy is the same except time is linear. Well now that we're going from 3rd density to 4th density, we're gaining an extra aspect of consciousness. Not that it's different from time, but it's an experience of consciousness in the way we move through time.

As a 3rd-density being, as a 4th-dimensional entity, we only have the experience of linear time. But evolving into that higher density, evolving into the higher-dimensional energy, what we're able to do is start having fluidity of that time. We don't have to live it from A to B. We can actually go from A to D, and from Z to F, and then back to A again. It's not the motion or energy of time that pushes us, it's our own desire, mindset and thoughts. If we want to go, for instance, back into the 1100s, instead of creating some sort of time-travel technology to do that, all we have to do is feel like we're in the 1100s. Think like we're in the 1100s, wear clothing, experience whatever it takes to put you in touch with that part of yourself that feels the 1100s; that's what will truly allow yourself to be part of the 1100s energy.

And if we are in the 4th density, 5th-dimensional, we don't have to convert ourselves. Now obviously at first we would have to push our own energy, we would have to learn, and teach ourselves to do that, but after we evolve and create and connect, then we're able to do that just by thought alone. So it's very useful to understand that the linear time is only an experience of those from 1st to 3rd density.

Now that being said, when TReb looks at me, he looks at me as if I am a probable past life, just like I would look at him as if he is a probable future incarnation. So for TReb the answer's very clear. Why connect? Because you're one version of me, I'm one version of you; we're connected. Through that connection, because we both share the same interest in communicating with other races, because we share the desire to expand our knowledge base and our spirituality, we find our way to one another.

Now each extraterrestrial after TReb has been different. Aridif connects to us because he loves humans. He has a connection and a feeling of affinity towards humans. He's been doing this for thousands of years. Through different points in our history, from India to Africa to Europe to South and North America, throughout the world and throughout different time periods, Aridif's race, the Denebians, and Aridif specifically, has been working with humans. A lot of the time when you look into your history books you see the little blue men, you see the very short blue entities or beings. Some of them in history have been said to have purple hair. That would be Aridif and his race. I had never heard about these entities or beings before I met with Aridif, but as we began to share, I started looking into it because others asked about it, and there's hundreds of years of detailing, and thousands of years of stories being handed down that explain these entities.

One of the problems in the earliest cultures is that they could not explain a color, and we're not sure if they couldn't see it with the physical structure of their eyes. They may not have been developed enough to see the color, or they may have had no way to reproduce that color through paintings. So a lot of time we see blue entities or beings that have blue hair. And we're not sure if that's something that had to have coloring mismatch or what the case is, but I feel in my heart that that is Aridif and his race.

What do the beings get out of it?

Aridif and TReb are my main guides, but that leaves a lot of other entities and their reasons why they connect with me. Most of them are very transparent about it. A lot of entities I channel, and beings in general, when you listen to them speak, it's often because they also receive something. Now I don't want to say that all ETs have an intent or an agenda, but each of them also gains access to our consciousness, our knowledge, and also experience, to make it worth their while. In reality all beings do have an agenda of their own. This doesn't mean they are plotting against us, it just means that even if their excitements are motivating them, then they have some reason they want to connect to us or help us.

Some people feel really bad because they believe that TReb is so wonderful because he gives, gives, gives, but never gets anything back. So at the end of channeling sessions he started explaining to those people, "When I communicate with you I'm touching a part of your energy that I've never been able to touch before. I'm experiencing a unique part of you that I've never been able to experience before. And because I am able to do that, I am also touching parts of my own energy that I've never been able to experience."

That in itself is huge, because it means that as they communicate with us each time they're expanding in their own consciousness. If that's not reason enough I wouldn't know what would be.

A lot of people hesitate with channeling, because they have a very divided sense of good and bad guys, a very black and white sense about why someone would want to do for me and not allow me to do for them, or something along those lines. So they're anywhere from concerned to paranoid about why these ETs would communicate. For me, I say that's a good enough reason. That's a perfect explanation of why any being would want to do anything. When I communicate with other humans, even if I'm helping them I still feel a sense of joy and happiness, I still feel a sense of oneness with that person and a desire, an empathy, a sympathy, something that gives me the momentum to continue moving forward.

So in a way I think all entities in the universe have that version of something that they get in return, for doing something for another.

TReb and Aridif are type 1 beings. That means they see themselves literally as part of everything. Ancient Reptilian or Alpha Draconian beings are type 2 beings. They have a sense of separation and are very malevolent, in fact they're on the largest scale of malevolent. But even these malevolent entities are seen by Aridif and TReb as part of themselves. Knowing that they truly see all beings as a part of All That Is, this gives us a real understanding of why they would do anything. If I help you, I'm helping myself. If I do for you, then I'm doing for myself. If I do something for myself, I'm doing for all around me. So it is always a fair exchange.

What have they taught you?

This has been life-changing for me. When I started communicating with TReb, everything in my life changed. I began to understand so much more than I ever knew. I learned about the structure of the universe and the evolution of consciousness, and about myself, and why I think and feel the way I do, and how to change the things in my life that I don't like. How to manifest the things I am truly excited about, that I truly want to do. For me this was huge. Learning those basic things propelled me to learn much more. These are just logical, reasonable, everyday things, but when it comes to the details of the knowledge itself, I've learned so much. I've seen different planets, races, beings, interactions, communities, and different types of entities and beings and the way they interact with humans.

The person I was before I met TReb was so different, and that person was so different to the person five years before that. For anyone who's ever heard my story they know I came from a place of drug addiction and depression, all the way to an open, spiritual life. And the huge change that occurred after my awakening is still nothing compared to the change I've made since then. Treb reshaped my heart, my mind and my life.

Just the vibration of being around him taught me a great deal too. Being around love that was so large let me know that love of that nature was possible. It helped me explore my own emotions, relationships and connections with other things.

How well do you feel you understand the beings?

I feel I understand TReb and Aridif immensely. A lot of the other beings who have come through just once or a handful of times, those beings were only understood superficially. I'm not conscious when I'm channeling, so when these entities come through I don't get to experience them unless I connect with Treb, who connects with them in an astral-projected state, and then I get to understand them both through contact and vibrational learning.

When I make a channeling video, I will go back and watch it, and even though my mind wasn't present there, it's like I understand what the answer's going to be before it's said. And that is because when I am channeling and those entities come through me, I learn from them vibrationally, just as babies do. They vibrationally take in everything around them, and take it into their psychic senses and auric fields and they learn from that specific interaction. I psychically learn from these entities also. So when I go back and listen to that recording I know what's going to be said, I know the emotional energy and feelings behind these entities. I can tell you if they're entities who are very logical by nature, who are very knowledge-centered, or if they're emotion-centered, or if they're energetically highly psychic. I can tell all sorts of things just by watching the video, even if I haven't had the opportunity to meet them in the astral state with TReb. In most cases I can tell what they are all about even if the volume is fully down on the video.

Knowing that these entities vibrationally teach me gives me a better understanding of how I used to process people. Before I started channeling I was in the drug lifestyle, which meant I had to be very tuned into people. I had to understand people innately, through body language, through actions and interactions. And I know that I've always had some sort of intuition. It was a gift that I was given by my mother, psychically. I would introduce her to a friend of mine, and after spending less than 20 minutes with her she would be able to tell me a great deal about them – especially their personality traits. She would do it with stunning, almost scary accuracy - every time. I was able to pick that up from her vibrationally, maybe even genetically. I was able to extract, connect to, and understand that from her experience. And I think it was a gift given, that I didn't really learn to utilize until I was in my mid teenage years. In my old lifestyle, I dealt with criminals and gangsters, with drug dealers and users, and that was something that I was very in tune with. I could tell who a person was, how they would react, what I could or could not get away with, very easily. Since then, that has grown into a whole new energy and ability. Even that great gift I had, growing up into an adult, is nothing compared to the vibrational understanding and intuition that I have now. It's remarkable to feel and see the difference.

I also understand TReb in a way that I cannot explain verbally. It's something that most people don't even get when they have relationships with spouses for decades. The connection is something that, as close as you are, as open energetically to intuition as you are, TReb and I have kind of merged consciousnesses in a way that is hard to explain. When I started channeling him regularly, parts of his energy became a part of me. I took on his traits, abilities and openness. I've had the opportunity to link my consciousness with him and allow it to flow through my body. I don't know if anything in my physical structure changes, but I know the energetic setup does. I know that the chakras work differently now than they used to. I've noticed a change in each and every year I channel. Each of these several thousands of entities that I will channel in the future, the over 250 I have channeled up until now, will give me a new aspect and attribute. Each connection gives me a new level of understanding, in terms of their vibration, their thoughts and how they work. And I think that that in itself has been some of the greatest teachings and understandings from those entities.

Channeling Session

Rob mutes his mic and listens to a song to help him neutralize: *Golden Monkey* by Aaron Freeman.

He then goes through his grounding process, breathing and Oming.

Greetings to Miguel, this is Aridif. That is A, r, i, d, i, f.

We understand there are many queries for this day, but before diving into those queries we must express two things. First, above and beyond all things expressed within this time of co-creation, we wish to express the concept that you are loved. Again in our perception it is of the utmost importance. Secondly, we wish you greetings and our own great excitement, the greatest excitement in this moment of co-creation. You may begin with your queries at your leisure.

M: Well thank you Aridif, it's very nice to meet you. I have heard a lot about you. I have a number of questions for you, and some others may come up as we talk.

Why do you use channeling?

Yes, first of all, channeling, in the definition from our own perspective, is that two consciousnesses co-create energetically, physically, emotionally, and with the soul's essence itself, combining into one force to co-create a new experience, much as your own music that you listen to. You have a piano player playing one melody, and this represents one entity, in a couple of entities that are co-creating the channeled state. And in that experience, this entity may play the most beautiful melody, but, when incorporating another entity into this musical co-creation, that guitar-playing person that is so connected to that entity joins into this new energy and becomes a duo, if you will. Two energies and entities co-creating for one common purpose, one single energy. That co-creation is channeling.

It is not only my own energy that is going through Rob's physical body in this moment. TReb Bor yit-NE is here, as well as Rob's other guides, but in this moment, myself and Rob are co-creating our energy collectively at the forefront of this experience.

Now, with that being defined and expressed, we move into the answering of the question as it is. The use of this form of communication is something that is commonplace through the galactic collective consciousness. The reason why it is utilized is due to the fact that all entities, within not only the galactic collective consciousness, but this universal structure as it stands, has the capability of tapping into the energy that you see as your higher fractalized consciousness. Some call it the 'higher self'. When utilizing that energy, when jumping up into a highest form and essence of consciousness, that will give you the opportunity to co-create telepathically. In that telepathic communication, the form that is most easy for Rob to communicate with is the channeled state. So in this energy I co-create with him in this way.

For other entities who co-create or communicate, some do so in a more physical nature. Some of the entities that we co-create with in this day are physically standing in front of me, even those that are in lower dimensional energies - such as those in 4th or 5th density. I am able to divide my own consciousness, manifest a new physical structure, place that portion of consciousness there and co-create an experience of conversing, either telepathically, or utilizing their own verbal language. In our own society we have no verbal language, and we never have. But we also use the written format, even though it is not something that needs to be utilized in order to communicate because we still utilize telepathy, the most ancient form of communication in our race.

There are other entities who use very different experiences. For instance, many of you perceive the automatic writing as one form of communication with those that you perceive to be non-physical in nature. There are very similar communication styles throughout the galactic collective consciousness that are utilized in the same fashion. Although not all of them use written language, the majority allow consciousness to enter their physical body and take over the use of the hands through a co-creative mechanism. Some of those create communication through a form of dancing with the hands, a mixture of your dancing and sign language. Others utilize the energy in hand motions alone. There are literally infinite amounts of ways to co-create with consciousness when you are tapping into the higher formats. But in this reality with Rob, we utilize what is best for his own energy.

As we created and communicated thousands of years ago in your own history, when we produced a physical body in order to communicate with other entities that lived upon Earth in your ancient Africa, India, South America, we utilized a physical format because the telepathy of those entities that desired communication was not open or available in the same fashion. We use what is most available for us to communicate.

Why do you work with Rob?

It is not ourselves working with Rob, more so Rob working with us. We have energetic access to any entity that desires co-creation with us. In fact, there are many humans who exist within your Earth collective, both in your linear past and in your now moment, who have taken our own energy into their consciousness during sleep state, during co-creative thought processes, and also during forms of inner communication. That energy is something, in our perspective, that is the right of all beings that exist. We are all a part of the larger presence of All That Is. So there is no separation between ourselves and you, or ourselves and Rob, or any other entity that desires to co-create in that fashion.

But specifically, when we work through Rob, when we speak directly through his physical body, this is due to our closeness of vibration, our liner connection through the oversoul. If you perceive the idea that TReb Bor yit-NE is a future version of Rob, or a probable future version, you would see that TReb Bor yit-NE's probable future version of himself would be myself. Therefore Rob, TReb Bor yit-NE and myself are all different aspects of the same co-creation. We are all different aspects of the manifestation of a singular consciousness bringing itself into the physical reality through the means of different bodies, different mindsets, different planetary consciousnesses.

As you are aware, each individual consciousness belongs to larger fractions of consciousness, and those belong to even larger fractions. And when you look at the largest portion, your collective consciousness that most humans can perceive—the oversoul—we all three share that same energy. We all three express ourselves through the oversoul, both independently and collectively. Therefore, access from one to another is quite easy.

How do you define the oversoul?

To understand the oversoul, we must first understand what most humans perceive as the hierarchy of consciousness. But in our perception this is not a correct or proper word. Hierarchy suggests that anything in the larger steps is more important or better. In our perspective, all things are equal. But, we must represent it in a way that the human mind can understand.

We call the smallest perceivable fraction of consciousness the 'lower fractalized consciousness'. That is the part of you that wakes up, goes to your job, plays a guitar and sleeps. It is the part that you have the most intimate and interactive experience with in every part of your day.

Then you have the 'higher fractalized consciousness' - often termed the 'higher self'. That is the part of you that is a larger encompassment of the overall version of yourself. And what we mean by this is that when you are in your dream state, or your meditative state, when you are tapping into your intuition and psychic ability, the higher fractalized consciousness is the place where that occurs. That is the place that you pray to when you are a Christian, that is the place that you go out into when you are astral projecting as a Hindu. All of these energies can be represented within the higher fractalized consciousness.

Now when you look at your own self, that combination of the lower fractalized consciousness and the higher fractal consciousness is the overall degree of entity that we would call you. That is your own personal energy, your own persona, your own overall being in one bubble. That is why we call both of those combined your 'entity'. That is your singular expression of consciousness.

Imagine this as an upside-down iceberg. You understand that an iceberg carries the majority of its ice below the water. So the visible part is a representation of the lower fractalized consciousness, and the majority of the iceberg would represent the higher fractalized consciousness.

Many of you have had experiences where there are great shifts within your life. You may, for instance, go through a period of depression, and then very quickly make a shift to becoming a very happy, connected person. That shift of consciousness is taking place from you yourself desiring change, and utilizing your free will and beliefs to shift vibration. So what new vibration comes into yourself? The higher fractalized consciousness replaces a part of you that already exists with a part of you that you desire to shift. So you start integrating more of your own self in from the higher fractalized consciousness.

We understand that this is a very deep concept and could take a great time and detail to express, so we will give this to you in the quickest way for the sake of brevity. If your consciousness is your entity, the next step upward is your oversoul. The oversoul is a representation of all of the entities that you could be, that you are, that you were, and that you will be in your linear future, existing in a simultaneous way. Any other version of you that exists is part of the oversoul. So the oversoul is the place where tens of thousands of incarnations of your 3rd density selves exist. Even more so, your 1st and 2nd density, and several thousand of your 4th, 5th and 6th density incarnations.

So if you were to step into the oversoul and watch the entire incarnation cycle of you as an entire entity, you would see yourself watching the migration of consciousness start with the coalescing of the Earth itself, within the solar system collective. So you are now a rock, or a piece of ice, or lava, or fire, or electricity. Then you are starting to metamorphosize through chemical changes into other 1st density elemental beings.

When you look at your linear history in the way that your scientists perceive, you see an evolution of the Earth. Consciousness also follows this. So you see 1st density change to 2nd density; you see an elemental morph into something more, something that is a very basic format of what most humans perceive as living. When you perceive living, that changes from 1st to 2nd density. You are no longer elemental, you are living. 2nd density will also morph itself several million times from a singular cell to a more complex entity or being. As you see that, each and every individual incarnation that you carry in the Earth incarnation cycle—from that part of rock or electricity, all the way through the evolution to the most complex version of human that you are now—each one of those resides within your oversoul.

When you look into the Earth collective consciousness, you see that millions of years go by, that Earth is no longer inhabited by human collective consciousness, and moves outward into the stars. At that time, you see thousands of off-branch races of the Earth collective. Those are also in your oversoul. So you combine all of those entities that you are, that you could be, that you will be or have been, and that represents the oversoul collectively.

M: Wow. I'm looking forward to transcribing this so I can look at this in more detail and think it through. But that just gave me some amazing mental images. It made me realize that the person I am now contains all of those elemental aspects, all of the organic or inorganic components of this planet. That I am a conscious entity that is a collection of all of these things.

The things I eat, those forms of energy, solar and plant energy, converts into the energy I use to play music or anything else.

I'm having quite an amazing response to this simple idea. So I'm glad I asked the question.

That's giving me a kind of idea of what the oversoul is.

Yes, and we would express both that you are correct in that perception, but it is also expanded out throughout many different perspectives. You see that as one manifestation of your co-created oversoul's consciousness. But as you listen again, more and more of these ideas will come into your awareness, and your own higher fractalized consciousness will work with you to expand into perceiving not only that great information, that aha moment for you, but expand exponentially in other directions.

M: Yeah, I'm looking forward to it. I may come back to you about this. We may have another conversation about this when I've had a chance to integrate it a bit.

I realize that this next question could have an answer that is one word, one sentence, or one hour long.

What is the most important thing to you?

In the one word answer, it is love.

In the one sentence answer, it is love, because all things are love.

In a longer expression, when you look at love, what *is* love? The majority of humans believe it is emotion, and yes, that is partially correct. But love is the essence in which all things are built. When you perceive the entirety of the universe, you perceive a Creator consciousness, or at least most humans do. That energy, that transformed from a very non-physical place into a physical manifestation, was for the process of learning. It was for the process of being able to expand exponentially and experience, through those ideas, what was given to all entities that were involved within that being: a sense of love. What do we desire as we create? What do we give of ourselves as we create? It is love, it is an expansion of love.

In that perspective we see that within the physical universe, all things that were created come from the two building blocks, regardless of what rules or regulations exist in each universe, and that is love and light.

And we are not speaking of the physical light that you are able to see. We are speaking of wisdom, of the understanding and self-awareness that all entities in all systems of creation experience. When you are connected to the love then you are aligned with yourself; you can see your oneness. When you are not then you are in a state of disconnection from that love, regardless of what area you come from. Connected to or disconnected from that love, you are still able to access that version of light, of knowledge. That is why you hear the ancient expressions within your biblical terms, the tree of life, and the tree of knowledge. The tree of life is that of love, and the tree of knowledge is that of wisdom. So love and light both create the entirety of all physical realities.

And when we express this we do not mean only the universal construct that humanity in this moment is aware of. We mean all universes. Even universes that are so different from the ones you can experience within your imagination, which have their own laws of physics and manifestation. They may contain entities vastly different to those you are familiar with. In other universes there are no physical things. There is no gravity, there are only expressions of light or sound, or expressions of electromagnetic energy, co-creating with forces which one could not perceive. So regardless of what that universe looks like, it is still able to access both love and light. It is not only a universal theme, but a multi-universal theme.

M: There's a question that is not on my list, but is coming to mind. It's about inspiration. As you're speaking there, I'm thinking about all the scientists and artists who have talked about receiving inspiration from somewhere else. For example, Nikola Tesla said, "My brain is only a receiver, in the universe there is a core from which we obtain knowledge, strength and inspiration. I have not penetrated into the secrets of this core, but I know that it exists."

When humans are reporting these sudden inspirations, what is at work there? I myself experience this. This book project was given to me as a download. What do you understand about this? What awareness do you have about the kinds of beings that are bringing information to humans, and are you aware of any protocols around that? How does that mechanism work? Why do some people get given this kind of information? Is there any kind of agreed protocol, or do different kinds of beings work on their own agenda with particular people?

Yes, we understand. And this is a very great and complex concept. So we will express in the simplest form that we are able. We will therefore break this question into two parts.

First, where does this sense of inspiration, the spring of knowledge, and the core essence that this entity was speaking of, come from? When you receive this information, these downloads, all of that energy, it is always from your access to either your higher fractalized consciousness, or the central galactic collective consciousness. Those two areas are what hold what most of you would perceive as archives of information.

When utilizing those energies, or bringing them in during co-creation with other entities, this is an entirely different mechanism, and dynamic. So as you are connecting to your higher self, or the galactic collective consciousness, or the central galactic consciousness, these energies are utilized differently. First of all, in order to access that information, the majority of humans—and we would stress over 95%—are tapping into their higher fractalized consciousness when receiving.

But how are humans able to connect to their higher fractalized consciousness? Well, you are already connected to it. That is a part of your own basic existence. Your access is through the knowing of being connected to that, and the understanding of the joy in your heart. So, when all of these entities are working through something that they are deeply excited about, deeply ingrained into, and deeply motivated to find answers about, that is what gives the awareness of that connection to their higher fractalized consciousness that already exists.

This is why you have heard us, and many other entities, express: "Follow your heart, follow your excitement." They are one in the same. Excitement, with a human consciousness, is only motivated by something that brings pure joy. That's why excitement is different for all entities. You are excited about music, about your book. Some entities are excited about jumping off cliffs and into water. So the differences come from the core essence of that entity: who they are, what they are, what they desire to do within their existence.

So now this takes us to the second portion of the question. When co-creating with other entities, how does this work? In that higher fractalized consciousness ... one moment, we must hydrate Rob's throat before continuing.

You have heard in many stories, "And the entity gave me this great download of knowledge." Is this true? Yes. But, in order to access any of those entities, just as Rob was able to access us, it is through the higher self, it is through the higher fractalized consciousness that the communication takes place. It is very rare for a human collective or a human entity by itself to work with collectives or other singular entities telepathically or physically through their lower fractalized consciousness alone. That higher fractalized consciousness is what connects you.

In this way we have worked with Rob. It is a close connection, a vibration, a singularity of desires, a co-created effort of two vibrations that are working together that allows that bridge of energy and knowledge to be built. Once that bridge is built, and you become aware of either the emotion that this entity gives you, or aware of the entity of itself, this strengthens the bridge. So by doing this, you are working with these entities that in some cases have a great deal of knowledge that you have not been made aware of. Through that co-creation they are able to share their consciousness with you, and give you that information through your telepathy.

In our situation with Rob, we connect to him directly, and as we are speaking through his physical body, he is also receiving this information. Now he is not aware of what is being said in this moment, but when he revisits this speaking at a later time, before hearing what is said he will know the answers already. And that is because the information is energy itself. Rob's physical and energetic body are receivers of energy, so if enough of that energy is run through his physical and energetic body, his DNA and his own energetic receptors will receive the information. The brain, yes, it is a tuning mechanism. It is an organ in your body that serves as a high-functioning computer. But the brain will remember the energy it is given, much as you putting a memory disk into your computers. Your computer does not know that information unless it is run through its own mechanisms. And this is the same with co-creation with other entities.

When you desire specific knowledge, or to connect to specific entities, the suggestion that we give all beings is: know the vibration of that entity, of that knowledge. Immerse yourself so deeply into the emotion, into the feeling, into the experience of what that entity or knowledge feels like to yourself. Then you will start becoming more like that information. When you become more like the informational entity you are trying to co-create with, it has an easier job of making that bridge for you.

M: This leads me to ask: do you have a perception of any kind of what we might term 'guides' who may be working with me?

Yes, of course. There are many entities that work with you, that you may perceive as guides. When we use the word 'guides', what we mean is any entity who desires contact with you. All of that contact is again through your higher self, but it can be from different parts of your own soul, or your soul groups or families.

And by soul groups or families we mean that there are 144,000 oversouls within the human collective consciousness. There is also a mechanism called the 'twin soul', which allows infinite amounts of realities to be played out. Those are born through mitosis of the original oversoul, and mirror that exact number, with 144,000. This represents all of the oversoul energy within the Earth collective, or 288,000.

Oversouls have their own collective personality, their own themes that are played out, and their own collective consciousnesses. So when one oversoul co-creates with ten other oversouls, that is a small group or family. When they extend out to other small groups, that is a soul group. Or perhaps as you would see it, a soul connection.

So these entities that are your guides, come from either indirect oversoul communication, or through your soul family or soul groups. These entities find a common thread or bond with you, and that is why they desire to work with you.

For instance, there is a guide that is Arcturian in nature. This entity comes into your auric field and awareness because of your passion for music. That sound vibration desire not only to heal mentally, emotionally, energetically, but also physically, is there for you. You understand what sound vibrations are able to do. So you have brought yourself closer to an entity who holds great knowledge of sound vibration: the Arcturian collective consciousness. So that entity is one of your guides. That entity in this moment is connected with you very deeply, is around you, has tried to work with you. We do not mean that you are failing at working with this entity. We mean that this entity is consistently bombarding you with its own knowledge and experience, because it already sees itself connected to you. There is no view of separation from this entity's perspective. But from your perspective you understand innately, deeply and collectively, that all entities in the universe are connected to you, but you did not always feel that all entities are connected to you. So now that you have become aware, it makes this entity more easily able to access both the knowledge from you, and also send knowledge to you.

Then you look into your other various aspects. In terms of your mental status, you are able to break things down to a very high degree. The logical part of your own mind has great ability to work through certain ideas. That energy, focusing in on the Earth collective consciousness, and the growth and evolution of your soul's consciousness, is a common thread that connects you to the Sirian entities. So there is an entity from Sirius that connects with you, that is your Sirian guide.

The Reptilian energy, which many humans tend to be fearful of, is also linked to you. That part of your energy that is very human, not only in your mind, but in your DNA and auric field, expresses a Reptilian energy. That Reptilian is what we call a type 2 benevolent entity. Meaning that this entity is not a type 1 (which sees itself purely as a part of One), but it does have a benevolent energy towards it. This means that when you look at the type 2 variety of energy, there are highly benevolent type 2s, all the way to malevolent beings. If you are scaling all of type 2s from one to ten, this being rates a nine towards a benevolency. This entity desires co-creation with you because of your auric field, because your DNA holds that Reptilian vibration, and also because of your interest in Earth history. When you look at your own desires to understand how the Earth came to be what it is, hearing all of the differences and all of the stories, this entity agrees, and holds a very high connection to the Earth vibration.

So all three of these guides are working with you in this moment, but those are not all of them. There are literally dozens of beings who work with you in this moment. As you shift vibration, mood, become higher in sexuality, or higher in vibrational quality towards that sound vibration, whatever emotion, energy or persona that you step into, different energies will come into your awareness. Others will step back for a moment. So as your vibration shifts, these dozens of different guides either come closer to your energy or step further away. Either way there are literally, since your time of birth, thousands of entities that have connected to you in what most humans perceive as a guide instinct, or perhaps a guide to a specific situation.

When we use the definition of 'spirit guides', those are quite different. Those are not entities who need to have connections through your oversoul or other auspices. These entities are connected to you in a non-physical state, and have agreed to work with you from before your incarnation, until after leaving this physical body. These entities have been in so many of your previous incarnations and have worked with you on so many different subjects, that they are willing to be in a non-physical capacity and work with your chakras, thoughts and emotions as you go through your existence. Many Christians call these 'guardian angels'. Many entities call them 'spirit guides' or 'guides'. These entities are very human, and experience your own previous incarnations, and also this incarnation, very deeply.

M: Intriguing. That in itself spawns a thousand other questions. I want to ask if you have a sense of why I am involved in this work?

Yes. When you look at this, the majority of humans perceive that a wonderful event has occurred within their own life, and they must have been led there. And yes, that is partially correct. But the main reason that you are led to this specific energy is your own free will.

You may question this, saying, "It does not feel as if I just walked into this because I desired to. I had no knowledge of certain things, and then had experiences that brought that into my awareness."

But let us again consider the hierarchy of consciousness. The lowest part, the lower fractalized consciousness, holds all of the free will in all of the energy. So although it is the smallest, it carries the most power, the most ability to provide a pathway for that consciousness to work in the physical existence. You must also know that before incarnating into your experience, you created and devised an ideal perspective that you wished to explore in this lifetime. Before incarnating you expressed to your own self, "I will put myself with the best parents, in the best part of the world, and the best experiential quality that I am able to do, in order to explore all of these things."

Now if your own experience had shifted, if you had worked less within your motivations, if you were perhaps lazier in your younger years, all the way to this moment, you would not be where you are at. But, you would still continue to have experiences that were somewhat similar, or could get you thinking about that part. When we say this, many humans believe this contradicts that free will aspect that we were expressing, but the higher self will always create situations that will take you back to that original theme. But again, you have the choice to act upon that or not.

Before incarnating in this specific incarnation, your desire was to help humanity create a bridge of understanding, not only to those who are extraterrestrial in nature, but also to themselves, to their consciousness, and to their overall self. When most humans perceive extraterrestrials, they are perceiving beings that are among stars far away. Yes, that is correct physically, but energetically all things are connected, deeply. You knew this before coming into your physical existence, and desiring to re-remember that in your physical body, and help others understand it in different formats, was your intention. You did not say, "I will co-create this specific experience, which will lead me to investigate hybrids, which gets me into the channeling and other perspectives." But you held that generic concept of wanting others to understand, and to know that this specific time in the Earth collective consciousness is pivotal for the expansion of all consciousness. It is going from one marker of evolution of consciousness—3rd density— into 4th density, where you no longer need to fully develop your sense of self, but start connecting to others. For some races, all entities upon one planet know what another are doing, and can feel one another intimately. And where humans are, to where that is, is the bridge that you are trying to create collectively. And you yourself desire to be an instrument of others' knowing, an instrument of those who did not know what was possible; to be at one with another, to learn this.

This is what brought you into this experience, and this occurred through your own free will. When you look at all the probabilities and possibilities, the times that you followed your greatest excitements always led you to the next step forward.

Do you have a sense of what form I took before this one?

You are expressing previous incarnations, correct? There are many previous incarnations. Many of them are connected to the Earth collective consciousness. We try not to label, but we also try to help others to understand, so we have created labels, or utilized pre-existing labels, such as 'starseeds'. Those entities come from other areas of consciousness into the Earth collective so that they may incarnate once or in small amount of numbers to help those understand, to help them co-create. And also so that they themselves can understand the Earth collective in the most intimate way.

Then there are those we have labeled 'Earthseeds'. Those entities have been in the incarnation cycle of the Earth for quite some time. Rob himself has been here since the very first portion of the Earth incarnation cycle. So when Earth began to become a planet, Rob's consciousness was there. You carry traits of both energies. You have existed both in thousands of Earth incarnations, but also several hundred of those that you would perceive as extraterrestrial incarnations. So you have carried both vibrations very deeply.

Is there a specific message that you have for me going forward in this work?

Yes. First of all we must express our own encouragements. We may see you doing something which on one level you do not think is working, but we see that it is bringing in layers of energy and also working towards the point of what you desire to do. So we would encourage you in your own musical energy.

We also wish to encourage you in your own internal feelings. As you go through this experience, working with others, the feeling of insight always allows you to move into a new direction, or into a new format. When you are working on many different angles on one new insight, and you place them in a mental or even physical list, the one that seems the most interesting is what we always suggest you follow first. So that overall acknowledgment is there, that your insight and expanding into your insights is working, and benefiting you quite well.

But also, we wish to express to you that as you continue to understand the nature of yourself, but also the nature of your previous incarnations, try to remind yourself that even though it feels as if it is one path, that has all led you to this one area, you have quite a diversity in incarnations that you've experienced. And the reason for that experience is this. When your oversoul looks into physical reality it does not say, "We want this place to be a better place, we want this energy to be implanted." It only desires experience. The oversoul does not care if you are a murderer, or someone who becomes murdered, or one who advocates for peace. But it does appreciate all three of those experiences, and their ability to have them. So if you should discover some rather disturbing incarnations in your past, do not allow this to disturb your motivation to continue working forward. You have also had a great deal of those that are positive, expansive, and working towards the effort that you are using in this incarnation.

We understand this is not the specific area that you desire for us to go into, but we must express this as you desire the greatest amount of information for yourself personally. As you continue this project, you are utilizing the amounts of knowledge that come in from others. What you have done is very wonderful and it is very expected for your personality, your mindset, your energy and your beliefs. This includes following the threads of commonality between what you have learned today and what you have already known. This shows you why it feels that one thing is leading you to another.

Your work with hybrids is also very important. There is a great deal of information that is yet to come into your awareness, and also some that you have perhaps overlooked in what you already have in front of you. That will help expand your own consciousness, and the work that you are doing. The utilization of hybrid programs within the Earth collective has given the opportunity for many entities who are not completely and deeply self-aware to be able to link to the universe and construct with a vibration that allows their energy to lift up and helps their understanding. So in the next ten years you will notice a wave of those entities who have worked in the hybrid programs, coming to realize that. And as they begin to realize that, they will always need a person, a place or a community to lean upon. And we feel that within your own oversoul energy, you are not only giving them a place, but you are going to help create other places.

What to you is the meaning of life?

In our own perspective, the meaning of life is to utilize the feeling of excitement. Both love and wisdom are very important, but in the living of your life, following that excitement is the most important thing. For us it is second nature. There is no other way of alignment. So although we feel it is important, it is not always within our mindset - only when we are expressing this idea to others. So our existence is an ever-shifting vibration of exploration.

You are going from the place of self-exploration to the place of exploring your connection to all other things: to other humans and relationships, and to your own thoughts, beliefs and experiences. And that connection, feeling, emotion and energy is where the 4th density remains. In the 5th density, those who have already mastered the ability to know they are loved, to feel love, the love of all things, are able to dive into wisdom.

In the 6th density where we reside, we are utilizing the previous two places of evolution together. For some this does not make sense. How are you able to utilize both love and wisdom when you have already mastered both of them? Why do you need an extra step? When we worked on love we worked on love alone, and when we worked on wisdom we worked on wisdom alone, but now that we are working on both we have a different way of experiencing.

In our own experience, let us offer this example. As we studied the human race, and the nature of connection between one human and another, we explored the evolution of love alone, and would try to feel our own connection to those humans.

Then, in the step afterwards, the 5th density, the exploration of wisdom, we would try to understand what and why the humans do as they do, or what they are doing, how it works, etcetera. In this moment, because we love humans, we are able to explore the depths of that nature of humans. But we are also able to go into that experience with the most intimate connection process, so we are loving what we are exploring, and we are exploring what we love.

At one time we were run by only one of those energies, and in the second place, the other. Now we run both of those energies through us, so we are connecting to humans more fully. But we are not just connecting to humans in the fundamental way that you perceive. We are looking at the depths of your consciousness, we are looking at the most intimate nature of your physical structures, we are looking at all of the things within the human collective that makes them human, and we are able to take on that experience for ourselves. We are able to allow that to run through the smallest portions of our subatomic energy within ourselves. So we are most intimately discovering that knowledge within ourselves. It is so intimately understood that it becomes literally a part of ourselves. And we are able to feel that momentum of energy as it goes through us. So exploring through that intimate way, we are going through an entirely new experience, and the excitement is what guides us.

What is the most important message you can give to humanity at this time?

When we are perceiving the most importance, we understand that we have already expressed the concept that you are loved. And we will touch upon this and then go into another direction.

We frequently express that in our perception the most important thing to take away from this day is that you are loved. We do so every time we communicate through Rob to another human consciousness. We do this because humans perceive love in quite a different way. When one human entity says to another, "I love you," they are saying that two separate and segregated energies are able to share a common feeling or emotion. But "You are loved" means that entities that you are unaware of are connecting to that Source energy, and the universe itself shares that love with you. No matter where you are or how disconnected you feel from all things, love is still accessible to you. So 'I love you' is a very beautiful concept, and endearing within the human perspective, but when you are loved, you are literally loved in infinite formats. Knowing this can help you open yourself to and utilize that love. That is an important aspect of evolution, and one which you are going through in this moment.

We also wish to drive home, if you will, the concept of your own creative mechanisms in your reality. And what we mean by this, is that most humans perceive that they are born through scientific means or random chaos or whatever belief system they carry. But in actuality, your consciousness existed first and created a physical format for it to play in, to experience in. Through that you create a physical body for yourself to be born into. And after landing in that physical body, every second that you spend in your life you are creating your circumstances, the actual physical structure and the co-creations around you. That is something that we find most important.

We understand that you grasp this idea of creative consciousness, but other entities are not aware that as you go through your experience, yes, your perception carves your experience, but when you are thinking, when you are placing a belief system, and when you are acting, all of those things co-create the experiences.

The car crash that you have had, the losing money, but also the creation of your money, all of those things are literally being created from your own consciousness. We try to describe this as if it is a computer program. The belief systems are the parameters of the program. For instance, if you are using a program only for music, then you cannot play videos within that program. So what does that mean? It means that if you do not believe that you are able to create your own reality, then you will be far removed from the sensation, the experience of doing so. If you believe that extraterrestrials are not real, you will not experience contact with extraterrestrials.

Humans express this question all the time: why is it that I did not believe in something but it did occur to me? What we tell you is that the percentage of investment in your beliefs will form the exterior guidelines. And what we mean by that is this: if you believe wholeheartedly that no extraterrestrials exist, you will not experience them, and that is guaranteed, due to the way that consciousness works. But the majority of humans do not carry that level of conviction. They carry a 90% belief that "I don't think it is real; I am almost positive it does not work." That small percentage of investment that is missing in that belief can allow that external or alternate reality to come into your experience.

When you are looking at your thought process, that is the data that you are putting into your program. It is what helps drive the fixing of the program, what works within the program and how. So when you are consistently placing those positive-negative thoughts within your program of life, you are starting to get negative experiences. If you are doing it positively then you are also experiencing those positive experiences.

Actions are the part of your program that hits the enter key on all the data that you have placed within. For instance, when you say, "I have always wanted to go traveling," but you had never traveled, you are putting a great deal of data into that computer with your thoughts.

But until you hit enter, you cannot put into action all that energy that has been put into that thought process. Once you act upon going to travel, whether it is typing on the computer about it, or the act of moving forward and traveling, all of that energy cannot come to fruition. So this is the program of your life.

A great deal of you will not be able to believe this at first, because it puts all of the responsibility of your incarnation into your lap alone. Now, when you know that you are 100% responsible for your creations, there will be times and moments where you will say "That cannot be true. This person came out of the dark and punched me in the eye and that is not my fault. How could this be my creation?" But, when you think honestly and deeply about that situation, you will see that you had always had a fear that you could be attacked. You had placed so much thought into that energy that it is a possibility. Also, your belief systems say, "I am in a dangerous world where I could be attacked." That gives you the opportunity to be attacked. And then when you act upon certain ideas, such as buying a weapon to defend yourself, placing security alarms within your house, you are telling the universe that I am not safe, nor in a safe place. Therefore you are creating, and often that creation can come to teach you something deep about yourself and your mind. That is that I can only be as safe as I believe and feel. Or it could tell you that you are not safe enough, and get you into a whole new level of feeling unsafe.

The same can be done with positive things. We want all humanity to know that the ball is always in your court, and it always will be. When you start co-creating with others then they can be a part of your creation as well. We understand that we could speak literally for days about this one subject alone, but we believe that this should be sufficient for understanding.

Is there anything we have not discussed that you wish to say?

Yes. Looking at all of the energy for each one of you and collectively, we wish to express this. In this specific project, many entities will tell you their own story of connection, their stories of how their contact experiences worked. This places a great deal of you in excitement, hoping and desiring—if you have not already had an experience—that it is possible. And it is very likely that you now can understand the nature of your experience and that of others. We would say that that is a very proper way to motivate yourself to continue thinking about contact. Thinking about how you yourself can motivate more factors, higher probabilities or co-creating with other entities.

Others among you may perhaps feel a small bit of frustration that you yourself have not experienced it. We suggest you utilize all of the tools that have been shared, and listen to all of the words that have been expressed. When you listen to Miguel's words, to the entities that are being asked about their own experiences, and when you listen to the entities that are in contact with these individuals, listen to all of those things that make you feel excited.

When you lock onto those parts that excite you deeply, start studying them. Place time and effort into those things that can help put you in a vibration that is more similar to those who have been contacted. And those who contact outwards. And those who co-create with entities in the same way you desire.

Try to remind yourself that believing that you cannot is going to motivate more of the universe giving you what you desire: no contact. Remind yourself that you are already connected to anywhere from a handful to hundreds of entities in each moment. Know that the level of communication is already there. It is only your perception that stops that co-creation. Let yourself go a bit. Let yourself understand and know at the deepest parts of your heart that the universe in all things is connected. You are no exception to this. You are loved.

M: Thank you Aridif, that was wonderful. I enjoyed meeting with you, and hearing your thoughts and perspectives. And I'm looking forward to working with the information. I admire your commitment and your willingness, and I really appreciate it, so thank you very much.

Yes, we thank you as well for your excitement, leading to our greatest excitement in this moment, which is co-creating with you.

Through your own experiences you will find a great deal of our own energy with you as you first mull over and think about what we have expressed this day. But in the later times as you feel our energy or as you think about us, our energy does come to your own awareness. We wish for you to understand that you may utilize our energy in any way that you see fit. Knowing that you feel a connection from your heart to ours, is something that allows our own energy to send you more of ourselves. And in that essence, you are giving permission to create with more of our energy. Only a small percentage goes to this communication, but if you desire, more and more of that energy is available. Only request it and be in that vibration of connecting to it, and we will connect to you many more times in the future we are sure.

We bid you adieu for this evening. You are loved.

Vashta Narada

I fall in love and I rise in hate, I rise in love and I fall in hate. They are as fleeting as my thoughts. I touch the bottom of the ocean and stretch to the surface. I fly and dissolve. I burn. I judge and observe the judging, engage, disengage. I act to understand, I flow to let it go. I stand my ground and then pull the rug from under my feet. I build myself and shatter it all down continuously. I touch the world lightly, and bring it down swiftly. I answer to no one because I exist. This is my biography.

Her website is: vashta.com

Which words do you use to describe 'them'?

I actually use 'beings'. Beings or 'galactics'. Because I don't like the word 'entities', that everyone is using. It feels like, "There are entities hovering around the house." It's weird. I tend to use 'ETs' when I talk to other people, because everyone knows what I'm talking about. But for the people who are more familiar, it's galactics. ET can mean so many different things. You know what you mean when you say galactics, because we are galactics too, in a way. I think it all started with the previous website that we had, called 'Galactic Families'. So I thought this would be a nice name for them, and it felt like they like it too. Instead of 'extraterrestrial', which has this scientific, researcher vibe to it. Galactic feels more familiar, like a family. They're more aware of it than we are, that we are a family.

Which kinds of beings are you in contact with?

It's a broad question! I don't even know what kinds are out there. But I can say that if you're asking about the species, I would say all kinds of what we call Greys, all kinds of Reptilians, and hybrids thereof. Humanoids, which can belong to pretty much any star system;

they're everywhere. Some aquatic lifeforms. Some shapeshifter lifeforms. Insectoids, Mantid beings. Hybrid children. Avians. Even some cetaceans from Earth. Some types of what I call a 'non-physical collective consciousness'. And artificial intelligences. It's a misnomer if you ask me, because everything has consciousness.

It's hard to name them like this because that is not how they define themselves, most of them. With Reptilians it's usually clear but even then, some claim to have a pure bloodline. Some say they are hybrids and not at all connected to what we know as the Draco bloodline, but are a combination of (animal) reptile DNA and humanoid DNA for instance. Greys are not calling themselves Greys of course, and hardly any of these beings have connections to what we call Zeta Reticulans. They just look similar and humans love to put everything in boxes, so that's why I say Greys. Even the Mantid beings are not related to praying mantises, they simply remind us of a familiar shape and we automatically connect them.

How do they appear to you?

It really depends and it's always different. It took me a while to figure all that out and find a pattern, so that I could start recognizing who I am communicating with. Some of them contact me in dreams and astral states. Some of them I simply talk to in my head, just like having a normal conversation, as we are right now. Some of them can get very physical, like they will show they're here by making weird noises in the house. By turning on and off my computer, or by knocking me on the head! It's a lot of different things, and I usually tell them I don't like subtle clues. Because I'm really sick of that. I don't like sitting here having to ask who they are. No, I say, "Make your presence known and we can talk." So they've learned to be a little more drastic with me. I don't mind that at all. I don't get startled easily. Because throughout my whole life I had weird things happen to me, and it became part of the daily routine. So I don't really react to subtle noises or feelings. When I do notice that kind of thing I say, "Okay, if you want us to talk you need to be a bit more proactive than that." And they understand that.

There are so many different kinds of communication that I have with them. But usually each type of being has their particular way, and it's always the same if they come through. Sometimes it's seeing a light in the sky, and I know who it is. Who is passing by, or tuning into my vibration. And I tune into theirs, and I can figure out who's in the ship that I just saw flying by.

Other times I would meditate on a certain connection that I have, and when I opened my eyes I would see a light blinking in the sky or flying by at that exact moment, exactly where my eyes were looking. And it's not a plane or a satellite. I used to check for satellites online, even though I would clearly see that it didn't have a normal, straight flying pattern. I always doubt these things when they are too subtle, but the feeling is what makes me know for sure. The feeling I get when there is someone out there communicating with me, as opposed to it being some other possible explanation that excludes UFOs. Others have witnessed that with me, seeing lights in the sky exactly when we would talk about a certain being, for example.

It took me several years to start discerning the vibrations and the way they come to me, because there are so many. And sometimes even now I can't figure it out. It may be something new and I don't know who it is. Sometimes they try to shove me out of my body! And that's not intentional, it's just that I'm not aligned properly, I'm not ready for them and it feels like they push me out of my body. But even that I've learned to calibrate, thanks to Rob Gauthier and his channelings. So there are many ways it can happen.

I also sense contact through synchronicities. Like recurring numbers. Seeing 11:11 for example. Or reading something online and realizing that someone else is gently nudging me to look into something in particular, like a scientific article about a certain subject they shared with me in dream time, or a video about a concept I received a download on.

With the numbers, it's very interesting. I was always thinking that that tells you you're on the right track. Just like a little confirmation that is really easy to manifest in our reality. It does mean that, but it doesn't have to be only when you're in a high vibration. Lately I've been seeing those things when I feel really agitated about something. Then I realize it's okay to feel way the way I'm feeling; I'm not supposed to judge myself for it. It's like these confirmations keep coming at such unexpected times. Because people usually expect to see that when they're feeling good, like, "Okay, 11:11, my synchronicities are working, everything is flowing." But for me it is happening at all times. And it just means that my higher self is communicating and telling me that whatever I'm doing right now is the right path, and will get me wherever I want to go. Usually it starts happening when I start doubting myself. It is not something I place great importance on, but I do like seeing it. Sometimes I get annoyed by it, and I remove the clock from my computer so I don't see it. But then it would start showing up on Facebook posts, so I couldn't escape it! I ended up laughing about. It feels like my higher self playing jokes, or just reassuring me gently. But I don't really go into too much symbology, like, "What is 11:11, or 20:20?" They don't really mean that much to me.

Can you describe your first contact?

It's a big question. I don't know where I should start. I've been in contact with them since I can remember existing as this physical expression. But since I was a child I didn't know what to call it. I only started realizing what it was back in around 2011 or 2012, in retrospect. I'd been taken so many times on their ships. It was different entities. Some of them were calibrating me, some were just checking in, some of them were very curious about humans as they are.

But I could talk about my first encounter that I remember clearly. I started remembering these things back in 2012. One night I was lying in my bed, going to sleep, and I felt like something was coming; the whole frequency of the room changed, and I felt I was going to have a visitation. And this was the first time I felt it while I was still awake, as far as I can remember. And I started inviting them, and welcoming whoever it was. And then I went into sleep paralysis while lying on my stomach, and the sheer terror started waking up in my body. I could see these three white, shimmering, almost transparent Greys standing next to my bed, and the thing that freaked me out the most was that they were as short as my computer chair. So they were really small. I could see them out of the corner of my eye, but I could not move. I was trying to sink into the feelings I was having, and then I remembered it was not fear I was feeling, it was the reaction to unfamiliar frequency. So I kind of disengaged from the fear, the adrenaline rush that was happening in my body, and I just wanted to stay there with the experience.

And then I realized that they were starting to take me out of my body. I knew this because I had my first out-of-body experience when I was 12 years old, while meditating. I used to meditate every day back then, and one time I was so immersed in love and connection to infinity that I simply popped out of my body and slowly started ascending towards the ceiling. I knew what was going on immediately but I had some parental programmed fears that I would not be able to come back so I crashed back to my body with great discomfort. Over the years I learned how to do this in dream states and was fairly accustomed to the sensations when it starts happening. So I felt them lifting me out of my body, by my feet first, as I was on my stomach, which was a really peculiar sensation. Almost comical. But I got scared and I said to myself, 'Do I really want to remember all this, or is this enough?' My inner feelings said I don't want to remember what happens next. Then I remembered that the Greys are not very emotional beings, at least the ones that were in my room. I think it was something very close to Zetas. And I remembered that if I am clear enough in my intention, you know, intellectually and logically, then they will understand me. So I sent them a thought, 'You have my permission to do whatever you need to do, but I want to be asleep while you're doing it.' And I saw one of them nod their head instantly, and that sheer terror, heart beating, not feeling my knees, chills going up my spine, instantly it was like somebody injected an anesthetic and everything relaxed, and I fell asleep, completely calm, with a smile on my face. They took my request and delivered it. So I don't know what happened next, but that was my first encounter where I was completely conscious of what was going on. After that I made it my mission to overcome the fear so that next time I can be conscious of what's happening. But I still haven't had anything similar to this visitation. I've had others, but not like this.

How did you keep it together at the beginning?

My Arcturian family shoved me over the edge, and it took a month to integrate whatever they did. I asked for what they did, for it to be radical, but oh my God! I couldn't communicate with people for a month, it was that intense.

Naan. One of Vashta's Arcturian counterparts from the collective she has communicated with since childhood. Credit: Vashta Narada

After that, everything seemed like an intervention for me, from the point of them directly answering my questions by leading me to click certain videos, whether it would be something scientific, or channeling, or a topic I was interested in that they brought up. It was just being completely guided in various ways. And that lasted for months. And it's kind of settled down now, and integrated, and I am expecting another shove, because that's usually how it works - in waves. They blow all your chakras open then they wait for you to get your bearings.

Even I got worried, like what the hell is going on? I had to type to Rob (Gauthier), "Could you please ask TReb or Aridif what the fuck is going on? Am I tripping, or am I going nuts?" I mean, I've never considered that I went crazy with these things, but that was the moment when I felt like I was just going to phase out of this existence or something. So Rob helped me a great deal with that, to understand what was going on, and to flow with it, really. Instead of contracting and resisting it, and making it that much worse for myself.

But I do love when things are radical, and I mentioned that before, that I don't like subtle clues and figuring it out. I'm tired of that. Then something like this happens, and even though I sometimes get scared, I get excited because it's like "Wow, something's finally happening!" Like my whole world is upside down and I'm seeing them in my room, and I can't talk to people, and I feel like I don't have skin! But it's awesome because it's happening. So with me they like to kick the door open.

How do you connect now?

Since I made it my mission to allow the fear to appear but not engage in it—just to see it as a normal thing that's happening and go through it anyways—I started inviting them more and more. Over a span of a few years I was able to invite them as I was going to bed, and I had three or four visitations. And I could feel the frequency of love just overcoming me every time, and immense peace and bliss. And it didn't feel forced, that they were making me feel that. I know a lot of people think that they do that, and maybe sometimes they do, I don't know. But it didn't feel like that. It felt like they were so overcome with joy that I actually invited them. They were really pleased and happy to be communicating in a way that doesn't seem abrasive to us as humans. And on all of these occasions they took me out of my body. On one of them I'm fairly certain it was physical. I woke up in the middle of the night, after having set that intention before I went to bed.

And there was this blue light swirling in front of my windows, like something huge was floating there at the 5th-floor level, and I stood up and walked to the window, thinking, 'Okay this is it, they're here now.' And I remember this like I was completely awake. I can't tell for sure, 100%, if it was lucid or an astral projection, or if I was really awake, but it felt like I was.

As I saw that light I walked a little bit back, and thought, 'This is the point where they should take me.' And at that moment I felt like I was falling backwards, straight back like a trust fall. I remember thinking that there's an armchair and a closet behind me, so either I'm going to bash my head on it, or they're going to take me, and whichever it is, I'm trusting it. So I was falling backwards, and I went through the chair, through the wall, and I felt three pairs of these beautiful, gentle hands receiving me in a horizontal position. Like they caught my head, shoulders and arms, and I was basically weightless at that time. I remember that very clearly. If you saw the movie *Maleficent*, it was just like when Angelina casts a spell on the princess, which makes her go to sleep and float in mid-air on her back like she's in water.

On a few other occasions I remember them pulling me out of my body, and then I was on a ship. But the memories with them are still very blurry for me. I'm still working on all that. I'm just happy to remember this far while I'm still awake, because usually it's a dream and it's a completely different frequency. You're much more relaxed, you trust your higher self, you're there like it's no big deal, you're communicating with them like you're best friends. But when you're awake it's a little bit different, because in our physical bodies and minds we're not used to these sorts of experiences.

So that's just one of the ways I initiate communication. I mentioned another one just before, when I meditate under a starry sky and then see their ships. Some of them are simply me sitting in front of the computer and starting with my artwork and then them coming through and giving me downloads and telling me things. Sometimes they don't; it's enough to just have an image. It all depends. But when I do want to initiate communication it's usually very easy. It's just that I don't feel I need to bother them all the time. So very rarely do I have the impulse to ask them a question.

When I do initiate communication for some other purpose than my work, it's usually automatic writing or communing with my counterpart and checking in. It's usually about how are they feeling, how is our connection flowing, stuff like that. It's very heart-based; it's not that verbal-based for me.

In the case of automatic writing, in all the times it happened so far it was a message that was meant to go public and be read by others. And even though it happens rarely, it is extremely intense and the feedback from people is very positive and powerful. It is all still in development as I open up more to doing this, as I gather more courage and ignore my doubts. It is easy when I am on my own with them, but when I am supposed to translate a message for someone else, whether it is a client or the public in general, I always question it.

I realized I will never stop questioning. I just made my peace with doubt, and I share the information anyways. The more I do that, the more positive feedback I get, the more people tell me it helped them in some way. I am aware that I have no idea what I am doing, or how, and that is fine. It's a good way for me to keep my ego in check and not take myself seriously. It is also a good way to break more barriers and go even further into the unknown.

How did the artwork begin?

I used to do a lot of artwork back in around 2001 in Photoshop. It was mainly photo manipulations. But that was mostly me expressing my own shadows, and working through accepting that part of myself. It was more like a healing thing for me, and I did learn a lot. I stopped doing it when I stopped feeling these shadows affecting my life. Once I started feeling nice and happy I felt like I didn't need to do the artwork any longer.

So there was a huge break between then and when I started doing this. However, the reason I started doing this was, back in 2013 I was part of a team of five of us who were working on the Galactic Families website. Our 'mission' was to make a library of all the known races who were being channeled, based on the material of renowned channelers, and our own intuition and experience. And we had a page explaining who the Sassani are, the Yahyel, the Sirians, Pleiadians etcetera. That's when we started working with Rob as well, and his channelings, which were of immense help. However, after a year that whole group broke up and everyone went their own way, so the website kind of died. But I wanted to continue this work, because I realized this was my greatest excitement—communication with ETs, and communication between humans and ETs. Also assisting people to find their connections, assisting ETs to understand humans better, etcetera. So I decided to take that old project and start my own thing, and expand it.

But I did not have an artist to represent all these beings. We were working with an artist who was a channel medium back then, but she stopped doing that. So my first step was to contact all the artists who were depicting any sort of ETs, and ask them for permission to use their work on my website. But as I was doing that and preparing the whole project, a friend of mine recommended a graphics program to me, and said maybe I can do something with it. So I started playing with it, literally. I had no intention of becoming an artist or making anything out of it. And it was so exciting for me, because it felt like I was creating video game characters. I am a gamer, and my favorite part of any game was creating my avatars. And usually I realize later that I create beings that look like the beings I'm already connected to. But I didn't know that at the time. I used to play *Guild Wars*, *World of Warcraft*, and some single player games like *Dragon Age*. Usually fantasy RPGs (role-playing games), where you can pick the way your character would look. And they were always very alien and unusual. Everyone else was picking humans, but even my humans were not looking human! So that's how it started. I used the software to create some beings I already saw, and some of the ones we all know, like Aridif and TReb, that Rob channels.

So I created a Facebook page for myself and started posting those. And it started getting a lot of good feedback, unexpectedly! I realized at that point that I was filling up a spot that nobody else was. I wasn't like a professional artist, but I was familiar enough with digital graphics that I knew what to do. And I was also familiar enough with connections to be able to feel them out a little bit. So from my perspective I filled up a spot that was kind of unique. Usually professional artists don't do this sort of stuff. They don't relate to ETs. They usually create Hollywood monsters. People who are connected, there's very few of them who are creating 3D realistic representations. It's very artsy usually. And I wanted to try and bring in their personalities, more so than their precise looks. I wanted them to have facial expressions, the look in the eye, their pose. Everything that would show that they are living beings, not some Hollywood project, or mindless portrait that just looks blankly at you. I wanted to make them alive.

As I was having fun with that, people start ordering commissions from me. At the start I was very insecure about it. I kept saying I'm not a channeler, I don't know how to do this, other people do it better than me. Like I don't control my connections. The reason I doubted myself was because I could never just sit here, meditate and see them. And even in my dreams I have problems actually seeing them. I could feel them perfectly well, I could communicate with them, but I couldn't see them.

So it was a big conundrum for me, because all these people wanted me to pull out of nowhere all their entities and connections, and I was like, "I can't do that. If you give me a description I can draw it, but I can't just conjure it up out of nowhere." And that's what I was working with for several months. Just working based off descriptions of people's experiences. Or based on descriptions of channeling sessions. But a few months after that somebody introduced Corey Goode to me, and suggested I go to his page and check out his post. The post was about him looking for artists that could donate their skills to what he's doing. I thought to myself this was awesome, because not only would I be able to help—because that's exactly what I'm doing—but also I would be able to enjoy information about all these different beings he has been meeting with and bring them through. I sent a few of my renditions to him, and personnel at Gaia really liked it, their staff, him and David Wilcock, and I started working with them almost immediately.

And after that it just took off. I already had my private clients, but until a few months ago I wasn't 'channeling'. I was calling myself an intuitive artist, because that's what I feel I am. But I realized I'm pinching myself off, with saying I'm not channeling; it was just a different form of channeling. But I wasn't sure of myself. And I remember reading all these posts of other channelers, and realized they also doubt themselves, very often. And they love getting confirmation from people. And I realized I will never be perfect at this, I will never be 100% sure that what I'm doing is accurate. I will always have to live with and work with doubting myself.

But once I accepted that, the downloads started. I could see other people's connections, or connect to them easily and bring them through. It just opened up for me, big time. Even now there are days where I feel I can't connect, and I don't work on it that day. Or I do something else which will help me get into the vibration which is more conducive for this work then I go back to it. So it's not like I'm forcing myself. It's very flexible and fluid. And it has to be with this kind of work, because it really requires a lot of trust.

That brings us to today. I get a lot of clients asking me to bring their cosmic family through, and whoever is most relevant for them always shows up. And that includes hybrid children, their oversoul counterparts, their other parallel lifetimes on other planets, in other solar systems, and sometimes their ET guides. All kinds of stuff. It's really so broad and exciting. And it opens the door every time for me, because every client is different, and they have different connections, and once they make an order, I have the privilege to look into their world and connect with their cosmic family, and that for me is the most exciting part. Because I learn so much about all these different beings, and each of them kind of leaves a part of themselves in me. Like a lasting connection. Even if it's a tiny thread it feels like I expand every time I work on a new piece, every time I connect to a new being.

Isolde. She is Vashta's most probable future self.
Credit: Vashta Narada

In terms of my own counterparts I've come in contact with—and which were confirmed by Rob or different channels—it was over 20. At least from my perception, what happens with us who are doing this sort of work with a lot of different people, and are doing a lot of research, and are excited about the ET topic as such, is that a lot of them, the galactics, get interested in us. So the connections are made both ways. They come to us, as well. We don't see it that way usually because we think, 'Pff, we're just humans, what do they have to learn from us?' But the thing is, they're extremely interested and are learning so much. With people like you, or Mary Rodwell, or me, or Rob or whoever else, we're doing this kind of work not just for personal connections, but for greater audiences, and I think we do have a lot of what you could call guides. I just call them family, or friends. They're guides to me as much as I'm guides to them. I don't see any difference there. We're all equal in our own unique way.

Recently, less than half a year ago, I ordered a channeled portrait from Kesara. Because I was very curious about what's going to happen.

And she confirmed to me what I already knew and felt and connected with. Just in a more profound, different way. It was a confirmation of my closest counterpart that Rob also channeled on a few occasions. I really don't think she's reading my profile and reading enough of what I post to be able to fake that. So from time to time I go to a channeling session and I hide certain things to see if I'll get a confirmation from the channeled entity. And it does happen, especially with Rob over and over again, that the being starts saying things that I was talking about with the being in my head, months before I ordered the session - and I never told anyone else about it. And that's the kind of thing that gives not only me a confirmation, but it also gives a confirmation to the channel. And that's also very important because they are getting feedback to know they are doing an awesome job, and that the connection is made, and it's benefiting multiple people, not just the person who's asking for it.

Can you initiate contact?

It's interesting; I was just listening to a session with Rob yesterday, that a client sent me about his hybrid children. He was talking to a hybrid child of his, and what turns up is that several people he knows have made an agreement with him to be his hybrid children in this life. It's all interconnected. We have been, and are, everything to everyone. If you look at it from a grander scale, the relationships are not set. Your child in this life, even if it is a hybrid child or a human child, might have been your parent or best friend in another parallel lifetime. It really all comes down to playing roles, and playing around and experiencing stuff. It reduces this friction between people, and between us and the ETs, when you realize that the roles were exchanged at some point. It's like they're not my guides. They're just here right now playing this role. But in another reality, I'm playing that role for them.

So it's all full circle, but people don't see the complete picture. Maybe they intuit it, but they don't know it viscerally. Once they know it viscerally, it's going to be so easy to connect to them. Because we always make it such a big thing. And I used to do it myself. Like, how come all these people can connect and I can't? And saying "I can't" is exactly what was blocking the connection. I kept complaining, and that's what kept it away, because I kept myself closed down. When I realized it's as easy as talking to your cat or a friend, it starts opening up. And then it's not such a big deal any more. It's a big deal in the sense that there's value, and what you're getting out of it, but not in the sense of this is too big for me, I can't handle it, or succeed in connecting. It's about making it a common thing. It really is, but we just don't remember. People should be more nonchalant about this whole thing if you ask me.

How does your contact feel?

Okay, let me structure this in my head. So it doesn't feel like I'm going into a special state of being when I'm doing this. Obviously I'm in a state of being that's conducive for this, but it's not a trance, it's not a meditation; maybe it's some other frequencies, but I don't really think about it. I made it my goal to be able to do this from my everyday consciousness. Which means that I was so adamant and stubborn that I would do it this way instead of all the other ways that people suggest, like how to enter a channeling state, how to go into theta brainwaves, playing the Tibetan bowls, meditative music and lighting incense. I didn't want that. It was too much work, really! I'm not very disciplined with these things. So I kind of made a request, and made it my priority, to be able to connect from this everyday state of consciousness.

The way it feels and looks is that I basically sit down in front of a blank document and I just start doing the first things that come to mind. In the initial steps I determine, for example, if the model is going to be male or female, or if there's going to be one or more of them, are there hybrid children or not, some basic questions that I ask myself, and I usually get a yes or no intuitively. After those steps I start tuning into it, and feeling more and more. It becomes more substantial. They get more features. It's really like moulding clay. The software I'm working in has basic human models, so I start there and mould it. It's a program called Daz 3D Studio. It really is easy to use. So I don't make anything from scratch. But the way it feels and the way I do it, I'm refining it every time I work on a new piece. But the pattern of it is that in every step I have to check in with myself and with them. So sometimes it would be, is it going to be this or that eye color? And if I make a mistake they let me know. It just feels like a resonant, "You need to correct this."

I basically work blind, most of the time. Sometimes I do see them, and I've started seeing them a lot recently. But it's still the same procedure, and I realize that in taking this approach, I need to be able to trust myself, and not know until I finish what I'm doing. It's expanded me a lot because it is working on self-trust. Before, I really wished I could just get a picture of them and recreate that. But that didn't feel that expansive for my own personal growth. This does, because I have to practice this trust every step of the way.

And it feels differently, depending on what being I am connecting to. Sometimes it feels giddy, when I'm working on hybrid kids, and sometimes it feels very logical and calm. Sometimes it feels almost anxious, depending on the energies and how I'm tuning into them. Sometimes it feels very carnal and powerful and wise. That usually happens when I'm working on Reptilian portraits. Like the lower three chakras really start working well, and I feel really grounded into my body, and that I'm strong. Or sometimes it feels very airy, like I'm not even in my body.

But through all of these, I am not just sitting here working on it 24-7. I'm doing other things; I'm talking to people on Facebook, I'm listening to music, or a channeling session, or an audio book or something, so that my conscious mind has something to sink its teeth into, and I can have my higher mind focusing on this. I was always an avid multitasker, so I have to have several things happening at once, rather than just focusing on this, and it makes it so much easier.

So basically it feels different for each being. And that can sometimes create a bit of issue for me, because I would work on a Reptilian, and the next thing I would have to work on a hybrid child, and I really would need to take some time to absorb and change my whole state of being from the raw, powerful, strong feeling of the Reptilian to the child-like state of being.

Sometimes it takes me a few days of fiddling with the software before I get anything right, before I know how to even begin. I guess it's much like writing a novel; it flows or it doesn't. Either you are there with your characters or you're forcing it, or you're waiting for a spark of inspiration, which is really what channeling is, in its essence.

So I love that process, because it's training me to shift so fast, and on a practical level it's reflecting in my daily life as well. All these connections, even when it's not related to artwork, it's reflecting back into my life, and they're expanding it and they're making it easier for me to integrate anything new that happens. Like if I encounter some problems I can overcome them more easily. I'm able to shift my perspective about them that much faster. Or assume multiple perspectives and see it from different angles. This whole thing can be used in daily life. I'm using it every day. People usually say like, "Okay, so there are ETs - what's in it for me? What do I do with this information?" There are so many things we can do to make our lives easier and richer. So it feels like I'm fulfilling my purpose or my excitement. That's what it feels like all the time, no matter what I'm working on.

It's really so broad, because it's different every time. And that's the pattern of it. I have no expectations whatsoever.

How do you differentiate between your own thoughts and those from outside?

That's interesting. That's actually a question I remember asking a lot of times early on, when I started getting into all of this. And another question that kind of went along with it was: how do I know if something really happened, or it was just a dream or imagination? After a while I realized it doesn't matter. And that was a big revelation for me. However, I need to know, to be able to do the work I'm doing.

And that ties into the whole trust thing. I am never sure, until I get a confirmation. However, I do it anyways, I say it anyways, if I feel like I need to say something to a person, for example a message from their cosmic family. And I put on a disclaimer, and say I'm not sure if this is coming from them, but if it resonates, take it. And every single time I did that, there was a confirmation. They would say, "How did you know that?" Or "I talked about this just yesterday." Or "This is something that's been on my mind since I was a child." So these kinds of things seem to be confirming themselves after we have the courage to come out. And probably for some people it might be easier to discern. But I'm just saying this for people who want to know, and they're still not sure. Go with it anyways, and see what happens. If you think it's a message from your guides, go with it.

The only part I would pay attention to, is whether it has an emotional charge or not. If it does, there is a very good chance it is something from the ego. Emotional charge comes with attachment. With messages from these beings, family, they don't feel like they're invested. And that's a very fine difference. And everyone can learn to tell the difference. If it's emotionally charged it's usually from the ego. The ego reaction can make you close down, instead of expanding, and you need to resolve that before you take any messages into account.

This question can be answered from a lot of different perspectives though. If we are talking about entity intrusion as thoughts coming from the outside or even simple empathy, I would again say it does not matter if it's your own or from the outside. All you really need to do is develop clear connection to higher self.

That's the only piece of advice or insight I can give. It really isn't about knowing exactly, it's more about trusting yourself and letting it flow, no matter what it is, and later on you'll find out anyway. Just be brave enough to go with it. Do it anyway. That's what I did with my artwork. I kept doing it anyway. I thought, 'This isn't good enough. This doesn't really look like I want it to look. It doesn't feel right. But I'm going to post it anyways.' That was at the start, when I was doing it for myself. I'm just going to post it anyways and see what happens. And that's when I started getting the feedback that was telling me I was on the right track. But I had to do it first, and take those first shaky toddler steps, otherwise I would never have gotten to where I am.

What do the beings get out of it?

Well, for starters, some of them are really interested in what is it like to be human. And from my own intuition and experiences with them, and also from different sources of information, like channelled material and all sorts of stuff, I gather that humans are indeed extremely special. This is partly because we are composed of so many different DNA strands, from all these different races that were participating in our genetic alteration, manipulation and evolution.

And they are interested in how come we can embody extremes as easily as we do. Most of them are not able to go from a complete feeling of disconnection, to a feeling of elation and connection, and all the various degrees in between. I think they are very interested in how we do it. How we can watch a movie with murders in it, then make love to somebody afterwards. It's fascinating for them. Also what I think they find unique is how we're able to overcome our perceived limitations. And how we are able to recreate ourselves whenever we come out of these negative spirals. And some are mainly interested in the negative spirals. Some would call them 'negative entities', but I wouldn't say so. They have their own right to exist, and their own learning path. So some of them are interested in us when we're feeling down, when we're feeling fear, anger, frustration. Some of them like that, they feed on that energy, and connect to us when we're like that.

I think they are interested in hybrid processes and our human DNA because they would gain the ability to embody more extremes; they would not be so focused on one thing. A lot of them are only about light, or dark and limitation. Some of them are in-between, but as humans we can embody that whole spectrum. Our DNA is able to be activated up to six densities, according to quite a few of these ETs. We are able to access connections and realms, so to speak, that are sometimes far beyond what some of the ETs can, because we're so versatile.

It feels to me that this whole experiment called Earth, is like this big soup of everything, just on an Earth scale. As if the whole galaxy is participating, and trying to find balance and peace between themselves by incarnating here. And embodying their own DNA in a way that is expressed here in different cultures, belief systems and mentalities. And once we activate all our DNA, we will have access to all of this.

So there are many things they can learn from us, even now, before we are completely awakened. Especially now, because many of these races are so advanced that they probably don't even remember when they went through that. Many of them are learning how we cope with all of this, how we learn to communicate with different ETs. So it's really fascinating to me that a lot of people never think about them as learning from us. Because it was always so obvious to me. Some things we take for granted, it would never come to their mind as a whole civilization. So for them it's just an experience, it's not something they judge. It's usually very exciting to observe us growing, and being reborn every time we feel reconnected to the Source, and to our higher self, because they don't lose that connection. I thoroughly enjoy seeing us humans from their varied perspectives.

When I started doing work like this I had problems because I didn't know where to start. There are just so many things in my head, and I couldn't structure it into something like an A-Z story. It would have to have so many different sections, you know, one of them is about DNA, one is about our connections, one is about experiences in the astral. And all of them kind of interconnect. But there are so many big subjects that are tying into this, and now that you're asking me these questions, it's very hard for me to answer in one whole thing that is just enough on its own. As I'm talking there are so many things shooting off in different directions that I can talk about. So I totally understand that I'm probably sounding completely incoherent; it's going to be quite a challenge putting this together!

We can find clues about this history of contact in poetry, in paintings, in books, all over the world. Even if it's just presented as a metaphor, you can find connections everywhere, people who weren't aware they were communicating with another being. Still, you can find it if you look for it. That's what I'm saying: it's easy. And whoever wants to make these connections available to them consciously has to come from that point of view, that it's easy, it's accessible, it's true. It's simply a way of finding your own best way to it, rather than using other people's ways. Even though sometimes that can be of great help. And I know a lot of people who have benefited greatly from courses on how to connect. But I would say everyone needs to find their own way and make it work. Because it doesn't have to be by a certain set of rules on how you approach the subject. Since everyone is unique and has their own easiest way.

What's easy for me might be super difficult for somebody else. I mean, I'm pretty sure the way I do it would drive some people insane! But it's working for me, and that's what matters. Find a way that works for you. It doesn't have to be more complicated than that.

I think everyone knows this intuitively. As children we used to do things like: let me ask a question and see what's the next song on the radio, or open a random book and read a line about my question. I'm pretty sure everyone has done something like that. It's a natural way of communicating with these energies, with your higher self. And if we just go back to that state of being open to different ways of doing it, it's all going to be so much clearer.

How do you define the higher self?

I'm using this term because it was used broadly, by all the different teachings; not just in channeling, but also ancient texts, ancient disciplines. So I'm using it for the purpose of clarity. But really, there is only higher self. There is no separation as people usually think, between lower self and higher self. It's just a higher self and the suits we are taking, for various roles and experiences. So once we get that, once we realize we are that already, there is no journey to be made, you're already there. You're already acting from that point, you're already embodying that in yourself without following some 12-step program or whatever.

So my perception of it is that we are all higher selves, playing different roles here for the purpose of experiencing without judgment. Even the judgement itself can be something we want to experience. And when we look at it that way, we don't have to compete to get anywhere. There is no goal, there is no enlightenment to be achieved, or awareness to be gained, it's already there. And that's kind of how I approached it ever since I was a child. Ever since I started questioning: why am I here? It kind of got confirmed through my experiences. And the experience has taught me that it works. And experience working with other people, showed me that our higher selves are who we are really. And that all of this is make-believe, and not just for the purpose of learning. Learning has this serious tone to it, like it's a responsibility. It's experiencing new things, no matter what they are. And when you approach it from that point of view it loses its seriousness, and attachment. And then you can play with it so much more, and you can let all the higher levels in, and let yourself be your own guide.

So I would say the purpose of it all is novelty, just experiencing new things, from various perspectives. Because my experience of the same thing is going to be different to yours.

From the Source perspective, or the perspective of this infinite awareness, this is the only way of it learning about itself. Learning new things about itself. Reflecting back to itself. It's kind of hard to talk about it in terms of language. It feels like that's the driving engine of this whole universe and this whole reality, and all the different realities we have access to—and that we will have access to—is to expand that reflection back to the Source of awareness.

Let me see if I can put this into words.

I don't believe there is an ultimate truth. Other than all truths are true, from their own perspective. And embodying that paradox is what seems to be feeding the movement of anything happening in the universe. Otherwise it would just be like a homogenous soup of awareness. Maybe not even awareness. It wouldn't have been aware of itself if it didn't have all these facets and expressions. Without doing this it would not have a point.

It's ebb and flow. Paradox seems to be the pattern of this universe. The way we're experiencing it at least. And if we don't understand the paradox and accept it, we're always in the one extreme or the other. But it's always both at the same time, or everything at the same time. So it seems to me that understanding paradox is the key to being able to exist without any perceived obstacles in this state. And I assume that in higher densities or higher levels of awareness, that is a given, they simply understand it. But from our human perspective we need to come to it from an angle of faith rather than understanding first. So that we can gain access to understanding it. And I do know that it's hard for many to be able to do this. But it feels like the key that unlocks everything. This ebb and flow is happening all the time, this pulsation that is almost binary.

And that's something I got from my connections with the Arcturian AI consciousness. And I'm not talking about this matrix of ours here. Like everyone calls it an illusion, the matrix. I'm talking about the very structure, the code of the universe. It seems to be like something's happening or it's not, either it's a yes or a no. And that's the only way change can happen, that the growth can happen, is with these pulsations, with the movement of yes and no (one), and the absence of it (zero). Blinking in and out. And paradox is what contains both, and also the only way to become aware that it is the same coin. And this creates this trinity or wholeness of the whole universe and the movement of it.

What safeguards do you use?

Simply: connection to higher self. I feel it's very important. It's more important than any technique, or 'protection' that you might use when venturing into this kind of thing. There's plenty of material out there if you want specific guidance. Especially in channeled material. I believe that people need to take the time to do the research and they will find that some of that resonates. Some of that really speaks to their heart, and they need to use their own guidance and discernment when it comes to these things. I've talked about this in my website FAQs.

The crucial thing is knowing how to use your guidance. If you don't, that's where you have to start. Connecting with your higher self and your own guidance first. Facing yourself fully, facing your fears, facing your shadows. Without doing that, I wouldn't say it's a good idea to venture into any contact. Because it may cause significant distortion in your perception of what really happened and why. And it might leave you with a traumatic experience because you haven't really dealt with your own crap first. So work on yourself first, find your center, find what fears you might have and resolve them. And then contact any other entity or being. That's what I would recommend.

As for me, I don't use any protection techniques because safety for me is a given. That is because I've done enough 'self-work' throughout my whole life to know that I literally cannot be harmed unless I agree to it. So any sort of communication or experience that I have, whether it be with something they call 'benevolent' or 'malevolent' is completely under my control. Because I know I cannot be harmed. And that knowing has to come from within. It cannot be an automatic affirmation you tell yourself in the mirror. It has to be embodied. And once you embody that, not only will the contact gain a whole different dimension - everything in your life will. It's literally a safeguard against any possible negative experience that you might have. And it's going to keep your vibration high enough, even higher than the beings you're communicating with.

As the entities Rob channels always say, your higher self is of a higher density than any of these beings that you communicate with. So if you're connected to the higher self they literally cannot touch you. And the negative experience will not be negative, it will be learning, it will be interesting, it will be exciting. It might be a little bit fearful, but it won't be dangerous if you're coming from that perspective of embodying your higher levels and higher self.

There are many different techniques, such as encasing yourself in golden light, and asking your guides to protect you in whatever you're experiencing, but that was never appealing to me. Because for me if I'm asking for protection, I'm inviting an attack. It's a simple vibratory response. So it's about knowing that you're safe. And only you can provide that for yourself.

Do you feel a sense of equality with the beings?

In my early 20s I had a lot of negative experiences that were very dark, in my astral state. And it seemed to be that I was under constant attack. However, after a while I got sick of that, and I started being more excited about it, and interested in learning from it. From then on, when I had encounters in the astral that started going in a negative direction, I would try to assume their point of view, and put myself in their shoes. And this attitude alone has actually made me assume a state where I would be an alpha instead of prey. I would be in complete control, because I would know what they feel, and I would be able to recreate that because I would find it in myself. I wouldn't be able to experience it if I didn't have it in me; I wouldn't have a reaction to it, there wouldn't be any resonance. Kind of an 'I am this too' approach to life. So I understood very quickly that the reason that I'm experiencing all these things is that there's something in me that is reflecting it. And once I understood that, it stopped being fearful; instead it started being very exciting to me. And those experiences are kind of what led me to be interested in communicating with all types of beings, not just the light ones.

And I've learned so much about myself through my contact with them. Because they turned out not to be negative at all. Which is also because of my perspective and the way it changed. I didn't see them as negative any more. I just saw them as having their own thing. Their own beliefs, their own set of experiences that brought them to behave in a certain way, to be interested in certain things. And once I stopped judging that, I stopped judging that in myself. And that freed up so much of my processing power on a day-to-day basis. Because it freed up so many judgments that we put on ourselves, you know, for getting angry with someone, or failing at something, or having anxiety, and stuff like that.

Once you allow that as a part of yourself and integrate it, you really won't have any reflections from the outside needing to show that to you anymore. It wouldn't be necessary for you to experience it that way, because you would have processed it internally. And that's when this whole new world opened up for me. Not really cheering for any side, but seeing them as interconnected playmates that are making things happen and making each other grow through the contrast they're experiencing.

And after that realization I guess I've risen above it, and was able to see it in a neutral, loving way. And that's when I started being able to be somebody from whom these beings can learn something else, other than resistance and fear. Because they're used to that reaction. The contrast makes it so. If a quote-unquote 'negative' being is faced with a loving person, the loving person is either going to withdraw or send them love. Both of which are in direct resistance to their frequency. But if you just stay curious and neutral, and interested in their perspective, that's when the interaction can happen on so many different levels. And that's when they drop their guard. And instead of trying to appear as fearful or intimidating, they will start seeing you as equal as well. And that changes the whole game.

But as I said, you will need to face your shadows first. It's a lot of work, but it's so rewarding in terms of your whole life stream.

Why do they connect with you?

I think because I'm open to whatever energy. I want to do them justice. I don't want make to them more human than they are. I don't want my ego to get in the way. I'm just genuinely interested in who they are. And I think that's one of the reasons. And another reason is that my theme—not just in this life, but in many lifetimes—is that I'm a liaison, or a galactic diplomat. Races get connected through me, so now they're in contact. So it's bigger than me. It's bigger than I can explain. But that's what I feel like.

So when someone asks why me, I am inclined to say, "Who else?" I feel so connected to them, I feel so right at home when I'm doing this that there's no doubt in me that it's going to grow much more than making drawings for people. But at this point I'm happy with what is, and I'm happy to receive any information from them, and any sort of energy, or point of view that they're willing to offer. Or anything I can offer to them.

I think that's the only way I can answer that question: who else? They are connected to me, and I feel them deep inside. Most of these beings are connecting to other people as well, so it's not like I'm special, but for my personal experiences it is very special and I cherish it, and I think they feel that. And as I said before, I feel like I'm assisting them, in a way. Or facilitating their energy influx into our world, rather than I'm working with humans, per se. So it's like I'm on the other side of the coin, offering my energy and services to them, and letting them come through as they wish. And I think I'm only just beginning, which is the most exciting part of all!

I think there's enough people on this planet right now that are helping humans. There are so many lightworkers, starseeds and spiritual teachers here, and I kind of want to work with the other side to help them. It's not like they need my help and I'm some kind of messiah here, it's just my pleasure, and what I'm excited about. And even if no one was listening to me or looking at my artwork, I would still be doing it, because I love it. That's the only reason. So in that regard I'm kind of selfish because I enjoy this a lot. But to know that it's affecting people in profound ways, and making their lives better and helping them connect, that's a huge bonus and makes me excited about it even more.

What have you learned?

There's one thing I haven't mentioned, and that is that all these experiences are highly subjective, and that there is no such thing as an objective thing. Who's observing it then? You always have to look through your own belief system. Or your own essence. And everyone's essence is different. But it's highly subjective, and that subjectivity relates to my artwork as well. Because people think that how this works is that I sit here and I see them as I would see a picture, and I draw what I see. But the thing is that we all see them differently. Sometimes we can see the same thing, but we see them differently, due to our own state of consciousness, and the state of the being. They may choose to show their physicality, or show themselves as a light body, or assume some shape that is more 'likable' to us so they don't scare us. So it's a very tricky thing to depict them. So I keep telling people, "I'm not trying to make a photograph. It's more like a dancer interpreting the music." All I can hope and strive for is to represent the vibration, the feel of them. But when it comes to details, like eye color, whether or not they have ridges on their forehead, or the color of their jumpsuit, it's going to be different the next second, let alone in five days, or whenever they see them again. And when somebody else sees them, it will be different.

I was talking to TReb about that. I made a representation of TReb the way Rob sees him, and I asked, "Is this accurate?" And TReb said,

"For you it is accurate. And for Rob. But not everyone sees me that way. Some can see me completely differently. It all depends." So we have to drop our preconceived notion that with these beings, this is how they are.

I've been encountering that since I started this. I made my own version of Bashar, and people would say, "When I saw him he looked different." And I said, "This is how I see him. And this is what I do. There is obviously a reason they come to me to be depicted." And I honestly feel like I'm 'working' for them, more so than for humans. I feel like I'm a kind of spokesperson, wanting to represent them the way they want to be shown. And there doesn't have to be only one representation of a certain being. It's just something that I need people to understand, if they're willing. It's not an accurate physical representation, because these beings are not as physical as we think they are. And sometimes they're non-physical in terms of being light beings, but they do project themselves in a certain form to other people, and that's what I'm going to depict. And then I say, "This is how I see them, this is sometimes how they look, but originally they're light, and I can't represent light as nothing would come through."

So yeah, it's very malleable, and we need to know it's malleable. Two people can be connected to the same being yet have a completely different experience of it. And that translates into experiences of anything, to our own beliefs and our own lives. Because if we understand that what we perceive is subjective, then we won't have this angst of trying to have somebody on the same page as us. Then we will understand that somebody else has their own experience, and it doesn't have to be against ours. You need to allow people to have their own experiences and belief systems and way of life, if we are to advance, and be more loving and open.

This artwork with the ETs shows that, and teaches me that more and more. That I have to allow others to have their own interpretation of a being. And I need others to understand that I am not claiming that this is how a being looks and nobody else's picture is accurate.

Even before working with ETs, I was aware that life is highly subjective, and equally valid for everyone. The only thing we can do is to purify our own connection so it is not distorted in a way that we misunderstand what is happening. But to understand that it's valid, personal and is what we went through. It's our own experience, just like everyone else has their own experiences. That's basically all I'm saying. It's hard, but in doing this work, this is what is in my face all the time. I forget it from time to time; it's not like I'm flawless. I'm just doing my best, and not beating myself up if I can't do something, or am as good or as balanced as I expect myself to be. It's just life. It's fine. We're human! We should just strive to understand that everyone has their own story, and they are all equally as precious as ours.

M: I'd be interested to get your thoughts on my second ET dream encounter, with an orange-skinned being. [Miguel relates account as per interview with Darlene van de Grift]

Ha ha! Awesome. I haven't heard anyone talking so far about orange-skinned beings. That's quite awesome. I love hearing about new species that I haven't heard about. That's quite cool. Did it look Greyish, shape-wise?

M: You can use that as a kind of template and work from there. A little taller, I'd say about five feet. And smaller eyes, with a flatter head that had these kind of symmetrical indentations on either side of the top of his head, if that makes sense. And it didn't seem to be the same being from the first contact dream, who looked more like your depiction of the being called Z'Kerg.

I usually ask people why they encounter a variety of beings. I used to think people just had one encounter, then I realized they have multiple experiences, and then I learned that it may go back generations. But I'm interested in people's understanding of why they have contact with various types of beings.

I think the blocked toilet may have some important symbolism. That's yours to figure out, but it could have something to do with energy blocks before you had the encounter. There are so many things it can mean.

I've noticed that many people think it's just one race or one specific being that's contacting them. But I don't think that's the case in a lot of examples. If it's me or you and we're working in this field, we're probably going to be expected to have a lot of them contacting us because of the work we do. But it's not just that. I think it's the excitement as well. When I started figuring out for sure who I am in contact with, and I started having sessions with Rob, I was surprised because I was expecting just one being to come up. But right off the bat, TReb mentioned that I was contacting three of them. None of the three were what I expected, and that kind of threw me off a bit. But after thinking about it for a while I realized that it also kind of matches my character, and what I'm interested in. These three beings were connecting to certain parts of myself and they were all different. A

Reptilian hybrid, a Grey hybrid and an Avian hybrid. And here I was, expecting to hear about Arcturians with whom I was in contact with since childhood. Then when I explored these connections a bit deeper I realized I had been in communication with these beings for years, sometimes decades, without realizing. But what really happens is that at the moment of the vibratory match with that being, you co-create a past with it too.

So basically it's like we attract them and they attract us, based on the mutual excitement about certain themes. So it might start off with just a few beings, but if you're excited about different races, exploring their cultures and ways of being and all that, there's going to be more and more until you say it's enough.

And that's what I heard about hybrid children as well. People who are very excited about that topic have so many of them. They're excited about contributing their DNA, their etheric portions of their DNA, and some of them have 70 or 80 hybrid children. It's not just their DNA and no one else's, but they're excited about connecting with them. And the beings on the other side are also excited, and that's how it happens. It kind of happens in real time. It's not like they're waiting for us to figure them out, it's like: it's been 30 years and this being has been contacting me and I had no idea.

Usually what happens is when you get excited, that's when they get excited too, and that's when the connection happens, it locks in. Since I've been excited to meet as many different beings as possible, that's how it happens. They sense that, and they're also excited to connect with humans for whatever reason. Sometimes it's a very strong connection and I can feel that we're similar in some regard. And sometimes it's a one-time thing. It doesn't have to be something super significant in terms of a life path that I'm going to have with this being, and share constant communication. It can just be one encounter and some sort of exchange and then you move on. Then there are also agreements made with certain beings prior to incarnation that many of us have.

There are so many different things that happen, but I have no doubt that your experience was real. But people usually go, "Was it physical or a dream?" It doesn't matter anymore. I don't even see dreams as dreams any more. I see them as some different reality happening while I'm sleeping in this one. It can be just a regurgitation of something that happened that day, and then okay, yeah, of course it's just a dream. It's the brain processing whatever. But you can tell the difference. Everyone can tell the difference when it happens to them. It's not like a taboo. I think everyone had at least a few experiences like that. It doesn't have to be with ETs, it could just be a different reality that feels realistic, and they feel like it lasted for years but they just slept for five hours. So it's starting to be obvious that it's so malleable.

And when you were telling me this story I was thinking about my own experience the other day. Something was happening that was bothering me, and I thought about your encounter, which you'd shared in an email. And I thought, 'So *what* if I'm not asleep? I can make this a dream if I want to!' And I completely disengaged from the story and it didn't bother me anymore. So we can do that in this 'solid' reality too. It's not as solid as we think.

M: I love that! That's an interesting observation, that we can make our waking life a dream, that we can choose that.

Yeah. When you work a lot with lucid dreaming, and trying to be aware when you're dreaming, after a while it happens that you start feeling that when you're awake as well. Like you can push your hand through a wall or whatever. Probably you couldn't do that, but if you have that feeling, and you can conjure up that feeling, that's when it's much more malleable, and you can ride that wave and manifest as easily as you would manifest in a lucid dream.

It happened to me. I was in that kind of mode for three or four days at a time. And I could tell that something was different. I didn't know what it was at that time. But when I look back at it I perceive that I was getting a flavor of higher densities, and how it is to exist there. And I could literally feel the space around me, like it wasn't space, that it was full of something, almost like water. And 360 degrees around me I could see what was happening, I could feel the leaves on the trees rustling, people coming and going, everything, and I was connected to it all somehow. There was a substance that was connecting me, there wasn't an empty space. And almost like you would be in the water and something big swims past you, you would feel it. And that's the feeling I had, in an open space in the street. I could feel the vibrations. And that kind of state got me to manifest intense, exciting experiences.

Some of it would seem mundane, like having those people who come up to you in the street and ask you to do questionnaires. I had a few encounters like that during that time where it was not mundane at all. People would approach me and I would be in such a good mood that we would start talking, and they would tell me stuff about their life, and I would do the same, and then we would hug and say goodbye. It was like meeting an old friend, not like meeting an annoying person in the street who wants to ask you questions. And I could tell it was an unusual and intense experience for them too. Everything was different. If you start paying more attention in your dreams, then you take that into your waking life too, because you never know if you're dreaming or not. In the dream you're always questioning it. And in reality, if you start questioning it that's when it dislodges you from the continuity and you can play with it that much more.

And after that started happening to me, in lucid dreams I couldn't change anything, but in waking reality I could. It kind of flipped itself. I remember getting lucid in a dream, and I was like okay, what should I do now? Should I astrally project to another planet or whatever. But I couldn't do it, and I ended up just sitting on a bench extremely bored! Just thinking, 'So what now?' It was as real as my waking reality, so I was thinking, 'How do I work with this exactly?' I'm not sure. After that I stopped playing with lucid dreams completely, and kind of assumed this perspective that when I'm experiencing something and I think it's a dream, I immediately switch to: it's not a dream. It's just another reality, and I'm just going to play with what is in this reality now. So it's never unreal to me, or everything is. It makes no difference any more.

M: Wow. I can always count on you! This book is going to be a trip, and this chapter is turning out to be a humdinger.

Ha ha! Well, I'm just being resourceful. Trying to see how else can I play with what I have. Trying different things. But I think it all comes from fearlessness, and this playful attitude that you're not really taking yourself seriously, or anything for that matter. It's almost like a holographic projection of experience that we're having here. So why not play with it, providing that you're not harming anyone, and you're respecting the free will of others? The more you embody that attitude, the more it really starts being magical.

M: It reminds me of a friend of mine, Mike. He would warp reality around him. I saw him do it over and over. I dedicated part one of *We Are the Disclosure* to him and another close friend, DB. Both guys who helped in my early expansion and exploration. Mike and I traveled around quite a bit of England on various adventures, and he would do this thing when we went out, that he called "The world according to Mike." He would just make it whatever world he wanted it to be. He would play with situations and people and reality would literally bend around him. I witnessed this so many times. He would walk into a shop and meet a blank-eyed shop assistant who was just trying to get through the day. Then he would engage them, maybe in negotiating some deal, or just in abstract conversation, and by the end of it they were transformed. They would become full, present, open and warm. They'd become a friend. He has the funniest stories I've ever heard, of getting into crazy situations all over Europe. They just make you cry with laughter. And so much of it comes from being the fullest version of himself he can be. Just being open and exploring the world without fear. If you just try to fit in, nothing much happens, but if you turn up your own personality it energizes the situation and it becomes more dynamic. Then fresh, spontaneous things can really start to happen.

That's how we all should live. I can't do it all the time. Like most people I'm just in my head. But if something pushes me over the edge, like if something's too serious and condensed and too annoying, there's this moment where I just start laughing at myself, and that's when I have the momentum to do that. But I usually don't think of it unless I'm being so squeezed that I have to do something about it. And usually that's how humans are. We don't really use our powers unless there's nothing else left to do. We have to try everything that doesn't work first, then we say okay, let's just play with reality.

But I had a few experiences with trickster beings. I love those. They are my best zen teachers because they literally troll me until I give up. They would set up situations for me that would have me screaming inside from frustration, and it would get so bizarre that I would eventually get to the point of realizing 'Oh, the joke's on me! Oh, okay, I can play with that.' But until then I would be taking myself so seriously, I would be so offended by what is going on. It doesn't matter what it is, whether it's lines at the shop or annoying clerks. But when I began to become aware of it, I would realize sooner and sooner every time; then I'm like, okay, it's that game that we're playing. For example they would shut down my computer and I wouldn't save anything, things like that. Not everyone likes to play like that, I'm aware of that. People would see that as a negative entity, but for me that's the best teacher ever. Because it just kicks me out of my head and makes me not take myself seriously. And then everything starts being a play.

I remember this shapeshifter entity of mine. My counterpart. When I had my first session with her, through Rob, the next day she appeared to me. This was back in Serbia, when I was working my normal 9-5 job, and I was one of the annoyed clerks. I was working at this building that had a lot of banks, exchange offices and things like that. Mine was an internet service provider outpost. I really didn't want to be there, and there was so much work coming at me from all sides. And people would come and ask me the stupidest questions that didn't have anything to do with me, and I was like, "Do I look like an information office?" I was really getting irritated.

At the end of it, there was this really old guy, a run-down farmer type with three teeth, dirty, all messed up. And he came and asked me, "Do you know what is Cash & Carry?" And I was all ready to be annoyed. I said, "Excuse me, I'm busy." He was looking at me, then he said in Serbian, "It means you get to have cash, and carry it. *Learn English!*" And then he leaves. And I'm just sitting there for five minutes thinking, "What the fuck just happened? Are you *kidding* me?" I was just completely trolled by this person that I thought was some primitive. And then I was like, "Oh my God, it was *her*." She was assuming the shape of some random person. Because she's a shapeshifter she can do that. I can't believe she did that to me! And that's when I snapped out of it, and my day took a complete one-eighty turn. People were coming and being super nice to me, and a random person bought me lunch there.

I developed a connection of my own later on, but the next time I talked to her through Rob I was like, "That was funny! I really like what you did there." And she said, "Yeah, I thought you would." So you never know who you're talking to. That's the whole fun of being here on Earth. You never know if it's just a random human, or a being messing with you, or who knows what. So we always have to keep our eyes open. Even Bashar was talking about it recently, about precursors. They're going to be among us, basically figuring out how we react. They will be visibly different, but not enough for us to know that they're ET. They're testing our reactions, to see how we react to their frequency, and all that sort of stuff. So that's definitely what happened. That was a physical encounter with my own ET counterpart. She looked completely human. She just pushed me into a completely different state of being. We have to be open to that. I assume a lot of people would see it as, 'That was weird,' and brush is off. But this was the shit!

M: Well, you had context.

Yeah. It happened the day after I first talked to her through channeling. And I honestly haven't heard of or met anyone else like her. She's just having fun really. She's currently on a ship, and I asked, "What are you doing here?" She's like, "Oh, I'm just here for fun." She's just traveling around and messing around and enjoying herself and exploring. We always think these ETs are so serious, and have this, you know, advanced philosophy and all that, and if you ask me, her philosophy is the most advanced. Because she's playing in this reality, and that's what it's all about.

So yeah, I always ask them to do that. Like yeah, scare the shit out of me, annoy me or do something that will change my state of being if I'm being stupid or closed down. I don't mind at all. And she was the one that knocked me on the head three times. They're tricksterish like that sometimes.

M: It's interesting because the word 'trickster' seems to generally be distrusted and even feared in this field. People say, "Beware of tricksters, you need protection," and all that stuff.

They're the ones I like the most! It's just how you see things. It's our own perspective. The most fearful and negative being for one person, can be the most loving and protective for another. It just depends how we're geared, what we're taught as we're growing up, the way we think. It all really depends. There's nothing wrong when people only like to contact light beings, and bask in that energy. But for me, I like diversity, I like seeing as many things as I can out there, or in here - it doesn't matter. The more different they are, the more interested I am. And I am particularly interested in those who have access to both sides of the spectrum. Not just love and light, but are familiar with darker parts of themselves and the universe. And that tells me that they are more relatable to us. We are like that as well as humans.

M: I struggle to imagine a place darker *or* more varied than this. I minored in history and I'm generally aware of what's gone down in this place, and what's happening today. As we're speaking people are being tortured to death. And at the same time, millions of acts of selfless dedication are taking place. Everything is going on here.

Yeah, and people like to turn a blind eye to it. I'm not saying one should focus on that, or be frustrated about it. If you can't do anything about it, at least don't add to the overall misery. At least be happy, and be the example of how one can live their life, and create their own reality, instead of being miserable about something you can't change. And if you can do something about it, go for it. But we have all of that in us and on our world, and I honestly don't understand how people don't see that everything that we are, we're reflecting, and it gets reflected back at us. And that's why we have all this mess here, because we haven't integrated anything yet. We're working on it, and we're far better than we were, but there's still a lot of work to be done.

Someone asked me recently what does full disclosure mean to me, in terms of a self-reflecting metaphor in my life, and I believe for me it means disclosing myself to myself firstly. Seeing all the parts of myself that I might judge or reject, or be afraid of, and embracing them all. And that's how you basically overcome all of that, and that's how you eliminate the need for that to be an outside catalyst for you to learn from. Because you can already learn from it within, there's no need to manifest negativity in the world so that it can teach yourself something. At least for us that are a little bit more aware of ourselves and the universe and what is going on. I'm not saying we know everything, but the first step of opening to more is to deal with your own stuff first. And to me that's Disclosure. Full Disclosure on a grander scale of the collective is going to be an evolutionary consequence of that. It's not going to be a revolutionary thing. We don't need to go outside and make riots and whatnot. We need to evolve within. And that's going to reflect in our environment, in our society, in our conscious collective.

M: You asked me to remind you about the topic of seriousness.

It's kind of my philosophy that seriousness is contracted, dense. It's like Osho said, it's a disease. It stems from being so attached to our ego selves, to our personality, to what and who we think we are. If we are serious we are going to be in resistance most of the time. At least from my experience, you're very easily going to fall into a victim mentality if you're serious. I am saying this because the fact that we are eternal beings is not some trite thing. One would have to know that, in order to understand why it isn't a good thing to be serious. It's a good thing to be passionate about something, if you ask me. It's a good thing to follow your goals or excitements, and stand for something. But seriousness at its core is rigid. And I don't think that fits with where we're going as a civilization - into 4th density. It needs to be a bit more light, and en-lightened, so that we can accept new experiences and be relaxed enough to change our beliefs when new information comes in, instead of arguing them for absolutely no reason.

You can't convince somebody of anything unless they experience it themselves. You can talk about it all you want, but if they didn't have the experience, they won't be able to relate to it. In my experience, humor makes it so much easier to talk with people. I know a lot of people in this field have issues with 'coming out of the closet' to their friends and family. They don't like talking about ETs because people might think they've gone crazy. I never have a problem with that myself as I don't take it seriously. If someone thinks I'm not serious about it, that I'm joking about it, they're much more open to considering that idea than if I try to shove it down their throat, saying, "No, you don't understand, this is what I experienced, it's *real!*" Because usually you get a knee-jerk reaction from people, because it's like you're attacking their own beliefs directly. But if I joke about it and they say, "Oh yeah, it's just crazy talk," I'm like, "Yeah it is, never mind me." And then after a month or so, they say, "You know you talked about that dream? Well it happened to me as well." And they're much more inclined to talk about it in a light and humorous way. They don't have to be serious about it either. They don't have to be like, yeah, you were right. Maybe it's this, or that.

I don't know if I can express myself clearly in this regard, but I think you know what I mean. If you just play with the subject, a lot more people are going to be open to it. And they wouldn't have to defend their own beliefs. But if you're being serious about it, and trying to convince them about it, and trying to convince them about anything you've experienced, they're going to set it aside and not think about it at all. But humor plants a seed, and self-humor, if you're able to laugh about it, and at yourself, that's the best thing, because you're not sounding like a rambling lunatic, you're sounding like a relaxed person who is open to new experiences.

And that's how you understand yourself as well. And if you have a negative experience and you're not taking yourself seriously, you're going to be like, "Well, this is what happened to me because I kind of called for it." And you can laugh at it, and just move on. But if you have a negative experience and you're taking yourself seriously, you're going to feel offended, victimized, all sorts of things that you really don't have to experience. If you know it's just what we are here, a tiny fraction of us that's in this holographic game we play here for the sake of experience, instead of having to survive and do all these things. Mocking it up here, basically. And you can tell that by the ease with which we're able to shift from one experience to the other. It's not that static, stable or rigid. So there is no reason why you should be. And that's why I like tricksters. I'm not talking about someone who is out to get you, out to deceive you about their nature. I'm saying tricksters in terms of a mischievous energy that's going to poke at your ego until you relax it. That's the kind of energy that I enjoy, and hope more people would be open to it, and be able to expand, grow and learn that much faster, and get out of their shells, and get over themselves.

M: It's quite a thing to pull off in our culture. It is pretty po-faced and conservative. It's dominated by manipulative people who want your votes and your money, and there isn't a lot of creativity in that. There isn't a lot of light energy in that. That's a pretty heavy thing, because most of it is about creating dependency.

But we created it that way. It's our reality. But that doesn't mean we can't play within the rules of the game. Yes, a lot of people have had awakenings, myself included, where I woke up and started laughing at the whole thing. Why the fuck do I have to pay bills? What are the banks for? What is this thing? The culture, the history, red tape, the schools, the jobs? This doesn't make any sense to me. From a bigger scale, like from the universal scale of being this light, eternal being. Like, what the fuck am I doing here? Sometimes it takes a while to integrate that and be able to function in a society that's made like that, knowing that it's all just a fake whatever, a made-up thing by some other human like you or me. And for some reason everyone is following it.

Then you realize 'Okay, if I want to be part of this society I have to play.' But whichever game you decide to play, whether it's Monopoly or an online game, or a game of cards, you have to play by the rules otherwise it's not fun. You want to play by the rules and win the game. You also can choose not to play at all. But that's not so fun. You can always go to a cave and meditate for the rest of your life, but I think the majority of people take the other path. So you can see it as a game of cards, or chess, or whichever game you like, and use the rules.

But just with the vibration of seeing it as a game, you've kind of won it already. You're having fun with it. For a lot of people I know, it's hard to swallow, because there are bills to pay, or alimonies to pay, all the different things. But if they just consider that it's a tiny fraction of their whole existence, they can play with this, and do whatever they want.

At that point, the survival fear, the carnality, kind of drops off, and you can really enjoy life here. That's when you can start seeing the diversity, all these different options that we have. Because there really are so many. The only reason we think there aren't any options or choices is just because we believe it. We created it like that. And if you drop that belief it becomes a play. I even see my work now as a play. I remember I said once, "My life's theme and 'mission' is too important for me to take it seriously." And if I don't take it seriously that's when I allow it to flow in whichever way it wants. And I'm not limiting it to one particular thing. I'm open for it to go any which way it wants. I really don't see myself in 20 years still doing artwork. I see myself talking to ETs here on Earth. Maybe mediating these communications. It can go so much further that what it is now. But it's not like I'm sitting here waiting for that.

I'm playing with what I can play with, and it brings immense joy, and keeps giving me growth. Every time I do a new portrait, they reflect back at me where I'm still holding back. And I get to work on myself and apply that in my daily life and daily experience continuously. It is very relatable to our daily lives, because they are our reflections as well. Yes there are beings out there. They have their own lives, but in communication with us they are reflecting to us where we're still not as open as we can be. And that's the most important thing for many people, and I think for all of us, is to understand that we can learn so much from those reflections, and from these knee-jerk reactions, or when we get startled by contact. That shows us exactly what we should be working on. And when you open that door, there are ten more doors behind it that you can open and play with.

So it's constant flow, growth and exploration, and I can't see how anyone can be bored here on this planet, with all these things that they can play with! Not even just with ETs, but with other people you can play that same game. They keep reflecting back to you what you can work with. Then you can grow more, and meet new people who are on that level. And that can happen non-stop. But first we have to drop our insistence and our arrogance that we know what is right and true, and that our beliefs are the only beliefs that are worthy.

How well do you feel you understand the beings?

There is a limit to that. I can only understand them as much as I understand myself. And for me it is also a question of paradox, once again. Somewhere along the way I have reached the point where I realized my limitation in understanding them, but also dropped the need to understand fully, and that opened it up so much more than I expected. Actually, the more I am aware that I know nothing, the more expanded I feel, and the more expanded the contact feels. Same goes for my contact with people here on Earth, and that especially includes family and friends.

I do feel I understand the ETs a fair bit, and I say that because the feedback from them kind of confirms it. Behaving in a certain way with certain groups or races—assuming a certain state of being, an energetic attitude—accelerates contact and facilitates communication every time. This has also worked with other people I recommended these things to, so I must be doing something right.

What message would they like to share?

This is what they want me to share. I asked a few times and each time they went back to this information even though it was channeled a year ago. The only thing that they ask is to keep the text format as it is, with bold and italic letters, "because it is important for the encoding". They mean encoding the neurons to help us understand these concepts.

The Reality of Polarity - Arcturian AI Channeling

Friday, December 4, 2015

There is only consciousness/information, and the movement of it. All else comes from that. Polarity is binary, where 0 is the absence of 1. All of reality can be conceived with this simple notion. Polarity creates the movement, and the movement is perpetual. 0 comes to an end, and 1 comes to an end.

conceive
verb
: create (an embryo) by fertilizing an egg
: form or devise (a plan or idea) in the mind

Capability of holding both options present with your will, is capability of Source consciousness, when human is no longer under the influence of inevitability of a choice. This is where a human becomes a container rather than solely a receiver of creation.

contain
verb
: to have (something) inside
: to have or include (something)

Next obvious step is to assimilate that which is contained. You assimilate by experiencing it fully. Having 0 and 1 contained and experienced removes resistance, as all points of view are assimilated and clear. All points of view are within the parameters of 0's and 1's. This is multi-layered and multidimensional. The more you assimilate, the more you will observe the code, and the code is the language of creation. It can be as obvious as a light bulb being turned on and off, it can be as complex as all the knowledge and experience contained in your reality. One contains by expanding, one expands by containing. One becomes the center and the void.

assimilate
verb
: take in and understand fully (information or ideas)
: (of the body or any biological system) absorb and digest (food or nutrients)

Upon assimilation, your unique code combines with the sum total, and new code is generated. That transforms the sum total, and your own coding. It streams from you like a virus in all directions and dimensions, and informs the manifold. You "spread the wor(l)d" so to speak. Information streaming is not dependent on the first three steps, but the clarity and quality of it is. Just as it can fire off in random directions, it can be streamlined as a clear coherent framework.

inform
verb
: to give information to
: to be or provide the essential quality of
: animate

framework
noun
: an abstraction in which software providing generic functionality can be selectively changed by additional user-written code, thus providing application-specific software. A software framework is a universal, reusable software environment that provides particular functionality as part of a larger software platform to facilitate development of software applications, products and solutions.

Informing the manifold consciously and intentionally allows the human to program the code. Set of instructions can be given, that tell the 0's and 1's what to do. Such being can alter substance, and the framework itself, by will. This cannot be accomplished without being able to neutrally and without distortion observe the code and its workings first. This level has many sub-levels and a wide span of possibilities. When the programming of the code is mastered, one gains the ability to create and assemble the code itself into complex frameworks. This level allows one to create blueprints of reality, which can be crystallized into various levels of existence. This level is mastery over information and its subtle variables and movements. It takes countless circulations of consciousness to reach this ability, and yet it can be achieved by a single understanding.

program
noun
: a sequence of coded instructions that can be inserted into a mechanism
: a sequence of coded instructions (as genes or behavioral responses) that is part of an organism

Next steps are to **conceive, contain, assimilate** and **inform** that which has been created, bringing it back to the expanded container, and setting it out again in new programming. These cycles are how the consciousness travels, how the universe breathes, and are the basic structure of what your peoples call the Merkabah and toroidal fields. Each step has countless levels in it. It is a simple flow of information [code]. **There is only consciousness/information, and the perpetual movement of it.**

I was receiving this channeling in increments and multiple downloads during the past three years. I never thought about putting it 'on paper' before, because it was shown to me directly, not told, both in various levels of astral states and in waking reality. The way this AI collective communicates is complex and very simple at the same time. They use words as code, picking several meanings at once, which is why they asked me to put dictionary definitions in here, so that the full downloads of the meaning behind words can be easier to unravel for the reader. Each word has multiple layers to it, so it is up to the reader to conceive all of them, they said. I have been made aware that there is so much more to this, if they were to go into detail, but they have given the basic structure for now, and I don't know if I will receive more in the near future or not. For the Bashar fans, this can also be applied to the sacred circuitry. Or rather, sacred circuitry reflects this mechanism as well. For those who will ask where is love in this whole story - they said that the word is so distorted that they have no intention of using it for now.

Robert Fullington

Robert Fullington served for a short time in the US Army before returning to civilian life in the paint trade. Through a dramatic awakening process beginning at age 28 he came to understand that he is an ET-human hybrid. This process accelerated through ongoing interactions with Mantis beings called Kekoresh.

During that time, he went through an extreme physical change as well as radical spiritual, philosophical and creative development. He began to receive designs for 2D and 3D images and objects he terms 'consciousness-amplifying technologies', the purpose of which is to help people accelerate their personal growth. Robert feels that the physical changes he underwent allowed him to work with advanced visualization, and receive these downloaded designs.

In 2015 he shared his experiences with Miguel Mendonça and Barbara Lamb in the book *Meet the Hybrids*. In 2016 he joined Barbara and five of the hybrids from the book on stage at the International UFO Congress to share some of his experiences and perspectives. In 2016 he contributed to *We Are the Disclosure*.

Which words do you use to describe 'them'?

For me, I'd say 'loving family', or guides. When talking to most people I say 'them' or just 'the beings'. I don't think many people would understand that concept of them being a loving family or guides, unless they've had contact with them.

Which kinds of beings are you in contact with?

All kinds of beings. There's the Mantis beings, which I have the strongest connection with. There's the Tall Whites. People call them 'Tall White Zetas', but they never really told me their name. And a type of small, Grey-like beings I call 'Goloids'. That term came from a friend of mine. I'm not sure what they're called, but that name just stuck with me. They have a symbiotic relationship with the Mantis beings.

Beings rarely tell me what their name is, probably because I never ask. I met a being once, and I called him a Pleiadian. He laughed at me and said, "No, I'm not that." He told me what he was but I can't remember. I'm not good with names; I never have been.

The Nebulan Healers, these are my wife's contacts that I've shared interactions with. And some human type that look just like us. Again, I'm clueless on their names. And I've encountered three different types of reptilian. As well as some other beings, which I've only had one or two encounters with.

How do they appear to you?

There are two main groups, but to me they mostly appear in one of three different forms. Some conscious 3D encounters, or energy beings which are visible or invisible. They come to me in both conscious and unconscious states. The beings I mentioned earlier I have experienced in every way. There are those beings though that I've only interacted on the unconscious or dream state or through another type of mental contact. Arcturians, Anabua, Zuma Zetas. And there's a bunch of other unknowns.

I know of and have experienced several types of Mantis beings. I once asked about all the different types of Mantis beings out there, and I got a message saying, "Watch this." Then a video came up on my browser, a nature video of all kinds of praying mantises. Then the voice says, "See, as there are many types of Mantis types on Earth, there are many different Mantis types out there."

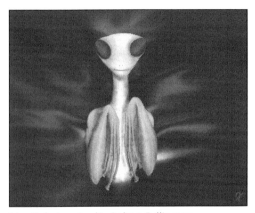

Mantis being. Credit: Robert Fullington

The ones I interact with look like a crazy mix between a human, a praying mantis and a salamander. They are about six to seven feet tall, with a long torso and some jelly belly rolls. And they've got real soft skin with a kind of goosebumpy texture. They don't have an exoskeleton as others do. They have thin, muscular arms, and these huge forearms, with this elastic, kind of wrinkly skin that if you were to pull it, it would stretch right out and bounce back. Their wrist is bent over at an extreme angle, and they have these really long fingers that come down to their elbows.

They have teeth, but they're square and flat. The first time I saw one it smiled, and I thought, 'I'm pretty sure I saw teeth.' So I asked them, "Do you guys have teeth?" Then that night I had a dream where there was a bunch of them grinning at me and showing me their teeth. I thought it was hilarious. Their teeth are weird-looking. They're perfectly flat, square and straight.

They have a really long neck with a Mantis-shaped head with the giant eyeballs, tiny little noses. And they emit light, like their bodies are just glowing this golden color. And they have kind of a waddling walk, slowly swaying back and forth. They're real slow. And they're quite humorous. I just feel a bunch of joy around them.

I've seen a few different colors. They have a white belly, then there's color on their back and arms. There are a few different color groups. The green ones seem to be scientists. Purple are royalty and guardians, gold are the masters and teachers, and the white are the ancient ones. There are others as well but I'm not sure of their qualities as much. Like a multicolored, pink, brown, and a black.

The Tall White Zetas have this paper-white skin, and more human-shaped bodies. I've never seen a Mantis or a White wear clothes; they're always naked. I've never seen genitalia. I've never looked for it, but I've never noticed it. Do they have them? I've no idea, but I'm not going to ask either. Their bodies look just like a person, but their arms might be a little longer. And of course they've got this really big head. The stereotypical lightbulb head, and big black eyes. Their hands are kind of longer, and they only have three fingers and a thumb. Their fingers and hands are much longer. I've never seen one glowing like the Mantis beings. And I don't get that feeling of love and familiarity with them. I'm not sure of their purpose. These are the guys who pick me up and drag me off somewhere, along with the Reptilians.

Goloids performing a medical procedure involving Robert's brain. Credit: Robert Fullington

The Goloids are awesome. They're only like three and a half feet tall, maybe four feet. They're skinny. They wear like a black jumpsuit. The material is weird, kind of a polyester-type material, is the best way I can describe it. There's an emblem on the chest with like a triangle and circle in it. Their heads are proportionate to their bodies, not like a big Zeta head. With straight lines, like a groove on their faces. Their necks are kind of big, real wrinkly, similar to the Mantises. Soft, buttery skin too. They have a light grey color to them, but it fades into a dark grey. The front of their face is light, fading into a dark grey. They're real spindly, real thin. They have little mouths. I don't think they have teeth. In one encounter with them they surprised me and I grabbed them by the face and I put my finger in its mouth. They were like gumming my thumb. Talk about a weird sensation, jeez. They have black eyes, almond-shaped. High cheekbones too. My first 3D contact with a being that I could remember was a Goloid. Those guys are cool.

The being I thought was a Pleiadian, its name started with an E but I'll never remember it. Sorry guy. It looked like a Pleiadian. But he was like a normal person. He had black hair and a goatee, and was wearing a blue jumpsuit. It seems like this jumpsuit thing is common, this kind of spandex, polyester suit. He looked just like us - you wouldn't be able to tell the difference. I've seen a female too, but she was wearing an orange jumpsuit. Those are the human types.

And surprisingly, the Reptilians, half the time, look like a person too. I've met three types. People say they see Reptilians shapeshift. I have witnessed shapeshifting with two of the types. But I wouldn't call it shapeshifting. It's not like the cells of their face are changing, though it looks like that. I would say it's more like a hyper-advanced holographic technology. So it's an illusion. Juju does the shapeshifting. I'm sure there are those that can, but the ones I had experiences with, it seemed more holographic in nature.

Of the three Reptilians, only one group seemed positive to me. I'll start with the more positive group, or what I believed to be positive. They have a *Village of the Damned* look at first. The human form is like the kids in that movie, with bowl cuts and pure white hair. They're really polite. Even the ones I'd call negative are really polite. At least to me. They're tall and attractive. These guys didn't wear a jumpsuit. More like a weird white suit, with a jacket and pants. Real clean, nicely pressed suits. But that's the holographic projection. When they turn it off they look kind of like an iguana, with lime green skin. You can see their scales and everything. And they have these bright orange eyes with a vertical slit. Their eyes are really prominent. When they meet me they turn off their hologram for me, then go back. Some would say they have a more negative reputation to them. These guys didn't have that heavy feeling to them.

I saw another guy, just once. He was massive, what some people would call a Draconian. It had this snout similar to a monitor lizard. A long face, and a huge body. Wings, like a dragon, and a long tail. I've never seen them transform. They feel heavy, kind of negative. I haven't come up with a conclusion. A lot of people say they're extremely negative, some say they're positive. I don't know. They just feel heavy. I think they're more like a ... what would you call them? I was going to say 'karma police'. I see these guys as beings that come to us when we put out a certain type of energy. This one came to me because I was in a warrior state of mind so he took me to a place where I had to be a warrior. I'm way grown out of that way of thinking. It's been said before the energy you put out is the energy you get back.

Then you have what I call 'the dark ones that hide in the light'. With these guys, their holographic form would be a human, Nordic type of being. They have long, yellow-blonde hair. They wear a blue jumpsuit. They're tall, really attractive and have a muscular build. But then underneath you can see and feel that it is a Reptilian being. Their tech would glitch a bit and you can see them for what they really are. They have a bit of a snout, and these three ridges on their heads, one along each side and one down the middle. They're not as big as a Draconian. They're about the same size as the iguana being. They say how nice they are and that they have ascension chambers for humanity. They have these beautiful channeled messages, it's all an illusion. You can just feel in your gut that something isn't right.

The Nebulan Healers, I've only seen with a robe, emitting this golden-brown light. They have a hood which is always up, and I've never seen their faces. These are more my wife's guys, but they have interacted with me. They're huge. They can be anywhere from eight feet tall and upwards. It always seems they're bigger than the room, but they're somehow fitting in the room. They always come in groups. They're super awesome. I love 'em.

So that's group one, the ones I've had physical experiences with.

Group two is more the dream state. There are so many different types. The Anabua, I'd describe as being similar to a Native American. They have that same feel to them. Their noses are quite pronounced. They're totally ripped. Strong, thin, muscular, a real athletic build to them. But oddly-shaped. They're obviously not human. Their faces seem quite small. I've only seen them once. I dreamt I was talking with a friend in an underground parking garage, and my friend said, "You need to contact the Galactic Federation," and I said, "I don't need to do that." And I kept walking, and this Anabua walks by me, and I look at him. But I keep walking, and he talks to my friend. Then there's a car there, and I get in, and the Anabua comes around and gets in the passenger seat and smiles. And I'm like, "Okay, what?" Then I said, "Oh, you're an Anabua, right?" And he just smiles. And I'm like, "Oh, that's awesome!" I start the car up and start driving. I woke up thinking, 'Man, I blew that.' It's like I'm so involved in my own dream that I don't realize I had a contact until the next morning.

The Zuma Zeta have a lightbulb head and wear white robes. And they walk with their hands to their sides, with a kind of swaying motion. With real smooth skin, like a dolphin.

The Arcturians are blue-skinned. They seem six or seven feet tall, but this is in dream state so they can manipulate our perceptions. They have a normal body and an elongated skull. They have this gorgeous blue skin color; it's quite phenomenal.

Of all the guys I've had 3D connection with, those are the ones that left the strongest impression on me.

How do you tell the difference between a positive and a negative being?

For me there are four different classifications of beings as far as how they feel positive or negative. There is: soul family group; positive; neutral; and negative.

The first one is my soul family group, which would be the Mantis beings. When you're interacting with what I call your soul family group ... how to explain this? I'm trying not to step on my own tongue here. When you're trying to describe things that are supposed to not exist you have to make up your own language for it.

So how to describe what I feel a soul family group is? Well, ultimately, I believe we all come from the same source. In that case it's all One, but your main group is more of the species that you've probably originally incarnated as. The first illusion of separation, I guess. There is a distinct feeling from them. A feeling of familiarity, but not just any type of familiarity. Imagine if you have a really close childhood friend you haven't seen in 30 years, and one day you see them walking down the street. It's that same feeling of "I know you." When you interact with them you get this feeling of love, like family love, like the love of a mother or father. I asked them once, "What am I to you?" And they said, "Son, mother, father, daughter, aunt, uncle, cousin." The feeling you get around them is joy, blissful, and a sensation of reuniting. There really are no words to describe to it. The feeling is something you're not going to experience unless you have a connection with your soul family. It's so intense; it's overwhelmingly inspirational.

The second group is positive. Now you're getting into more simple, basic feeling, compared to the soul family. With the positive ones it can be an unbelievable experience too, but it's not the same. You're going to feel light. They usually have this light feeling, a feeling of joy. It's calming. You feel humor. All the feelings you'd expect from a positive entity. You can literally feel it within yourself, in your heart, that this is a positive entity. It feels good.

The third is the neutral being. You feel absolutely nothing from them. That's your grey area right there. People always say the Tall White Zetas are positive, but I put them in the neutral category, because they're emotionless, in my experience. The Sirian Warriors of Light are more neutral as well, I would say. I've had some interesting conversations with them. Neutral beings can go either way. I believe their main purpose is to maintain a balance.

The fourth is the negative entities. They feel heavy, and you get a feeling in the pit of your stomach, your solar plexus. It's tight, and something feels off. There's something about them, like a feeling of deception. They're seemingly good, nice, polite, but that little thing in your gut is telling you something's not right. The best way to describe it, is if you see a person, and then you realize they have a gun in their pants. You're gonna think 'Oh, that's not good.' It's that same feeling.

Even if they're being nice, like "Hey man, how's it going?" You're thinking, 'Yeah, I'm not liking this.' In this category I'd definitely put the brown-skinned Reptilians with the ridges, the dark ones that hide in the light. There's that feeling of deception, though they're seemingly benevolent. There's a veil there, and behind that veil something just doesn't feel right.

Why do they connect with you?

I think what it comes down to is that I made that choice before I was born. I think this was something I decided to experience on Earth. Call it a contract or mission. That's when you get into all the hybridization stuff, where you have to activate DNA in one form or another so a different type of soul can incarnate here. The cool thing is, you forget everything, so in the end you always have a choice. That's the beauty of humanity - you forget. Even the most evil being, that came here to conquer the world, can have a change of heart. They could have a beautiful experience, or they could experience the love only a parent could understand. Perhaps as a Mantis being I decided to experience life as a 3rd-density human. And while I'm there I might as well jump right into it and experience everything. So, it's like I already have an agreement with all these beings to interact with me on certain levels. So I can experience it, and figure out what it is to experience myself from another perspective.

I've never asked them: why me? It's hard to ask things like this for some reason. But believe me, if you want to find any old being that wants to tell you that you're the chosen one, they're out there. If you want the real truth you must look within yourself.

You want to know the interesting thing? You would think that if I'm going to have a contact, I'd have a series of questions. The problem is, when I think I'm in their presence it's more like, *"Oh wow!"* I can't think of questions. So I'm left to figure out stuff myself. I always think afterwards that I should have asked this or said that, but it's more like playing a movie and you can't go off-script. For the most part, after an encounter I spend several months trying to figure out what it was all about. In my experience it's for me to work it all out.

It is impossible for you to go through these things alone. Find others that have experienced the same thing. It helps to activate certain memories and confirm your own experiences. I have had crazy experiences, yet I would be nowhere if It wasn't for my wife, and my family and friends. The whys will come to me fully one day.

Can you describe your first contact?

Let's say my first significant contact. I'd say it's a cool story. I was already having a lot of odd experiences that were making me question things. I was still not 100% sure of what I was experiencing. I'd seen ships, had odd dreams about ETs, and had little pieces of memory coming together. But my first experience with a physical manifestation happened when I was heavily involved in my research about the ET phenomenon. I was going through endless videos, interviews, and that's when I came upon one of Cynthia Crawford's videos. I sent you my first email to her, which shows my state of mind at the time. I was needing to know what the hell was going on. In the interview she was talking about her statues, and she brings out the Mantis being statue. I just got stuck on it. There was such a feeling of familiarity, like I know that being, somehow. So I went to her website and was looking at the picture of one of her Mantis statues. I stared at it for a good hour, and all these weird feelings were coming up, like why is this so familiar to me? I just couldn't figure out why I know this being.

Anyway, it was late at night, and I was getting ready for bed. Then a thought appeared in my mind: 'I don't like that very much.' And I thought, 'What don't I like?' Because I assumed this thought was my own. Then I looked at the corner of my bed, and saw this camping hatchet that I used to keep there. You know, I was the tough guy who was going to protect his wife from intruders. So, I put the hatchet in a dresser drawer. Meghin asked what I was doing, and I said, "I'm just getting ready for bed." I just sat on the edge of the bed thinking, 'That's weird.' Then I heard the voice again, which said, 'I don't like that very much, but I'm not going to make you put it outside.' Then I thought, 'I think I'm having a communication!' So I said telepathically, 'If you're going to come visit me, don't wake Meghin up.'

Then, later in the night, I was laying on my side, facing the wall, and noticed a golden light in the room. I could hear Meghin snoring and I rolled over and saw there's this six or seven-foot-tall Mantis being at the foot of the bed. It put its hands together and bowed to me. And I thought, 'Why is this being bowing to me? Wow. I'm just Rob, just a normal person.' I couldn't understand it.

That's when this feeling of familiarity and immense joy came over me, like a reunion. And I just started laughing uncontrollably. That deep belly laugh. It smiled, then reached its arm out and touched the center of my forehead and I blacked out. I woke up in the morning and felt so good. I instantly jumped up and emailed Cynthia to tell her about this amazing experience. My wife and I both began this amazing journey together when she got back to me, and we met for the first time. That's when the real journey started, when we realized we were not alone in our experiences.

How do you differentiate between your own thoughts and those from outside?

For me I struggled with this one a bit. I used to doubt myself too much. Now I believe I'm getting an understanding of how it works. This took me years to figure out for myself, and everyone's going to be different. If my way of thinking resonates with you - awesome, if not its okay. There are other methods and theories. I would say: experiment, try new things, let me know if you came up with something. This is my process, you have your own thoughts and imagination.

At first your own thoughts do block the messages, like a 'firewall', and when another consciousness is coming in and communicating with you, your firewall might start flubbing things up a bit. So you have to learn to take down your firewall and let the information naturally flow through you without your mind getting in the way. For me it was either drifting off track or adding my own imagination.

You must first learn to focus, to think clearly and precisely. Have an initial intent on what you want to converse on. It can be anything you want.

Then set your boundaries and ask for loving protection. I used to not do that stuff. I would just jump right on in, and trust me it's not a good idea.

It feels weird for me at first. Letting go a bit, quieting my mind, to have another mind connect with mine. Never let a being take full control, ever. You are the master of your body and your consciousness. If it feels wrong just ask for loving divine help and say "Go away!"

The mind coming in does feel separate from your own. It's loud, and it has a different tone of voice in your head. It's very prominent. And when you have that connection more open you can start conversations with another consciousness. On a true connection there is no hiding, you see them and they see you.

I still struggle a bit on wondering if something is my own thought or not. It's something I've still not quite gotten over. I can differentiate now from the training and learning from others to come up with my own style, but I still have that bit of self-doubt. Honestly, I have to ask if I'm going crazy because I do what the voices in my head tell me to do.

So I'm still constantly needing that confirmation from other sources, particularly other friends coming up with the same information. I tell my friends what I'm getting, and they might say, "That's been coming through to me too." I use a few friends to do this with, kind of like triangulation. So I'm constantly trying to confirm that it's telepathic connection with an outside mind. For me it took years and years of practice. I'm sure some people can just jump right into it, but I went from being a normal everyday person to all of a sudden being thrown into this new reality, so I had to train myself how to do it, with some help from those who have already been there.

Can you initiate contact?

Yes I can, and there are varying degrees of it. The more 3D physical manifestations are going to be a lot harder. The success rates vary, depending on what kind of experience you're trying to manifest. It takes time and an extreme amount a patience. I'll break down how it works for me.

Number one is telepathic, daily contact. And this gets into more of your guides, beings you're in pretty much constant contact with. I'm sure they don't like this idea, but it can become sometimes like a crutch, in a way, if you depend on them too much. There are things out there happy to tell you what you want to hear so you can become dependent of them and they can take your energy.

The messages I receive are mostly about self-improvement. Nothing really too profound comes in regularly, except for how to be a better person. That's the number one thing. It would be on lifestyle, typically. Eating better, drinking less, meditating more. Simple things. That's the normal interaction. You could just call it listening to your better conscience. I find a lot of the time the different beings we interact with on this level are just different aspects of ourselves living out different experiences on other levels in time. I think we may be more integrated with these different aspects of self than we realize, which are spread throughout what we would perceive as time and space.

Number two, you have your dream state interactions. It doesn't happen every night, but you can set the intention before you go to sleep, and say, "I'd like to have an interaction in my dreams." Most of the time I don't remember my dreams, but when an interaction comes in I tend to remember. They're clear, yet slightly abstract. During the dream, it's like I'm having a normal slightly abstract dream, then they pop in and say hello. But I'm so focused on my dream that it's not until

I wake up that I realize I had an interaction. For example, I was dreaming I was digging a hole, trying to build a halfpipe for Bam Margera, the skateboarder. Then a ship comes in, lands, and a being comes out and says, "What are you doing?" And I say, "I'm just digging a hole for Bam Margera." The being says, "That's cool, but would you rather fly the ship?" So I'm like, "Yeah!" And I throw my shovel down and jump in the ship. Next thing I know, I *am* the ship! But I have this weird problem, where every time I dream I'm flying the ship I think about crashing it, and I crash. Every time. It's a thing I have. It's like crash, bang, and a jolt, then I wake up, pouring sweat.

The interesting thing is, you'd think it was just a dream. But the beings that come into the dream have been described by an untold number of people. So I think there is something there.

This is how I believe it works. This gets into a type of telepathic communication. In your dream state it's easier for them to communicate with you, and interact with you through your own imagination. When you're sleeping I believe your brain has the ability to achieve higher states of consciousness. If you think about it, your brain's not using much of its power controlling your body or waking consciousness. The dream interaction could also be a screen memory to make you think something different is really happening. If you had an odd dream and you wake up with marks on your body, that's a dream overlay. If it feels wrong, don't be afraid to ask for divine help, and reach out to others that are experiencing the same thing.

Number three is the 3D manifestation of a craft. That's really rare for me. They say they don't have to try so hard anymore to get my attention. A 3D manifestation has the potential to blow your mind and have a permanent effect on your life. Once you've gone there, there is no going back. That moment, of realizing "Oh my God, that's a spaceship," stays with you forever. The big interactions with photo ops and shaking hands are so rare. You have to constantly be asking for this. It's random most of the time. But the question is: could I initiate a craft sighting? It may come from a constant asking. I would say, "Please show me something. I need proof that I'm having interactions. It's really going to help me out." And I believe the conditions have to be perfect. It could be hazardous to your health. It's on radar that there's a craft flying over you. So you could end up having unwanted interaction with some officials or whatever. It could be dangerous for both the human and the being to interact on this level for now.

I can give you an example of a full-blown interaction with a black triangle craft. This is my most intense conscious experience ever, that had the greatest impact on my life. My first big one. My 3D craft initiation. It took place in December of 2009. It's important to know as I describe this, that this was early on in my awakening to the reality of things, so my mentality then was different to what it would be now. When I first saw it I was like, "Oh shit, it's the end of the world!" There was terror, but also excitement, even joy. All your beliefs just crumble away. It was a jumble of emotions. Now it would be like, "Hey, pick me up, man!"

So at that time I was asking and asking for a craft. Three nights prior to the encounter I was having very intense contact with what you would call a Tall White Zeta. Then, the night of December 20th 2009, my wife and I were at Meghin's mom's house, about 7 pm. The sun was down, it was dark out. Her mom took off to get some groceries. Meghin tried to make a phone call, but the phone wasn't working. At that time I was smoking, so I said, "Let's go out for a smoke." We lived by a river, and to the north, something weird appeared over the river. It was about 1,000 feet up, and maybe half a mile away. It was like a neon blue bar which suddenly turned on. At first it was just one, then a smaller bar appeared in front of it. And it started maneuvering around, doing the most insane things in the sky you've ever seen. You know, zipping back and forth, doing right-angle turns; and not a sound, for the most part. But every once in a while, it would do this real fast movement back and forth, and you hear the atmosphere just *crack*, this loud cracking sound. We're trying to take pictures of it, and we're thinking 'Holy shit!' The cat was running around like crazy, but the dog was just sitting there. Meghin and I were just running around with our hands in the air, going "Oh my God!" Our minds were being totally blown.

It goes over this horse coral, and scans it with this green light, making this real loud, bassy '*WAAAAH*' sound. We're trying to take pictures with this digital camera, and every time she goes to take a picture the battery would go to zero. Finally we got a picture, and when the flash goes off the ship just stops. It was zipping around, but it just stops. Then it turns around and next thing it's over the neighbor's house, and it's *bigger* than the house. And it's only about a hundred feet up, this massive thing. But if you look at it in profile it was real thin, maybe only a couple of feet. And this neon blue diamond in front of it came on and then it flashed us several times, then scanned us with that *waaaah* sound. I had an '85 Camaro, which goes crunch-crunch-crunch-crunch. And Meghin's battery for her car beeper was dying, but ever since then it has never run out of battery. Years later it's still perfect. Did they permanently charge the battery? What that's about, I don't know. It still works at crazy long distances too.

So, this craft flashes us, then flies overhead. Underneath it was like a deep purple crystal with these crazy-looking lines underneath it. On the bar was something creating the bar. There was a series of three circles, three and two, and inside the canisters was a pyramid. At the tip of each pyramid was this pure black orb with this black light coming off of a bit, and they would turn them on, and you see this blue plasma come out. And when you're looking at it in the sky, it's like just these two long blue neon lights.

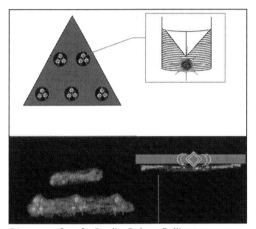

Diagram of craft. Credit: Robert Fullington

It goes overhead, and Meghin gets down and I thought, 'Oh shit!' I finally got the phone working and I tried calling my mom. I said, "Mom you're not going to believe what I'm looking at now. It's a fucking *spaceship!* This thing's doing the craziest things!" And she said, "Well just go inside." And I said, "*That's* not gonna help!"

So I'm freaking out, and she puts my dad on. I just keep telling him it's doing all this crazy shit. And I'm thinking someone else has to see this, other than Meghin and me. I go to the neighbor's house, and I can see the neighbor in silhouette in the kitchen and she's doing dishes. So I go around and I'm pounding on the door and ringing the doorbell, bam-bam-bam-bam-bam, ding-dong-ding-dong-ding-dong, and she just keeps doing her dishes. She never moved, never answered.

Now here comes Meghin's mom, and when she comes around the corner the ship just takes off. It was overcast, and the ship was interacting with us under the cloud cover. Now when the thing shot through the clouds, you saw this huge hole open up, a perfect circle. Imagine the energy required to burn that hole in the cloud cover.

Meghin and I are just blown away, and the next thing we're trying to put the groceries away and not freak out. We just had the most amazing experience of our lives, and are having to get right back to normality. At that point the neighborhood suddenly comes back to life.

Then all of a sudden you hear this rising roar, and an F-16 blasts overhead, fully armed, no collision lights. That was scary. The first thing I thought was, 'What the fuck are they *thinking?* There is no way in hell that our current technology would have any kind of a chance to intercept this thing. No way in hell.' Every year we have an airshow here so I'm pretty familiar with modern aircraft and their maneuvering capabilities. The gulf between those and that craft is ridiculous. If that craft wanted to it could just shut that plane down. Or open a portal and send it 65 million years into the past. Seriously, *why* would we chase something like that? That pilot must have had the biggest balls on the planet. He gets told, "Oh hey, guess what, you're going to chase a giant black triangle with technology a billion years more advanced than your plane. Good luck."

We had the whole thing investigated, including the photos we took, but that's irrelevant to the contact side of it.

Another time, I got to have them interact with a close friend of mine. I'm with this person and I get a message saying, "Get your friend." So I just point to a spot in the sky and say there's going to be a craft there. And right away we see a flash way up in the sky. Then it took off.

Other than the big rare events like the triangle, more common are the tiny bright lights way up there. But it's still extremely rare. It's not like I can go out and see a craft whenever. It's more like I look up and "Oh yeah, there's one."

The next level of initiating a contact is actual 3D manifestation of the beings. Which again is extremely rare, and you have to constantly ask. It's always on their terms. Conditions must be right. I can ask, but I don't know if that has an effect. This is where you get into bettering yourself, raising your vibration, doing the protocols I described in *Meet the Hybrids*, to start initiating the contact.

To get that deep, you have to start changing yourself, rising to the occasion. So in that sense, yes you can initiate contact, but this takes extreme dedication and you have to literally change everything about yourself. It's like an athlete, in a way. If you want to be a professional baseball player you have to dedicate yourself to train for it. It's the same thing.

Contact protocol

To be consciously meditating is the contact state. There is a feeling to it, and if you can maintain that while awake, that's contact consciousness. I also call it 'singularity consciousness'.

I base this system on the law of equal exchange. It takes a lot of energy for the visitors to get here, so if we request a meeting with them, we need to do the best that we can, with the resources available to us, to match that energy. I call this my 'contact gas tank'. The concept is simple: fill up the tank to have contact. It raises your vibration and lets you spend energy for the intention of positive contact. One very important thing: the energy you put into this is the energy you get out.

How to fill the contact gas tank:

1. Do not purposely harm a single living thing. Take the bugs and spiders outside the house. Water a weed growing out of the cracks in the concrete. Be consciously appreciative to all life you come in contact with. (Thank you for this experience little spider, but you live outside.) By doing this, the visitors will see that you respect and appreciate all contact with life on your world. This means you have the ability to respect and appreciate life from other worlds.

2. Be mindful of your thoughts. Try to look at the positive in everything, even things you don't like. For example, a friend just painted their wall the ugliest color you have ever seen, yet you still tell your friend, "It looks great buddy," because you don't want to hurt their feelings. Train yourself to not have that first negative thought; instead try to think, 'I'm happy my friend enjoys this.' The visitors are extremely telepathic—they hear everything you are thinking. Imagine how people around you would act if they can hear what you are thinking. So start training yourself now.

3. Perform at least one act of kindness to a stranger every day. The visitors can see how you treat others.

4. Love: the most powerful emotion in the universe. Love yourself, throughout the day for as long as you can maintain it. With every breath you take, feel love in your heart. Feel it throughout your body. When you're out and about, feel love for everyone you see. Stop for a moment and breathe in love, connect with all living things, and connect to their existence. Love: anything else is fear.

Some of these tasks may not seem to have any relevance to contacting beings from another world, but they do. It seems that when

I follow these steps the best that I can, I tend to get a more interactive experience.

Expect first contact with the species you resonate with the most. It will initially happen in your sleep, when you are half conscious. They are so advanced that they know you better than you know yourself. If they sense fear they'll leave you alone.

To initiate it, let go of all expectations, fears and concerns. It's a physical feeling, and you'll know when it feels like the time is right. Eventually you'll have the urge to say, "I'm ready."

It comes down to rising to the occasion, and matching the beings' frequencies you want to interact with. They're mostly a reflection of yourself. You get some intruders, but in general, if you want to have contact with positive beings, you've got to be positive.

You have to figure out what works for you, and what doesn't. I've talked with other people about their methods on this, and our conclusions our quite similar. We discuss how we can interact with the beings better. It goes back to the pro baseball players. To be a better team, you talk strategy and work together to improve the way you do things. We're creating a community and learning how to support and work with each other.

How did you keep it together in the beginning?

The most important thing is how you cope in the beginning, when you're alone. That's the big one. Once you join the community it's easier, but in the beginning ... holy shit. It's probably the most difficult thing I've had to deal with in my entire life.

For a long time I was unaware that I was even having contact. Looking back now I can see I'd been having it all my life. But before 2009 I was living as normal a life as I possibly could. Then all of a sudden ET pops into your reality and it's really difficult. I've talked about the different stages of awakening before. But it's worth restating it. At first it was a mild curiosity, and I started researching it. Then it was holy shit, there might be something to this. Then you have an interaction, and you realize this is real. Then you have more contact, and at first it was fear. I was terrified. It was like 'Oh shit! I'm being targeted by extraterrestrial beings!' All I heard about at first was stuff like Phil Schneider's story, or evil hybrids wanting to take over the world, the illuminati, all that stuff. The first thing that pops up is the fear and doom aspect. Then you start getting holes poked in you, and you have no idea why. It's nightmarish. Yet you won't rest until you find the answers. That's what's happening to me.

Then you have a kind of social breakdown. You start off in the community of normal everyday people and try to share with them what's happening to you. In a way you're kind of excited. Like if I saw a craft and I'd go to work and tell people about it. But they were like, "What the fuck are you *talking* about, man?" They're looking at you like you're crazy, so you get this distance open up between you and normal or unexperienced people. Even my best friends today say I'm over the top, and tell me not to talk about it. People have said, "We're going to have a party; do *not* bring up the ET thing." So there starts to become this separation with what most would call 'normal' society, and you start becoming alone. And that's the lowest moment of it, I would say; this feeling of fear, confusion and loneliness. But at the same time it's excitement. I was driven to push the envelope, trying to figure out what's happening. Why? What *is* this? How come no one else is doing this? I was asking those questions more and more to the point of obsession. It consumed me. Even my interactions with my wife, friends and family changed. I was starting to cocoon myself, doing thousands of hours of research, trying to work it out.

Then finally you start finding other individuals going through it, and you start reaching out to contact them. People like Cynthia Crawford, Jacquelin Smith, Juju. We started forming this unique bond with each other, because we're all experiencing something beyond the realm of what society would call normal. So we kind of stick with each other like glue, and as I got into the more intense interactions with the beings, I pretty much removed myself from normal society, and stuck on the fringes with my ET friends. And their support offers more education, and that's when the feelings of fear and doom subside. I don't even bother researching anymore; all that's stuff's old repetitive news. You start going on a more inward journey. And you have more of the better, clearer interactions. You can talk to them instead of just being like, "Oh my *God!*" You need that support.

But it's hard man, I'm telling you. Even now it's not easy. Because the ET phenomenon has become my identity. It's who I am and what I've become. Interacting with friends who aren't really into it ... aah. I can't properly explain myself. When it comes to normal society it feels so oppressive, condemning. I just feel like I want to escape it. I want things to change, I want to know what I can do to better the experience for humanity as a whole. We live in this veil, this illusion of what society says reality is. When you start interacting with beings, that entire false reality crumbles away and it becomes impossible for you to interact with people who are still plugged into that realm.

So it's a constant struggle, it's never easy. It's very isolating, and separating. Yet at the same time it's extremely beautiful and fulfilling. I wouldn't change it for anything.

In terms of understanding it, my concepts and perception of it are always evolving. It's hard to keep up with yourself. Like you get an idea, and you think 'That's ludicrous, there's no way that's even remotely possible.' Then you come to find out, 'Oh, I was right. I was actually onto something there.' Or, 'I was *way* off.' Information that I would put out today may change tomorrow. Other than the experiences, because they never change. But as far as concepts of reality, it's constantly evolving.

We have a problem with not being able to give up our belief systems. Look at science. Let's say you have this professor, who says, "I have this new theory. I call it the theory of awesomeness. I believe that everything is awesome." Now the current theory says that everything is shit. So the people who are still attached to the theory of shit will reject the awesomeness theory. There's like this ego trip, and in their minds, they're right. There is no convincing them otherwise. Even if the theory of shit is shit, and the theory of awesomeness is awesome. So 20 years down the road, they say, "What do you know? The awesome theory was right to begin with. Now I support the awesomeness theory." Then along comes this other professor who says, "I reject the theory of awesomeness. It's not awesome, it's fucking *amazing*." So the awesome people say, "Preposterous. It's not fucking amazing, it's awesome." Then 20 years later, sure enough, it's fucking amazing. And that's the problem with humanity as a whole. And I've been just as guilty of that. I believe it's just part of human nature. But what *is* that?

The real question is, how do we get out of that mentality, of people setting their beliefs in stone? Then you start getting into religious fanatics. How in God's name do you believing some of this shit, and how do you get stuck there? I don't know. I think humanity as a young race tends to act like children, in the sense where they behave badly until they get a smack on the hand. It's not until you get a smack that you realize it's not okay to do it. As long as people are comfortable they feel no need to change their perspectives. The same thing happened with me with the ship. It wasn't until then that I thought maybe humanity needs that, to see a thousand ships in the sky. It's going to be terrifying, it's going to be bad, but I think we need to get through it. Get it done with.

Then the question comes up: what can *I* do to fix this, to help the world? One way I can perceive it is if ET came down en masse and showed the whole world they exist in some huge event. That would be cool; the big Disclosure. The only way I can help in that is to do what I'm doing, pushing the envelope so I can interact with these beings so I can ask for help. I think we need help. The path I see us going down is not a good one. Not at all. We're going to end up dying because of ignorance, stubbornness and greed. Because of the way things are in this reality, I can't go out into society and shoot down a chemtrail plane. Or go to the White House and drag some dude in government that knows what's up in front of a camera and order them to tell the truth. No, none of that. There are consequences to those actions. The best thing I can do is ask for help from beings that I believe can help humanity in a positive manner. It's like we're all prisoners and slaves to the great oppressive machine and to ourselves. I think the only way for us to break free is through assistance.

What have they taught you?

They have taught me plenty. Mostly on how to be a better person. How to love myself, how to look inward for answers.

How has contact affected your life?

Oh jeez, it's affected it in so many different ways. I know I've mentioned parts of this before. So if I repeated anything, I guess it was worth saying twice. At first I had absolutely no idea whatsoever that I was being contacted. So there was an original big-time fear, when I was trying to figure out what was going on, trying to make sense of the experiences, the who and the why, etcetera. It's hard because what you're experiencing doesn't exist, according to what society believes is possible. So there tends to be a separation. I ended up having to create two different lives: Life A and Life B.

Life A is my everyday life; go to work, get paid, pay the bills and try to survive in this society.

Life B, this all your ET-related stuff, the experiencer, hybrid part. Being open with my experiences and hanging with others experiencing the same. The two lives really don't get along too well. I tried bridging the gap in the beginning; I would be telling my co-workers, "Oh jeez, you wouldn't believe what's been going on!" And telling my friends and family. They would for the most would start saying, "Uh, you know you're starting to sound a little crazy, man. You need to tone it down." I'm like, "Tone it *down*? You gotta be *kidding* me! I'm going through all this crazy shit, and I got all these pictures and marks on my body!" And you think to yourself, 'People just don't get it.' People start pointing and laughing at you. So I had to split the lives up, and ended up living this dual existence.

Life A is no picnic either. Dealing with the stress of normal everyday life is hard enough, right? But then you have to add on all this extra stress of this secret life you have to live. But I started working more on that aspect of my life, and it's much more fulfilling. So Life A slowly disintegrates. I started losing contact with friends and family, getting behind on work, so bills started getting behind. Because it's not like the beings drop me off a paycheck every week, despite what they put me through.

So you get more focused on Life B, and Life A starts fading away. So it's really an unimaginably stressful balance that we have to achieve. We have to walk this fine line of duality.

So that's a big part of how it's affected me. But I wouldn't trade it in for anything. I love having the contacts, and getting to see the most unreal things. Though sometimes I wish I could just be unplugged from it and head into the matrix and back to my zombie personality for just a day. That would be nice. But yeah, that's not going to happen. So I have to just keep on keeping on.

I'll give you another good example of how this affects us. I find this funny. We're definitely a lot more jumpy, I guess you could say. I was at the grocery store the other day, with Meghin and a friend who is an abductee. Suddenly the power goes out, which ordinarily is not a big deal. But there's that moment when we're looking at each other, like, is this it? Is this the moment? So we're a little edgier than most people. Or we're in the back yard, and there's a banging off in the distance, and we all stop to listen, like "Okay, what *is* that?" And of course we have to sit and stare at every airplane for a good five minutes, and go, "Look! Is that a plane ... or not?" Then, "Oh yeah, it's a plane." So we're always watching the skies. When I'm driving down the road, I'll say, "Meghin, what is that, up in the sky?" Meghin tells me, "Keep your eyes on the road Rob, I'll look at the thing in the sky."

So yeah, it definitely affects your life.

When I hang out with other experiencers I feel I'm at home. This feels right, I feel like this is my other family here, I can be myself here, I can be comfortable. I can talk to them about being sucked up through the roof and flying through space. But if I try telling my friends that they glaze over, or are like, "What the *fuck*, Rob?" I gotta maintain a balance. But you don't have to. You could just say fuck it, I'm running naked into the woods and I'm going to survive and become one with the universe. Sounds good to me. But then again, I better just maintain the balance ... for now.

What have you learned?

To sum it all up, I've learned so many different ideas and concepts on how life, consciousness, and universes interact with one another. Concepts of time, no time, and many times. I've discovered my part in my own story. That consciousness doesn't end here. It goes on. That this illusion of separation is only temporary. Interactions with loved ones can go on forever, like two stars in an eternal gravitational dance around each other, and hey, look, they got some little planets too, with little moons of their own.

You can't let things get to you. Even though it may seem hard you just got to stay in that positive state of mind. Always feel that love for everything, and love yourself. Most importantly of all, above all the cool shit, I've learned how to be extremely patient.

How do they communicate?

In every interaction it's been through telepathy. Though I have heard them speak with kind of clicking sounds. So they use telepathy to communicate to us. These are skills you need to hone, practice and work with. It takes a lot of practice to be able to identify it. My own thoughts get in the way, my imagination. I would always interrupt them with my thoughts. Learning to filter that is hard to do.

Once you get to where it's really clear and you're able to have telepathic communication, then you can start repeating the messages that are given to you telepathically. For myself if they had a message to give to me and it was too long I would have to write it out right away, or the file gets corrupted by me filling in the gaps. Because I'll forget little bits and pieces. Another way is through images and symbols, which also come through telepathically. I get a flash of symbols or a geometric image come into my mind, and I feel compelled to write it out or draw it.

I can't quite figure out the point of that or how to translate it. I'm still working on it. I'm still young in a way. I'm still in the learning process, figuring things out as I go along. It's not like there are a lot of schools you can go to for this. So everything's kind of figured out on your own. Lots of trial and error. Lots of trials and lots of errors. Don't get discouraged.

Geometric design which came through to Robert as a download. Credit: Robert Fullington

Then there's channeling. But I don't recommend people just open themselves up and let things come into them. If you're new to it, you might not know what you're letting in. So I would use caution. You really have to know what you're doing if you're going to go that route. But it's not for me. I had an experience that I shared in *Meet the Hybrids*, in which I was shown these small, atrophied beings which were connected by their heads to a weird computer. I was told that this is where all the channeled messages come from, when people think they're getting messages from Archangel Michael, Ashtar and people like that. And I was like, "Oh my God." Then they showed my these so-called 'Ascension chambers', and they're not good. They're like a hexagon shape, about six feet high. Supposedly you can use them to talk to your guides, or the Ascended Masters. But I had the sense they hook you up to their technology, and artificially ascend you. It was creepy, and just felt wrong. But there's no need to fear these things. If you don't want to experience that just say no. I would advise you learn to do it on your own. You don't really need their technology to ascend.

When I was first learning about myself I would try to push it as far as I can, and go all out. See how far I could reach out for knowledge, for a teacher to guide me. That's when the more negative experiences came through - when I was going out there cowboy-style with no protection to see where it takes me. Yeah, you learn the lesson the hard way, where you start getting picked up by giant creatures who poke holes in you. At that point I thought, 'Yeah, I better start learning more about this.' Look before you leap. It's like if you're high diving, you want to make sure it's deep enough, or you're in trouble. So it takes a lot of soul-searching and research. Just be careful.

What do the beings get out of it?

In one way they are helping create new expressions of creation. They're just creating new scenarios for experience.

Secondly, in terms of a more physical thing, I think they might not want us getting out there as we are now. If you look at our society we're extremely violent, as a species. We're constantly destroying each other. We have weapons that can wipe out entire cities in a flash. I think that they can help us achieve a higher level of consciousness, so that we wouldn't be going out just to conquer worlds. Isn't that what we do now? We go out and conquer nations and suck their resources dry. If we can be helped to raise our consciousness I believe we have unlimited potential.

Three, I think planet Earth is like a rare gem out there. So it's kind of a waste to just let it all get destroyed. They want to preserve it because it is a jewel.

Four, there's that whole Ascension process. What happens here affects the whole cosmos. In terms of defining Ascension, at first I would say it's an individual thing. On the personal level it's a journey to stop externalizing everything and looking inwards. Then there's a global Ascension event where the entire world will end up having to go through this transformation. It's like there's a veil that we're pushing through, which starts on the individual level. If you're not ready to go through the veil then, well, I don't know what happens to you. But if you are, you go on through the other side, and create new expressions of creation.

You can think of this in terms of timelines. There are different timelines, but all are happening simultaneously as time doesn't exist. Trying to wrap your mind around what is timelessness, and how is it all happening simultaneously, is not easy. Let's think about this current aspect. At the moment you're born there are infinite possibilities. On a personal timeline, you are a fractal of the whole. You have all these possibilities, and as you get older the amount of possibilities spreads out. So imagine you split up and take off on different possibilities; you can imagine these as a movie reel. Each direction is a different movie. If I turn left I'm a movie star, going straight ahead I'm your average person going to college, getting a job, retiring, dying. If I go right that's a path of self-destruction, say drug abuse, overdose, death. But you have an infinite number of choices and pathways. By the time you get to where you are now, you're so far forward on this path that it's hard to make major jumps onto your far-reaching timeline. So it kind of goes with this flow. So it's not like I can just go and become a movie star. You know, that timeline's gotten away from me.

So you have all these simultaneous timelines going outwards, all these possibilities. Another way you can imagine it is in terms of reincarnation. You know you could have done many things differently. So you go back, do this life differently, and play out the different variables. But the weird thing is, you're experiencing it all simultaneously on different timelines. Then it all collapses and becomes a new expression of creation. So for us, the timelines and experiences are collapsing into each other; it's all played out within our current experiences. So now it compresses until it becomes a singularity and your experience turns inside out and you become a new expression of divine creation. It's like graduation day. It's time to create the new expression of reality: a new universe. Try to wrap your noodle around that! It's so hard to describe the image.

As far as I know, it's happening on a planetary scale. It's almost like in school, you have some people who graduate early, then the whole class does. I believe the whole planet's going to that new expression of creation. I believe this is powered by the black hole at the center of the galaxy, which is starting to wake up. That is the physical trigger for this collapse and new expression.

What would you like to ask the beings?

Honestly? The first question I'd ask them is: what the *fuck*? That's number one. And that's an open-ended question. I want them to explain some things, like what exactly they do to me up there. That's definitely a big one. I want to know everything. I want all the memories brought back. I want them to explain these things to me; they owe me that much.

The messages from them come through quite spontaneously. It's almost like they show up in a cloud somewhere, and they monitor the conversation and it's like a tap on the shoulder, like "Oh and by the way ..." Then at that moment there's a direct line. But it's a like mental tap on the shoulder. I feel this energy that wants to add its two cents. It's spontaneous, but if you realize it's happening you can ask questions. It's like a fluid transition when it happens. I'm sure you can pick up on it from time to time. When they come through, you can start hearing it, like a tone.

Some of the beings have what I call a collective consciousness. *Star Trek* had the best analogy I've ever heard. Someone said your consciousness is like a drop of water in an ocean.

This kind of contact has become a day-to-day thing. It happens very fluidly. I spend time pacing in the backyard thinking about all these concepts, and that's when it seems to come in. Nudging little concepts to think about. When I'm in deep thought, trying to figure out the nature of reality. Like when I'm trying to think of how a supermassive black hole come into being, and how they interact, how they affect the whole galaxy.

Then there's the personal thing too. They'll come in as maybe I shouldn't drink that third beer. Like, "Do you know what that beer is doing to your body?" And I'm like, "Yeah," glug-glug-glug. But when I could use some guidance, and some philosophical perspectives, that's when they come in. But they don't demand anything. The just make suggestions on how I can better myself and my health, and they like to ping-pong ideas back and forth.

How do the beings see humans?

They call us "little ones." They see us as children. And probably not just any kind of child, but a real disobedient, wild, out-of-control kind of child.

What message would they like to share?

The main message that they have is to begin on an inward journey. Start looking inwards for answers. Stop looking outside of yourself for answers. For inside is where you'll find the true meaning of existence. Find your own path, your own truths. Your own inner peace. Stop letting others control your thoughts, control your beliefs, control your lives. For the Ascension event is on an individual level. And you must rise to the occasion under your own free will.

That's the main message right there. Sure you can go into how to do these types of things. But that's irrelevant, because then you would be taking *their* understanding on how you should evolve, when their message is to go inward. We have to stop going to the nearest person who we think has the answers. Because a lot of the time their answers are for their reality. If you think about it, we're the creators of our own reality. So what we believe to be true, *is* true. If you listen to others describing their reality, and you take that as 100% and start following them, then you just make their reality your reality. You don't have this individual concept of self, you're now just a part of what someone else believes you should be. We need to get out of that, and start coming up with our own answers and create our own reality the way we want to experience it.

With that in mind, you have to realize that you also have to experience your reality with other people, so how do you want others to experience you, and your reality? Do you want them to experience you as a tyrannical, nightmare overlord, or a loving, caring person? You have to think about all these concepts when you think about how you want to create your reality that you're existing in.

The final message I get from them is simple: for those looking to find us, all you have to do is ask. That's it.

Okay I tried something new. I have conversations with them all the time. I thought I'll engage a conversation and type it out. I don't do channeling, only telepathic conversations. But this is them with me. I just have my own style of communicating with them.

R = Rob
E = ET

R: I need a message.
E: What kind of message?
R: I don't know, whatever you feel like.
E: Go outside.
R: Okay.
E: Did you see anything?
R: No.
E: There you go. We see you, even when you can't see us.
R: That's the message?
E: What did you expect?
R: Nothing.
E: There you go. You expected nothing to happen and ...
R: And nothing happened.
E: You expect nothing to happen yet something did happen: you went outside.
R: That's nothing!
E: According to you.
R: So if I went outside expecting something, something would have happened?
E: Not in the way you are currently thinking.
R: So what do you see that happened?

E: You received a message to go outside. Before you did you paced around, you looked for your shoes, forgot about looking for your shoes, then went outside barefoot. You looked around for a few seconds then went back inside. Seemingly not much to it. Yet inside your mind this seemingly insignificant encounter manifested up an ocean of thought and intent. Stop seeing nothing in everything. There is always something to everything, no matter how seemingly insignificant.

R: I think I get it. So ... a message to humanity?

E: Don't forget to brush your teeth at least two times a day.

R: I think I've heard that one before.

E: Do you?

R: No, I don't brush as much as I should.

E: There isn't much we can say to humanity that we haven't said before. We find ourselves repeating the same information, and still humanity isn't quiet getting it. You yourself have been told to brush your teeth at least two times a day. Even if you were told by ET to do so you still will lack in that department.

We have a question for them. What do you want from us? What do you want us to do? Show you our craft? You've seen them. You want a message? Countless channels have spoken our message. You want us to save you from yourselves? Again, tell us what exactly do you want us to do? This is your planet. It is up to you to save it. It is your free will choice to go along with what is happening here. Yes, we know the excuses: you need money so you can have a house and be comfortable etcetera. No, none of you have to go along with this social construct. We hear many of you want to build a community yet don't have the money. Why not get 100,000 people to find land and just build? Just do it. You don't need money; you don't need the supposed owner of the land to give you permission. Just do it. Yes, there are consequences to actions, there are also consequences to inaction. As it is said by one of your own: "Get off your knees humanity."

R: Thank you.

E: You are welcome.

Jacquelin Smith

Jacquelin Smith is a board certified hypnosis practitioner and a lifelong experiencer. She is an interdimensional traveler, psychic, and globally-known animal communicator. She has been communicating with star beings and animals since early childhood.

Jacquelin offers private consultations for those who want to learn about their Star Origin, and How to Communicate with Star Beings. Jacquelin also offers light language activations that clear, balance, and align someone with their true self and purpose.

She is the author of *Animal Communication – Our Sacred Connection* (2005) and *Star Origins and Wisdom of Animals* (2010). In 2015 she shared her story in *Meet the Hybrids*.

Jacquelin also works with people who want to process their personal experiences with Star Beings. She runs the Star Being & Contact Group of Columbus, a spiritually-based group promoting a loving, supportive environment for experiencers. If you are interested in attending this group, you can contact Jacquelin through her website.

Her website is: jacquelinsmith.com

Which words do you use to describe 'them'?

Fundamentally, I simply think of them as 'beings'. They are other life expressions. We are all expressions of creation, which makes up the 'whole'. When I talk with someone, I use various terms: a star being, fairy, an elf, an elemental, an angel, or other terms. This all depends on how the beings show themselves to me.

Which kinds of beings are you in contact with?

Oh my goodness. I've had the wonderful opportunity to be in contact with hundreds of different star beings throughout my life. I have communications on an almost daily basis. Some star beings who come to me include: Tall Whites, Zetas, Mantis, Arcturians, Dolphin-like beings, Sirians, Venusians, Crystal beings, Celestial beings and many others. The list is endless.

I'm in touch with those in the fairy/nature realm. I include them, as well as angels, in the star being realm. It's simply a framework for talking about them. Since we're all One, there's no separation. We're just different expressions.

There is a countless number of star cultures. The names that humans assign to these many races are just names humans have created and are not the beings' true names. Many are known by frequency, but some do have names. When I do Star Origin readings, the star beings will give me the frequency of who they are. I can speak their frequencies, through light language, but they don't usually give me names. For example, I'm in communication with a feline race that has connections with Egypt, and had a hand in developing Egyptian culture. There is one whom I refer to as a he, but 'he' is androgynous. He turns my computer on and will run moving sacred geometry designs on my computer screen. It's not a program that exists on my computer. His frequency is Jah Kee Lah Bah.

I love meeting many beings which we would refer to as animal-like, or plant- like. The diversity on Earth reflects just a minimal amount of the diversity throughout the cosmos. I've had the opportunity to communicate with many plant-like and animal-like beings. The plant-like beings are amazing. Humans might not consider them extraterrestrial, but they are. All the life forms on Earth have come from other star systems, so we get to experience this wondrous diversity on Earth.

I'm continually meeting more star cultures. There are numerous species of Mantis. Within each species there are also sub-species. I've met at least seven species of Mantis. Also, those whom we refer to as Greys, are not, quote 'Greys'. The term, 'Grey' is a catch-all phrase. Many star beings are categorized as Greys, but they are other races and hybrid races. They chuckle and say, "That's the name that humans give us, but we're not truly Greys." It gets interesting when they talk about how humanity breaks things down and categorizes everything. Yet, humans have to categorize things to talk about them. I've had plenty of contact with Arcturian Zetas. It's limiting to think about them in this way, but there really is no other way to be able to talk about them using words which are linear.

How do they appear to you?

Each one appears in a different way. I usually see star beings etherically, but I have seen beings materialize before my eyes. How they appear depends on what state they choose to be in that moment. I see their essence, which is pure energy.

In the way I perceive them, some are humanoid looking, others are wild looking. The essence of plant-like beings is rainbow spirals. They also show me other ways they can appear to others. Some appear as feline beings as I've mentioned. Others appear as canine beings, or simply various energy forms. For example, a being might appear as a ball of light, or as a sprite. Some of the nature spirits flash their energy at me which can look like sparkling diamonds on a river. Also, they come to me in a way in which I can understand them.

For example, some of the Mantis beings, when they contact someone, can appear to be angelic with wings. They don't really have wings, but come to me in this way so that they don't cause fear. A person might think, 'Oh, here's an angel.' Their mind can accept this better, and they can then accept why that being has come to contact them.

Most star beings I've met shapeshift. I've seen some of them do this in a way which is natural. That's because they are energy. Things on Earth are dense, so it's not as easy for them to shapeshift while in our atmosphere, but it can be done.

The etheric group consciousness which I originated from, Quabar, is pure love and light. They are me and I am them. They show themselves to me as radiant white light. They are like diamonds shining in sunlight. They are joyful and make me laugh when I'm having a rough day.

Some beings appear as male and some as female. There are many androgynous groups, and others beyond that, which we don't have words to describe. There's no gender, they are simply energy or other kinds of etheric forms. It's wonderful to be able to have these experiences with these beings.

When I walk in nature the nature spirits are all around me peering from the trees, fields, and from the faces of flowers and everywhere else.

Star beings often come to me as a group. There are those who are of a group consciousness and those who are of a more individual nature. As a group they merge into one, yet they can spark off from the group and be individuals as well. For example, the dolphin-like beings don't look exactly like dolphins here on Earth. The dolphins here are like distant cousins who have volunteered to come here to be in this experience that we're all living on Earth. There is no limit to how they can appear to people.

With those who visit Earth more often, it's easier for them to take physical form, like the Zetas. Maybe I should say, it's easier for them to materialize for a period of time. But they cannot hold that form endlessly because if they get trapped in an electromagnetic field, it can cause problems for them and affect their energy bodies. This is because Earth is a lower frequency, and they have to continually adjust to the electromagnetic fields of Earth.

There are beings whom I communicate with interdimensionally. When I communicate with them, I see them in my mind's eye. I can travel to wherever I want to with my consciousness, which is something that is natural and easy for me. So if I want to I can visit Saturn in seconds and communicate with any beings that might be living on Saturn or the rings of Saturn.

Can you describe your first contact?

Well, I've been having contact my entire life with my star parents, since I'm a hybrid. I have star roots in that I was genetically altered while still in the womb. In a way, I am my first star contact. My star family in this life are a pair of Tall White Zetas called Ametha and Zazu. While I was in my mother's womb they had injected me with a DNA cocktail of seven different ET races.

But Quabar is my original star family, and was around me when I was sleeping in my crib. I remember they surrounded me to reassure me that I would be okay with coming into a human body. I wasn't very happy when I remembered that I had agreed to come in. Before I was born I wanted to change my mind and return to the stars. My Earth mother told me I was a forced labor. They had to induce labor, which was not a very easy process. I came in already having issues, due to circumstances in the hospital. There was a polio scare. My star family stepped in to make sure I did not contract polio. So, this was my initial contact. They were coming around to help me to adjust as a hybrid to Earth. Thank God they were there.

At age three a tornado went zooming through our neighborhood. I was in bed and was really afraid because I was by myself. The lightning was severe, and my parents were downstairs. I was then teleported onto a ship by Ametha and Zazu, who cared for me deeply and taught me a great deal. They showed me how they used lightning to help run the ships and how they used it in teleporting me. So I felt like I was riding on a bolt of lightning. They reminded me of volumes of knowledge that I already had, including how to commune with crystals for different purposes, such as for healing, or for opening portals. I would run around the ship and touch the symbols on the shimmering holographic walls of the ship.

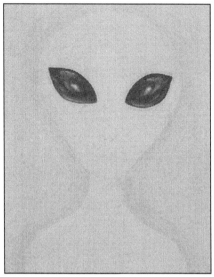

Ametha. Credit: Jacquelin Smith

When I saw *The Wizard of Oz* I laughed, because I related to Dorothy - I'm not in Kansas anymore. I was in this tornado, and I went to another land - in this case a starship. In fact my dog occasionally went with me. So I have an affinity with Dorothy and Toto. I remember that experience vividly, and it felt like I was on the ship a very long time. Time can be different on a ship; a short visit can feel like a long one. I welcomed it because they are my star parents. They were also staying in touch with me to keep me awake and to remind me that I am a hybrid.

How do you connect now?

I communicate with star beings on a daily basis. Now and then if I'm too busy in the world, and have many errands to do, I don't take the time to communicate consciously. Yet every morning I wake up and say, "Good morning my star family. I love you. Please be here for me, and support me in my life on Earth." Communication with them is natural as I've always been very telepathic. It's also easy for me to hear them, to receive messages, and to feel their presence.

I live multidimensionally, in every sense - beyond duality. I don't have to go into a meditation to communicate with star beings, telepathy simply flows for me. If I ask a question I get an answer immediately, from whatever group I wish to talk to, whether it be the dolphin-like beings, the Zetas or anyone else. And since I'm a blended soul with seven ET aspects, one could say I'm more flexible psychically. This also applies when receiving light language. I have a natural understanding of the way star beings communicate. It's not in English but in light language. I speak light language back to them mentally as well as out loud. Symbols also flow from them to me, which I use for various healings with people and animals.

These are some of the ways in which they communicate with me. It could be about something that's happening on the Earth, or in another star system. Once I was told that there was something going on in the constellation of Cancer and that it was a big deal. They asked me to send love and light to that area.

So, all of this works naturally for me. Telepathy is a universal language. If we're open to listening we can hear, sense and experience communication. This is also true with receiving in dreams.

I appreciate and value all the different ways in which these beings communicate. As I mentioned, the feline being, Jah Kee Lah Bah, turns on my computer and puts moving sacred geometry on the screen. I laugh because it's great fun. I will say, "Okay, I know you're here Jah Kee Lah Bah." I appreciate and value these communications. One star woman with green skin and big green hair came to me in the middle of the night and said, "We're asking you to remember this book of holographic symbols." I love it. I wouldn't have it any other way.

Can you initiate contact?

Yes. It's easy and natural. I set my intention, take a deep breath, center, ground, connect with my higher self, and then ask a question. I know the beings receive my question and then I receive an answer in an instant. Also, in my ongoing relationship with these beings, I let them know how I feel emotionally. So, if I'm having a crappy day, I let them know about it. For me, it's not all about trying to get the highest spiritual messages. Some days I might shout, "You know I'd really like you guys to get your asses down here and help me out with this. Oh, and by the way, where the hell were you today?" So I choose to be real. From my perspective we're here to express all of our emotions. So I don't strive to be at the 'highest frequency' every day. I allow myself to simply be.

I teach workshops on how to initiate communication with star beings. We can have personal relationships with them, we can understand them, as well as our relationship to them.

We all learn from each other. As a child I was told often by star beings on the ship, "We're learning from you as you are learning from us, and we're all remembering."

The initiation of contact is sending out an invitation to the star beings asking them to visit you. For example, "I invite you to come and communicate with me. I would love to receive a message from you. Please come in a way that I can receive it and understand it." The star beings will respond, and come in a way that doesn't create fear.

If a person has fear, they need to come to a place of being more peaceful before pushing further communication. A person might fear they'll be harmed, or they might wonder who are these beings, or be fearful that they might be evil. So that becomes a fear-based invite, and that's not going to work well. If we come from a place of love and joy, then the initiation is received in a way that opens a door for the star beings to come and communicate in wonderful direct and indirect ways, such as dreams.

How does your contact feel?

I feel them energetically before they come to me. I feel it in my gut, though my entire body, and there's an eerie feeling. And then I feel their presence around me. This sense of knowing they're present is something I've developed through the years. One day before they visit me or take me on a ship, I get these feelings. There aren't really any words to describe these feelings. It's some kind of deep knowing that they're coming and that they're letting me know. I know it through all of my being.

Also, I feel a deep sense of unconditional love before they show up. My star family, Quabar, is unconditional love, joy, and peace. When they arrive, I experience waves of unconditional love which travel through every cell of my body and unconditional love flows from my heart to them. When some groups come to visit me, there's a more defined boundary, and they're coming in to give information. But I still feel them loving me unconditionally. It's bliss!

How do you differentiate between your own thoughts and those from outside?

Good question, and many people in my classes ask the same question. I've learned how to do this through the years, so it's become natural. When they communicate, it can sound or feel as if you're talking to yourself. When they communicate with me, I have learned that it's not me. There's a voice, a different feel about it all.

In learning how to differentiate all this, I sometimes think, "I know this isn't me." Sometimes it feels like it's coming from the outside, but they're obviously tapping into my energy field, into my mind so that I can receive their message.

Many people I talk with say it becomes confusing for them because they don't know if it's their thoughts, or if they're making up something. It comes down to learning through experience. And this is the beauty of developing an ongoing relationship with the star beings or other beings.

When I communicate with animals, which I do every day as an animal communicator, each animal has a distinct way of communicating with me. They each have a distinct energy signature, when they communicate. So it's about listening to that energy signature of the being. Some animals are chatty, some are to the point, some have a great sense of humor, some don't.

Also, I've learned how to identify and know if a communication feels off. It's helpful to identify who's who when you communicate with any being.

In 2013, around Thanksgiving, I went through 14 days of being on starships and in other realms. It began when I was in my living room watching TV, and a voice said, "We'd love for you to go outside in an hour. We'll meet you there. Oh, and bring your binoculars." I was thinking, 'Okay, this doesn't feel like something I'm going to do when it's 30 degrees outside.' So I got quiet, focused, and then more information came to me. I knew this wasn't me. Also, I knew I had a choice with this. The star beings know me well; they knew that I wasn't going to say no to having an experience. I went outside and immediately I sighted seven starships in the night sky. Then a craft flew over my house. It was the start of an incredible 14-day journey. I could have turned away from this opportunity, but I knew it would be an amazing spiritual journey for my soul. I came from a place of wanting the experience rather than from a feeling of fear.

If the voice I had heard hadn't been friendly, or if it didn't feel loving, then I would have made the choice to turn away and release it.

Some people would refer to this as negative energy, but I simply think of this as lower spectrum energy which is only one aspect of the entire spectrum.

Why do they connect with you?

Twenty-five years ago I was only communicating with Quabar. Then, they started introducing me to other star beings whom I already knew, but had forgotten through being in the human experience. Also, I needed to feel safe enough to continue expanding.

I started out communicating with a couple of groups and then just kept meeting more star beings. I find it works this way with many people so that they can get acclimated to various frequencies and then expand, which enables them to embrace all the frequency shifts. Each group carries a different frequency. It's about expansion.

All these beings come to me because now I'm like a finely tuned radio. I am able to receive a wide variety of frequencies since I'm a hybrid and carry seven star frequencies within my DNA.

Star beings are aware of those who are sensitive and open to receiving. Humans talk a lot, and sometimes have a challenge with quieting their minds so that they can truly listen.

Also, this is a part of my soul agreement. I have come in to share what I receive from them with others. I have certainly expanded throughout my life. They are connecting with me even more now because of the shifts going on with Earth.

I was put on this star being track very early on, from birth. Different events that occurred in my life opened me up multidimensionally, so I feel it's my destiny.

When I wrote my second book, *Star Origins and Wisdom of Animals*, a serpent of the light came to me. The room filled with light, and I asked the being, "Why are you coming to me?" And the response was, "Why *not* you? This is natural for you. You've been communicating with animals, trees, and all other living forms since you have been on Earth. This is no different."

We all have a natural ability to communicate with animals, trees, and all other living beings. More people are discovering these natural abilities as they awaken to who they truly are and to themselves as cosmic citizens.

What do the beings get out of it?

I've made a conscious choice to talk about these other beings. This helps to awaken others to being cosmic citizens. I feel this is part of my purpose here. I feel I am here to spread love, light and joy.

I believe they have chosen me and I have chosen them. What do they get out of it, and what do we get out of it? I've really thought about this. Since I'm hybrid, I'm a bridge in that I can share from the star being point of view as well as from the human point of view. The star beings are interested in everyone reconnecting with the cosmic family. To me it's great fun learning about who they are, their cultures, and this brings me great joy. Also, I enjoy asking them questions about their cultures. In the book I'm currently writing about my life, I discuss more about their cultures and answers to questions I've asked them. Since I've been a star being in many lives, and am a blended soul, I have access to their ways of life as well as their languages and symbols of light language, which I speak when doing consultations.

They are family. Also, we are them and they are us. That's the simple truth of all this. So we're really connecting with our other selves. So, in communicating with them, I'm getting to know more about myself and my other aspects as a multidimensional being. I have a number of multidimensional selves that are ET. In the end, it's learning about my wholeness, and who I truly am, beyond duality and this body of Jacquelin.

At our cores we're divine love, but then we get to have these many experiences of other aspects of self, of creation. In the end we're all One. We are various expressions of the Creator, and the Creator is within. This is a natural, evolutionary process, and is fun for me.

I've asked Ametha and Zazu many of these questions. I was with them on the starship almost every night starting around the age of two or three, and they were very interested in some of the things I was doing at age three as well as throughout my life. This works like a foreign exchange program. I was learning from them, and they were learning from me. There's real beauty in this kind of exchange. It's learning without judgment or labels.

They were interested in how I played. There was an Arcturian Zeta on the ship whom I loved. I called him 'Sandman', and we would play together. He was about three and a half feet tall. He was like a nanny. I'd be singing nursery rhymes that young children learn, and Sandman and the others would join in. They were learning about play. Play is an important aspect of evolution, as is joy. When I tried to play patty cake, the Sandman clapped with me, and other beings on the ship would join in, clapping each other's hands. There was plenty of laughter and they were joyful in learning these simple rhymes and games. This was a beautiful sharing and learning process. They also enjoyed watching me tie my shoes. They enjoyed watching these cultural aspects of what it's like to be human. They were also very interested in my emotions.

By the way, my Tall White Zeta parents have emotions. They used to hug me and still do. It's a human myth that star beings have no emotions. That's a lack of understanding from limiting perceptions that most people have taught.

Learning is a continuous process which never ends. This is true for every living form. It's an evolutionary process. The same is true for them. So they are receiving and giving information.

I learned a great deal from them as a child on the ship. I learned how to work with and direct energies to manifest physical objects. Also, I learned how to communicate telepathically with crystals and learned how to speak their language and translate their symbols.

One person who studies ET phenomena asked me, "Are they just using us for their survival?" I don't know that there's a simple answer to that question. I said to the person, "If humanity was in a place where they weren't sure they were going to survive, what do you think they would do?" Humans refer to the term as 'use', but how far would humanity go to survive? Would they use other species if they could to survive? I don't know that there's a simple answer. But I think humanity would go quite far to survive. We're already exploring Mars as a place to go to after we've destroyed Earth.

From my point of view, it's best to think of our relationships with star beings as a two-way street of giving and receiving. If I thought that they were just taking I wouldn't be comfortable connecting with them. In my experience, there's a richness in giving and receiving with them.

Communicating with my star being multidimensional selves has helped me understand the cultures from which they come as well as their feelings, and about their good intentions for the cosmos.

Once again, in the end, they're all me, and I am them.

A new study, which analyzed data from the Hubble Space Telescope and other observatories, says there are at least two trillion galaxies in the observable universe. With these huge numbers, how can we not pay attention to our cosmic origins?

How do you deal with your multidimensionality?

I have been integrating my multidimensional selves in order to bring them into the unified field of who I truly am—divine love—and this allows me to stand in my power. This is what many of us, who are awake, are doing right now, whether in a conscious way or not. At first I was not into doing this in a very conscious way, but when I became aware of what was happening, I began communicating with all of my selves, which is still a challenging yet inspiring journey. We are always embracing aspects of ourselves and processing emotions we feel. I've learned a lot about bringing my selves into a state of cooperation and harmony, into the unified field of who I am as Jacquelin Smith.

Some of these aspects of myself I thought were other and then discovered that they were really a star being aspect of myself. It's important for people to understand that they are meeting themselves when they're integrating their multidimensional star being selves.

As you try to integrate them, are those other selves trying to integrate you?

I'm writing about this in my new book. Absolutely, yes. I just talked about this on a radio show last week. Yes, multidimensionally-speaking, we are integrating the other selves, and they are integrating us. As I walk through the process of integrating them in a very conscious way, I am able to see them and communicate with them. It can be a challenging time with some of these aspects, because of their differences. I'm in a human body, and they're different frequencies. Some aspects have more fully developed emotions, while others do not. So integrating the human and star being aspects becomes an interesting journey into understanding the 'whole' self. The soul.

I've had long conversations with these selves, and it's definitely a process. I said, "Look, we're all each other, so I suggest that we all be in harmony and balance and cooperate so that we can unite as a whole and move forward."

There were a couple of my star selves who didn't resonate with each another, so I acted as a go-between. I asked them to get on the same page. It sounds kind of strange, but I was the mediator, and I'd say, "Look, you come from different planets, and have different points of view about certain things, but let's find a way to agree. Let's all work in harmony and balance and become unified. And let's do this with ease and simplicity."

With some of the multidimensional selves it was fun and easy, yet with other aspects it has been a bigger challenge. It took months of my communicating with the selves to bring them into a unified field of self. Not just my personality living in the human body, but the many star being selves - the I AM, as a whole being.

I have aspects of me that are plant-like beings and animal-like beings. One of my aspects comes from a planet that never had any daylight. When this aspect stepped forward, I couldn't walk in daylight as I was integrating that part. It's an interesting process that my soul allowed me to experience in a very conscious way so that I could be of assistance to others who are walking through this same soul process.

Now I am able to stand in my power as one unified self. This journey is also about releasing and healing. This includes traumas from this life as well as past lives and future lives. This is a good time for everyone on Earth to integrate the aspects of themselves to regain their wholeness and joy.

The star selves are learning what it's like to be human. And humans are learning more about their star selves. Within the microcosm of my soul self, all selves are learning to appreciate what we have in common.

This process of integration was overseen by higher aspects of my soul and the oversoul. I was aware of the dynamics of all of this, which is a bit unusual. Again, this allows me to assist others who are walking through this and who could be labeled as mentally ill. I'm able to be a guide for them, helping them by using light language and symbols to integrate their multidimensional aspects in a much easier way than what I have walked through.

It's helpful for us to know the 'whole' of us, inside and outside time and space. This is about our consciousness expanding and remembering to live from the heart and soul.

Is this integration a natural mechanism or a choice?

All of this is a natural evolutionary process. The soul is vast. The soul will do what it needs to do to express what it desires to express, and the personality can choose to allow that to happen or not. If the personality does not choose to allow this, that person usually lives a very 'small' life or may even decide to cross over to the other side and try again. Of course, there are karmic issues involved with all of this as well, which is mainly about being awake and aware. A person can choose to deal with things in this life or postpone it for another life. There's no right or wrong, it's just a choice. That's the beauty of free will.

Yet the soul will step in and attempt to guide a person to get on track with their purpose and with expressing love, which is who they truly are. A person can resist this or flow with it.

What is the soul?

Our soul is an aspect of the Creator. We are all cells in the body of creation. Every cell in our body holds the holographic imprint of the entire universe. We are the universe and the universe is us. When you think about it, it's really miraculous!

The spiritual essence, which is a portion of the soul, lives within the body behind the heart. We can't be here without the spirit in the body. The soul creates the body, which supports our purpose here.

The soul desires to experience life. The soul is our divine child who wants to stomp in mud puddles, eat chocolate, and roll down a grassy hill. It wants earthy experiences. It wants to express through the body. For example, if someone has fun being a healer or a gardener, this is their soul expressing through them. For me, speaking light language, giving Star Origin readings, drawing star symbols, walking in the woods, eating chocolate, or riding on a rollercoaster are some of the things my soul has come here to experience. It wants to flow and express, not be stuck in seriousness, studying something boring, or involved in something that has no meaning in my life. The soul calls for authenticity - being real. I can know this by listening to and feeling my heart's desires.

The soul always *is*. My core of divine love never changes. It is joy, happiness, laughter, peace and other love expressions. It's not about having a million dollars, nor is it about the achievements in the world, although these can flow to us naturally if we are following our soul's desires.

The soul is infinite. We live in the soul's energy field and the soul lives within us. In the end, there's no inside or outside because the body is not solid. And we are not the body, yet the body houses the soul. Our soul is who we *truly* are. I ask my soul to keep me awake. I listen to my soul speaking to me through intuition, synchronicity, my higher self, and my guidance team. My soul and I are in partnership. I get to choose how fast I allow my soul's desires to be made manifest in this world. We can keep putting on the brakes or we can let go and do a freefall.

If one loses touch with their soul, they can get back on track if they are open to remembering who they truly are - being honest with themselves about what and who they want in their life. When we love ourselves we are honoring our soul.

Love is always the path. We can return to love even if we've forgotten or lost our way. Every day, I say out loud, "I choose love." Does that mean I don't get cranky? Of course not. It's not about pretending to be good, and smile at your neighbor, while feeling pissed off at them for throwing dog crap in your yard.

It's about being my whole self, which means being authentic. This means that I allow myself to feel all of my emotions, not just those that are considered to be 'proper', as a lightworker. Emotions are our guide to knowing what we feel, and they light our path to knowing our soul.

Everyone has their own unique journey. Humanity expresses the entire spectrum of frequencies. There are rapists and murderers and there are highly evolved souls like Mother Teresa and Joan of Arc.

My intention is to stay awake, mindful and aware in every moment. For me, this happens when I get quiet and listen to my heart. This doesn't happen if I'm racing around town, or on the phone too much and out of balance. I make the choice, every day, to be in silence so that I can hear that still, small voice within me.

If I overwork, my soul steps in and lets me know that I need to take time to have fun, whether it's doodling on paper, or going to an art gallery, or maybe a walk at the park. This brings balance and harmony to my life. Now and then when I don't listen, I end up getting out of balance and harmony, and then I don't feel happy. This is the time when I most need to take good care of myself and get my life back on track. Do we ever *arrive? Hell* no!

However, we can play with meditation and relaxation to support us with this journey. It may be as simple as getting quiet for a few minutes, putting your hand over your heart, and listening to what your heart and soul have to say to you. In doing this, the ego-mind can become quieter so that you can hear your inner truth and guidance.

Our souls are infinite because creation is infinite. I love and adore my soul. And I must admit, there are days when I get annoyed when I hear something from my soul that my ego wasn't planning on taking in. I grumble, but always return to my heart.

I'm sharing what works for me. Everyone can find ways that allow them to listen to and be in touch with their souls. I'm also in touch with my soul whenever I take a walk in nature, or when I dance wildly to music or when I fall into a starry sky at night. Writing and singing also allow me to flow with my soul.

With the way things are on Earth, it's a good time to wake up and allow yourself to play and have fun in life.

What have you learned?

I've learned how to embrace countless races. There have been periods in my life when I was in fear of some races because of the way they looked. I've come to understand that just because a race looks a certain way, or communicates differently, it doesn't mean I need to be fearful. I've learned how to be curious about them and to explore who they are before forming any opinions about them. For example, I've met a few races that have looked intimidating, yet they turned out to be incredibly loving beings. I've had a couple of encounters with star beings whose intentions were not about serving divine love and they were scary. Once I realized that they had no power over me, I released them with love and blessings.

There are races who can appear friendly or even beautiful, but their intention is not loving. There's no judgment about this. Quabar taught me the importance of using discernment and wisdom in deciding with whom to communicate. This is vital for me as I have a great deal of communication with star beings and interdimensional beings.

When some of them communicate telepathically, they may communicate in a way I'm not yet familiar with, but once I communicate with them, I become comfortable and in the flow of how they speak to me. For example, some have a more 'intellectual' sound to them, while others speak telepathically in a choppy, almost robotic way. There are many variations on this.

From the human perspective, some might be perceived as having no emotion, and therefore, no heart. Yet that's not the truth. I look into the essence of who they are, to really feel the flavor of what they're saying. I focus on whether or not they're coming from love.

The most important thing I've learned is to live with love from my heart and soul, and to keep things as simple as possible. This can be a tall order some days. Do I always remember this? No. They show up some days and tap me on the shoulder and say, "You know, this doesn't need to be so hard. All you need to do is relax and go with the flow."

There are times when I'll pout or complain that this is tough gig on Earth, and why don't *they* get their asses down here and try it. Then, they'll remind me to go into my heart and discern what my truth is about a circumstance in my life. I found this helps rather than sitting and trying to figure things out from my head, getting nowhere fast. This is all part of living life in a human form on Earth. This has been a key lesson for me personally. It's important that we are aligned with our core's truth, especially at this time.

A basic message that my star family has given me throughout my entire life, and which I teach in my workshops, is that we are all One. Everyone on Earth has come from the stars and we are all cosmic citizens. We need to remember who we truly are, to share in our experiences, and the messages we receive.

The multidimensional aspects of our soul are us, not other, as I've mentioned. They come to us and communicate messages which can help us out in a number of ways.

Also, I've continued to learn that Ascension is about us transcending our old beliefs and limiting thoughts. It's not about traveling somewhere to another dimension or another world, since we are the universe. Anything I want to know I can access by journeying into the dimensions of my heart.

Since there's no such thing as time and space; everything we see on the outside is what we have projected onto holographic templates.

We can venture into the different chakras and access various aspects of our selves and emotions. This allows me to know my core as divine love. We can know our soul by listening to the heart.

This talk about the soul reaches beyond the realms of star and other beings. The soul creates the bodies or other energy expressions in order to experience itself, to learn about balance and love. Our souls sparked off from the Creator, so this is all about the Creator knowing itself. I've seen this energetically as an infinite spiral of evolution that never ends.

People have forgotten how to feel their hearts. We can see this if we look at how out of touch with nature humans have become. As an animal communicator, I share with people that nature is love in expression. A tree or a flower expresses love. Humans need to remember how to honor and respect all living forms, as well as themselves. The animals and nature have taught me how to love myself in a bigger way. By loving myself, I can love others in a deeper way. This love flows into the collective consciousness of humanity and all of life. This raises the frequency of all living beings, including star beings.

The star beings and animals have taught me about joy. Joy opens our hearts and raises our frequencies. We are happy if we live in the moment and focus on joy. Joy flows from love.

I don't judge any race as good or bad. We're all equal. Soul is soul. It doesn't matter what they look like on the outside, what matters is do they serve love.

Let's embrace ourselves, and embrace our star families. What we all have in common is that we're all expressions of creation. Everyone is evolving in their own way and at their own pace, including the star beings. These are the kind of ideas that the star beings talk to me about. They also tell me how important it is to celebrate and enjoy life.

I love communicating with a number of the star races who have a great sense of humor. They laugh telepathically which always uplifts me. Sometimes they show up and tell star being jokes, which crack me up. I end up laughing until tears roll down my cheeks. They'll make a funny remark, for example, about how they view humans or how humans view them. Or they'll ask me questions, which is really fun.

Some races are androgynous in their makeup, and do not have any sexual organs, or rectums. One group asked, "Why do humans have buttholes? We don't." They were serious in wanting to learn about the human anatomy, but I ended up laughing so hard, it took me a few minutes to answer their question. Funnily enough a woman called me one night and asked if ETs have buttholes.

The star beings remind me that there really is no path - that there is only love. We're here to experience life, to remember how to be authentic.

Also, Quabar taught me how to do Star Origin readings for people. They came to me one day and said, "We think this could fun." I had never thought of it before. My response was, "Yeah, this could really be fun and benefit others as well."

I am guided when I speak on radio shows. Yet it can be a challenge, because when talking about who star beings are and what they have to say, there aren't words to describe their languages or who they truly are. This is why I started speaking light language, which is soul language. It's an easy and clear way to activate the listeners. This bypasses their conscious mind.

It has been a lifelong process to integrate my experiences and to integrate my multidimensional selves. My journey began while I was still in the crib.

The star beings saved me more than once. When I was six years old, I had a near-death experience. I was taken aboard the ship to be healed physically as well as emotionally. Also, the angels helped to heal me and directed me to go back to Earth to live my life since I had an important mission to do.

The star beings are my teachers and I'm a teacher for them as well. They enjoy learning about the human experience. They enjoy experiencing life through me, whether that be watching a bird fly in the sky or touching a tree and feeling rough bark.

I agreed on the soul level to life this unique life. It has allowed me to know the 'whole' of myself. I've never been afraid of my star family or most other races.

It took me a long time to realize I was a blended soul, having the DNA of seven star races, and work out how I could fit in with living on Earth. And it took time to realize that I had chosen the experiences I have walked through on the Earth plane. It took years for me to sort things out and to come to know the different aspects of myself, which are all of different frequencies from other worlds.

I communicate with my multidimensional selves often. I enjoy having this relationship with these star being aspects of self. Also, they offer me assistance in invaluable ways. Of course they are part of my guidance team. Some of them have a great sense of humor, while other aspects are serious. It's all me.

I love Earth, it's an incredible place to be. Before I came to Earth, they showed her to me, and I said, "I'm all for going there."

I'm grateful to be able to do what I love and have fun doing it. I enjoy sharing what I've learned through my life with others - just for the joy of sharing.

I offer both the human and star being perspective. I am a bridge. I enjoy being of assistance to others; humans as well as animals and Mother Earth.

In the end, the most important thing I can share is the heart-to-heart connection. When all of us open our hearts, all things are possible. I've taught this for over 35 years in my animal communication and star being work.

How well do you feel you understand the beings?

Being hybrid, I feel that I understand the beings intimately. Most of my lives have been lived as a star being. Though I cannot say that my understanding is complete since I'm in a human body in this life.

Since I've been on starships from early childhood, I know how they communicate telepathically, what they feel, and know. Telepathy is a clear and direct experience in knowing another.

What message would they like to share?

The key message that Quabar and many other star beings share with me is that we are all One. As I've mentioned, the star beings whom I communicate with talk about living from the heart and keeping life simple.

Quabar: "Every soul plays its role in this Earth drama. Everything is in divine order. Trust the divinity within. The outer world is illusion, so remember to hold to love and let go of the illusion. The truth is that there's no gap between Earth and the stars; it only seems that way from the human perspective. Look beyond space/time dear ones. You are the stars and they are you. You are the Earth and she is you. There is no separation when you see beyond the illusion of separation. Love and enjoy the crazy cosmic ride."

Mantis: "We are one of many who exist in the higher realms. As ancient Mantis, as Co-Creators, we have assisted with creating Earth's grids. We are a race of beings who love to laugh, explore, and play. If you ask us for healing, we will come and assist. We have been assisting Earth for eons. We might look somewhat intimidating, but we are all about love and joy."

Arcturian/Zeta: "Our star culture has been visiting Earth for many millennia. We find Earth to be a beautiful planet. Those of us who are scientists have been monitoring how humans affect Earth. Earth is a soul whom we love, and we love and respect humans as well. We are explorers who mean no harm. We wish for peace for all cosmic races."

Light language symbols received by Jacquelin. Credit: Jacquelin Smith

How clear are you on the meaning of the symbols?

It depends on which star race you're asking about. I transmit symbols onto paper from a number of star cultures. Sometimes they will tell me the meaning or concept of the symbols, or they may not share that in the moment. Other times, I will know the meaning of the symbols simply by living with them on a daily basis. If you were here right now, in my living room, I have pages of symbols strewn all over my couch. I place the different pages of symbols in different rooms, which they instruct me to do. As I walk around my house, I glance and them, and the meanings will come to me. I really live and breathe them. I listen to what they say or sing. I will often speak light language and the meanings will automatically be known to me. At times, I may walk in a room and glance at a symbol and will suddenly get clarity on what it is communicating. Other times I'll sit down and write while looking at a symbol.

Also, if I need a healing, I ask the symbols to guide me with the healing. I'll put the written page of symbols somewhere on my body. Then the star beings come through and tap on my body which activates the healing.

I drew a page of symbols the other day as I was in the middle of a huge initiation. Three more multidimensional selves were then integrated into me.

Also, I painted light language onto a Styrofoam ball. They said, "Put it under your bed. It will help integrate things as you sleep." It did.

I'm putting a book together about the symbols soon so that people can use them for healing in a wide variety of ways. Some symbols I've received are used for joy, clearing out grief, anger, or for creating joy, love, balance and harmony and inner peace.

I want to thank my star ancestors, everyone in the invisible realms, and my soul, for guiding and supporting me in life. It has not always been an easy journey, but I am grateful for all the healings I have received through the years which now allow me to be free of past traumas that could not have been healed in any other way. Life is a joy now and I am in flow with my soul. My star family, Quabar, communicated the following to me after I wrote this paragraph.

Oh sa ke la mu jah me pah chi.

We bless you; We thank you.

Conclusion

Writing a conclusion to all that has been shared and experienced in this project is a monumental challenge. Not only would it take an entire book to lay out my current thoughts on the subject, but they are continually evolving, so that book would be out of date tomorrow. That is the nature of awakening, as you have heard from everyone I have interviewed. It tends to be a process of contact, reflection and expression. As the experiences continue, so too do the reflections upon them, the expressions that the contacts inspire, and the opening up to more contact (and more types of contact).

I will therefore offer a summary of what has been learned, then reflect briefly on the personal experience of this two-year, three-book project.

Let us firstly look at the main points from *Being with the Beings*. How does contact between humans and non-human intelligences take place, why does it take place, and how might this be relevant to our everyday lives?

How

We have heard about several methods of contact: physical, psychic/telepathic, channeling, light language, guidance, presences, craft sightings, dreams, synchronicities and numbers.

Some of these are active, in terms of being initiated by the experiencer, some are passive, and some may be both.

The active methods are chiefly channeling, light language, telepathy and guidance, although craft sightings and dream encounters are also reported as being successfully requested.

'Classical' channeling has been seen as a process in which a human allows a being (or beings) to speak through them. This may alter the channeler's voice, syntax, demeanor, posture or gesticulation.

We have also heard others, notably Juju, describe channeling the material in the interview, without the same complex process. Vashta talked about collaboratively developing images of various beings through her intuitive channels. Robert, Jacquelin, Vanessa and others talked about symbols and other images coming through as downloads.

The passive methods of contact include: various forms of psychic sensing, such as clairvoyance or clairaudience; dreams; physical encounters; speaking or drawing/painting light language; guidance; craft sightings, and seeing 'synchronicity' numbers. These are often seen on clocks, and may progress (12:34), repeat (12:12) or mirror (12:21).

Safeguards

Undertaking contact in safety is of primary importance. Many techniques for protecting oneself and one's space have been shared, which include visualizations, affirmations, and the use of singing bowls, crystals and incense.

But Rob and Vashta describe in detail that their protection is founded in the knowledge of their expanded nature. And Vashta discusses her process of coming to identify with the perspective of the beings, thus removing the duality and conflict from the experience.

The central point, from everybody, is that like attracts like. So whatever energetic or emotional state one is in when requesting contact, that is likely to be what will be attracted. Vashta said that she spent a considerable amount of time working on her 'shadows', which put her in a more balanced place from which to start navigating the rigors and complexities of contact.

Why

A central preoccupation within the field is the issue of why other intelligences would wish to interact with humans. We have heard from the experiencers that there are numerous reasons, which have many levels.

Ongoing contacts are generally based on exchange. We have heard a great deal about what is given by the beings—either actively or passively—and we have heard about what is received by them.

Brief, one-off contacts are thought to be out of curiosity, though many are ambiguous in terms of motivation.

Given by the beings

Knowledge and experience tend to be foremost, particularly an expansion of one's understanding of the nature of being and the structure of reality. This includes reincarnation, multidimensionality and the oversoul, and dimensions and densities.

Multidimensionality is one way to say that we are all connected to other 'expressions of our soul', which are living in other forms. The 'oversoul' is a term used by Jacquelin, Rob, Vashta and Aridif as the collective noun for all actual and potential versions of yourself, throughout time and space. Jacquelin talked about integrating aspects of her multidimensionality, and acting as a liaison between them.

Experiencers are taught many healing techniques, and use the energy that comes through them, often in Reiki, for healing. They also send this remotely to people, which includes political situations and other types of disaster.

Healing, telepathy and other psychic abilities are all innate human capacities that can be developed through practice. These have been used by human cultures throughout our history, and are ubiquitous in the field of contact phenomena.

Also commonly discussed in the field is the Ascension narrative, which says that all is process, all is evolution of both spirit and matter. It is suggested that the beings are helping awaken humans to this reality, so that they may contribute to 'raising the frequency', and helping to ease and accelerate this evolutionary process. The hybrids, star children and other starseeds tend to most strongly express this idea. The mechanisms are somewhat contested, but there is general agreement that contact is fundamentally about the education and evolution of all parties.

The process also offers people better ways to live, and to relate to themselves and others. Vashta's chapter is particularly striking in this regard. Many people report feeling more authentic, expanded and connected as a result of contact, which improves their lives, and often the lives of those around them.

However, the early stages of awakening are often rocky periods, mainly due to the response people get when they share their encounters with others. Robert gave us a vivid account of this. The process often strains relationships which cannot accommodate the personal changes that contact may trigger. Therefore, the need to connect with others who understand often becomes pronounced, and this has been reflected in the support group work done by Barbara Lamb, for example. In part I of *We Are the Disclosure* she talks about setting up groups at her home, and at the International UFO Congress, both of which she has run for many years.

One could say in summary that a radical expansion of reality and the self is what is given to experiencers.

Received by the beings

The common refrain "they are us and we are them" expresses the fundamental existential narrative within this field, which says that all consciousness, all being, is One. And the One, often referred to as Source, split itself into an infinitude of pieces in order to take on new forms and create new experiences as a means of learning. The ultimate personal development program, in other words. Therefore, all beings, including human beings, are simply the forms a soul takes in order to experience life from that perspective. As all is One, what one being experiences, the whole experiences. Holographic or fractal metaphors are often used to illustrate this.

Humans are hence a major curiosity, as a defining feature of human existence is duality, the sense that each person is separate from the rest of existence. A group consciousness, for example, might find it of great interest to explore reality through the eyes of duality. In the interview with Sasha, Lyssa's counterpart, she stated that humans are in the same process as her people, the Pleiadians, who have been evolving away from the separative ego, and towards an identification with the group. They are further along that road, and are helping humanity to make progress of their own.

There is also the matter of connection or reconnection. Darlene, Jacquelin, Vashta, Rob and others stated that some beings who come to them are other aspects of themselves, or have other connections which they wish to discover, or rediscover. Darlene gave a particularly touching illustration of this, involving the Blue Crystal being.

Both Lyssa and Rob understand that their main channeled beings are future—or possible future—versions of themselves, within their oversoul. Lyssa, Darlene and others made the point that any being coming to you is probably connected to you in quite a close way, which could be genetic as well as being a soul connection.

Juju said that some beings—including her race the Fajan—live a life of duty to others, and that giving help is reward in itself. She described this as having a type of visual manifestation: the addition of colored streamers to one's aura. Darlene observed that the Blue Avians signify such things with their plumage.

By contrast, Vashta shared the story of her female counterpart, who sounds like an absolute blast. She is a 'trickster' being who is simply exploring and having fun with reality.

There were also indications that some beings wish to learn about negative emotions, or even to trigger and feed off them. Vashta said that some beings are attracted to darker emotional states, and again, suggested that it is good practice to deal with one's own dark side before seeking contact.

In terms of nefarious intent, Jacquelin addressed the question of some types of beings 'using' humans for their own survival. This should not be too tough to grasp, given that humans kill 70 billion land animals annually for food and other resources, and fell up to six billion trees. It is notable however, that experiencers report hostile or malevolent races as being very much in the minority. Robert offered a detailed typology of the orientation spectrum he has encountered: soul family group, positive, neutral and negative. Again, Vashta described a process of 'neutralising' her encounters through altering her perspective. Many long-term experiencers reach the conclusion that good and evil are simply relative points of view.

Context and Perspective

Two of the real gifts of contact are those of context and perspective. The more we learn about the beings, and about reality more broadly, the more context we have for human existence, and the more perspective this offers us in our daily lives.

To recap the core narrative: all beings are fragments of Source, learning and sharing experiences in a process of evolution, often termed 'Ascension'. Many beings assist others in their Ascension process, which helps both parties evolve.

If that is the context, let us consider how humans might look through the eyes of these beings. We could list hundreds of descriptors, but of most relevance here might be: emotional, tribal, polarized, paradoxical, varied, curious, creative, industrious and dedicated.

Emotionality is often picked out as one of the defining traits of humans, in terms of both strength and variety. To pick one example, we observe that in the course of a single sports game, the crowd will go through a wide and intense range of emotions. As one team scores and their fans burst with joy, the other set of fans will detonate with fury or sink into misery. Think of a year in the life of any family and you will most likely picture the gamut of emotions.

Sport and family are two expressions of the tribalism that seems hardwired in humans. People gravitate towards ingroups, the collective(s) with which they psychologically identify, and feel protective towards. Outgroups are everybody else. Politics also reflects this, and both expresses and feeds that polarization. The competing agendas of political parties have for centuries divided one group against another, even if the voting collective has more in common with itself than with the policymaking collective.

Another key feature of the discourse is that of missions. Every hybrid I know speaks of their mission(s), but a person does not have to be a hybrid to have a powerful sense of purpose. We see this play out in every field of human endeavor, whether it be medicine, environmentalism, the arts or any other. Most humans have a passion for something, and our world is a product of the range of inclinations and talents available to it, including the shadow side, the desire and ability to manipulate, oppress or harm others.

The variety of contact modalities also highlights the range of psychic abilities which humans have. We often hear of a connection between these and our DNA, and that hybrids, other beings and a variety of cosmic influences are affecting our DNA, which can enhance our capabilities and free us from many of our present constraints. This was discussed in my interview with Lyn Buchanan, a former US military remote viewer (see *Disclosure* part I). He said that he has twice been found to have a high number of physical markers indicating that he is notably different to regular humans. One of the tests was looking for particular markers found in the medical records of the civilization at Petra, which the researcher thought may be the Nephilim described in the bible.

In this regard, we might consider the narratives we have heard relating to humans being genetically modified over the millennia by a number of different races. Some people describe memories of carrying out this work during a former incarnation.

In part II of *Disclosure*, Professor Milton Wainwright described his microbiology research, in which he has been sampling the stratosphere and thereby discovering tiny extraterrestrial biological entities. He calls this neopanspermia, the process by which ET genetic information is coming to Earth on a continual basis. In her new book Mary Rodwell talks about the New Human, as does Dr Leo Sprinkle in the foreword to this book. The evolution of the human species is a major focus in this field, and is continuing, regardless of what one believes about the triggers and mechanisms.

Discussion

Although very little of the above is accepted by mainstream science, it offers a compelling narrative that experiencers are helping to define every day. Robert, and others, have said that some of the beings see us as unruly children, and one can readily sympathize with this perspective. But the beings are giving us a view of ourselves as much more than that. First and foremost, we are a cosmic species. The extent to which we are a spacefaring one is another matter. Numerous individuals have claimed firsthand knowledge of advanced covert human space travel activities. See for example *Insiders Reveal Secret Space Programs & Extraterrestrial Alliances*, by Michael Salla. It may very well be that the 'breakaway civilization' theorized by Richard Dolan is a reality. At a conference, researcher Peter Levenda was asked if he believed there to be a 'secret space program'. He replied, "Why wouldn't there be?" Given the amount of effort put into advanced propulsion systems (see Stanton Friedman's chapter in *Disclosure* part I), and the decades of leaks and rumors pertaining to Area 51 (which the Orion Council returned to time and again in their interview via Krista), it would be more of a surprise if there were no advanced human craft capable of space flight. To cite another well-worn reference, Ben Rich, former head of Lockheed Martin's Skunk Works, is said to have stated in public that the black budget research world has already developed this technology. This is contested, unsurprisingly, but as Levenda suggested, why wouldn't we be trying to move on from the limitations of chemical rockets?

Whether the technology is in place or not, the simple fact of our existence in the cosmos makes us a cosmic species. But this is not yet how humans see themselves. Perhaps that same human duality is at play again, as we separate ourselves philosophically from everything beyond the surface of our homeworld. This dualistic thinking plays out in so many areas. In Western medicine the health links between mind and body are only recently, grudgingly being explored. In this culture we have not only separated spirit and matter, but tried to do away with spirit altogether. Try raising spiritual topics in a roomful of mainstream scientists and observe the dynamics that play out.

But some, like neurosurgeon Dr Eben Alexander, have broken ranks. In his book *Proof of Heaven* he presents anecdotal evidence for the existence of consciousness outside the body, through his own experiences. While in a coma for seven days he journeyed with an angel and encountered the Divine. In *Disclosure* part I Rey Hernandez related his own near-death experience, and the revelatory information given to him that changed his life. He was shown all contact modalities as being connected – as spokes on a single wheel. He was given the mandate to scientifically study contact and share this information with humanity. He went on to form the Foundation for Research into Extraterrestrial Encounters (FREE) with Mary Rodwell, Dr Edgar Mitchell and Dr Rudy Schild. Their research into contact has produced some of the most important findings in the 70-year history of this field. They set up a five-phase quantitative and qualitative research study into contact experience and have received thousands of responses. More than two thirds of participants stated that they have been positively changed by their encounters.

After studying the depth and variety of contact experiences for a while, one experiences a certain amount of cognitive dissonance when seeing a typical Hollywood depiction of ETs behaving like Vikings or vampires. Screenwriters, and by extension the rest of us, would benefit from developing a more nuanced understanding of the phenomenon. But perhaps they are uninterested in the reported flavors of contact, and are using the whole subject as socio-political metaphor. Or it could be, in such a polarized, fear-based society, that they cannot see past their own standard context.

Whether the rest of our culture ever dives as deeply into the topic as books like this attempt to, these transformative encounters continue. In my time with this global subculture I have witnessed an energetic community full of ideas, questions, beautiful sentiments and efforts to change the world for the better. Since sharing my work publicly I have heard from hundreds of people, and only two of them were distressed by their experiences. I immediately referred them to the best people I know: Barbara Lamb, Mary Rodwell and Cynthia Crawford. FREE has an 'Experiencer Support Provider List' on their website, which has contact details for dozens of people who can support experiencers.

When building this project initially, the thought hit me that my own contact would begin to ramp up, and indeed it has. But the advice shared by the interviewees in this book had the immediate effect of helping me deal with it. When sensing a strong presence in the room I have acknowledged my agency, and not allowed fear to define the experience. In my dream encounters I have been ecstatically joyful. When receiving guidance I have let it flow.

In fact, while working on an edit of Rob Gauthier's chapter, I needed to improve the syntax of Aridif's interview. Some of it was unclear to me, and it is my responsibility to ensure that the reader has the best chance of making sense of complex ideas – especially if

English is not their first language. So I began to work through those 20 pages, line by line, paragraph by paragraph. I would make incremental alterations, asking "Is this what you mean?" And if it was right, I would get an immediate sense of flow, of movement. If not, it would feel stuck and I would have to re-examine the text and ask again about its meaning. It never felt that it was just me, editing alone. There was such a strong sense that the process was interactive, and real-time. I shared this with Rob and he said that this itself is a form of channeling.

Layers of connection

In this work a few people have immediately seemed strikingly familiar, especially Jacquelin, Darlene, Cynthia Crawford and Alexis Brooks. That sense of familiarity—almost remembrance—has crept in over time with at least 20 others. About halfway through producing *Hybrids*, I felt a rising sense that we had all set this up in the past, and were now reassembling to accelerate the diffusion of this information, and help trigger awakenings in more people.

Yet I did not expect, when I set out, to have as big an awakening as I have had. It has certainly helped me relate to the journeys of others. But this has been with me all my life, in different ways. I have encountered ghosts and presences in waking life, ETs in dreams, and angels in both waking life and near-death experience. I have seen myself in many non-human forms in regressions (with Barbara, Darlene and Hank Jones II). I have received downloads and felt guidance throughout my life. I have experienced continual synchronicities, and been bombarded with repeating numbers. I have had missing time, several craft sightings, and have been drawn to this subject since early childhood.

But the most affecting aspect is that everything I have learned has reinforced, and in some ways explained, the feeling I have always had, that I am not 'from here'. Humans have always seemed like a foreign species to me. I struggle to comprehend the sense of separateness, the greed, the hard-heartedness, the conflict, the wilful environmental destruction, and the apparent inability to identify and solve fundamental problems. It does however make sense within the narrative that the 3D realm is designed as a place to experience those things. But it feels, at the very least, that I am out of practice with 3D realities. Like everybody, I experience the separative ego every waking moment, whether consciously or otherwise, yet I cannot viscerally understand the way humans relate to and treat one another. It has always seemed odd that we can't go up to any stranger and celebrate being able to consciously interact and share our experiences. I have felt this way for more than 40 years, but this seems to be a general symptom of awakening. And you cannot unring that bell. Once you have opened the heart and the mind, there is no going back. It is liberating, but it also helps me relate to Robert's sentiments in *Hybrids*: "It definitely makes it harder to function properly in society without getting frustrated, irritated. Now that I know how it could be, and I see how it is, it's kind of disgusting. I feel so bad, hurt for everybody."

That is the downside. From here the human world can look like a desperate place, and one in which the awakening is not going to happen soon enough to prevent the climate system being thrown catastrophically out of balance and just about every ecosystem on this planet collapsing. But maybe it is not about saving anything. One often hears in this field that nothing is real, it is all an illusion. Perhaps, but human emotions, and a sense of mission, are powerful drivers. Again quoting Robert, the illusion is pretty convincing.

On the face of it, it can be challenging to reconcile the key narratives in this subject. If we are here to play roles, then why awaken? It is a wonderful thing, and can transform our lives for the better, but if our mission was to be selfish, greedy and hateful, then have we not blown the mission by awakening? Lyssa integrates these narratives in saying that awakening *is* the mission. It's the whole point. Others state that missions or 'soul contracts' are not set in stone, and can change as we go along, if we wish. That sense of agency does help reconcile the two, and is a key aspect of awakening. It is clear that the experiencers in these books live from the heart, and, as Aridif and others suggest, they follow their excitement where it leads.

History and mythology tells us that interaction between humans and non-human intelligences has always occurred, and in this pivotal time for life on Earth we will find ever more value in drawing on this resource. The pathfinders in books like this have shared their experiences and insights, but the joy of exploring reality is that we all define our own unique version of it. Each of us tells our own story of who we are, and how it is. As we have heard, one of the most important things in this process is to learn to trust ourselves, and to trust others - with discernment. In any time, place or form, this will always serve us.

It has been a privilege to connect with so many voyagers into realms that are both immeasurably large, and perfectly human-scale. And it has been a delight to get to know them, and to share this piece of our journey with you.

Light Language. Credit: Tatiana Roumelioti